Fictions of Advice

Fictions of Advice

The Literature and Politics of
Counsel in Late Medieval England

Judith Ferster

PENN

University of Pennsylvania Press
Philadelphia

Library of Congress Cataloging-in-Publication Data
Ferster, Judith, 1947–
   Fictions of advice : the literature and politics of counsel in late medieval England / Judith
Ferster.
      p.   cm. — (Middle Ages series)
   Includes bibliographical references and index.
   ISBN 0-8122-3332-8 (alk. paper)
   1. Didactic literature, English (Middle) — History and criticism.   2. Authors, English —
Middle English, 1100–1500 — Political and social views.   3. Great Britain — Politics and
government — 1066–1485 — Historiography.   4. Chaucer, Geoffrey, d. 1400 — Political and
social views.   5. Gower, John, 1325?–1408 — Political and social views.   6. Hoccleve,
Thomas, 1370?–1450 — Political and social views.   7. Politics and literature — Great Britain —
History.   8. Education of princes in literature.   9. Kings and rulers in literature.
10. Secretum secretorum.   I. Title.   II. Series.
PR275.D53F47   1996
820.9'358'09023 — dc20   95-53268
                                                                                         CIP

To Robert Craig Lane

Contents

Acknowledgments   xi

1. Introduction   1

2. The Context for Literature: Public Discourse in the Late
Middle Ages   15
England as a Political Nation   16
News: Information Exchange and Political Dialogue   22
Limitations on the King: Deposition and the Memory
    of Deposition   24
Limitations on Speech in Parliament   26
Limitations on Nonparliamentary Speech   31
The Poets Speak of Silence: The Trope of the
    Hidden Transcript   36

3. The *Secretum Secretorum* and the Governance of Kings   39
The King Governing   40
Governing the King   44
Deconstructing the Ideology of Advice   49

4. The *Secretum Secretorum* in Ireland   55
Deference and Challenge: Yonge and Ormonde   55
Ireland "Entremedelid": The Writer, the Patron, and the
    Patron's Patron   61

5. Council, Counsel, and the Politics of Advice   67
Still Harping on Advice   68
Edward II   70

Edward III   72
Richard II   79
Henry IV   85

6. Chaucer's *Tale of Melibee*: Advice to the King and Advice to
the King's Advisers   89

The *Melibee*   91
England in the Late 1380s   99
Chaucer in the Late 1380s   101
The *Melibee* in the Late 1380s   102
Chaucer in the 1990s   104

7. O Political Gower   108

The Languages of Advice   110
The Hermeneutics of Counsel in the *Confessio Amantis*   113
The King and His Counsellors   118
The King and His People   126
Sad (Hi)Stories of the Deposition of Kings   132
Appendix on Idioms   134

8. A Mirror for the Prince of Wales: Hoccleve's *Regement
of Princes*   137

Begging and Advising   139
Begging as Advising   147
The Discipline of Advice   150

9. Machiavelli's *Prince*   160

The *Prince* and the Medieval *Fürstenspiegel*: What's New?   161
The *Prince* and the Prince   165
Novelty Again   172

10. Conclusion   174

Works Cited   189

Index   205

ILLUSTRATIONS

Figure 1. University College, Oxford, MS. 85, p. 70.   48
Figure 2. Drawing, D. Reilly, *The New Yorker Magazine*, May
23, 1988, p. 33.   177

Acknowledgments

THE GENRE OF ACADEMIC ACKNOWLEDGMENTS echoes the mirrors for princes when they remind the king that he will make the final choices among options. The writer, too, is ultimately responsible, so that advisers are implicated only in a book's successes, not its failures of style or substance. It gives me greater sympathy with the writers of *Fürstenspiegel* truisms to realize how true this one is in my case.

Many friends and colleagues have offered just the right encouraging word, bibliographical reference, linguistic insight, or connecting idea at just the right time, among them Barbara Baines, Catherine Batt, Jane Burns, Michael Carter, Charlotte Gross, Graham Hammill, Elizabeth Hansot, Geoffrey Galt Harpham, Linda Holley, Deborah Hooker, H. Marshall Leicester, Jr., Lee Patterson, J. G. A. Pocock, Phillip Richards, Colin Richmond, Elizabeth Robertson, Jeffrey Robinson, Mark Sosower, Heinrich Stabenau, Annette Stoller, Edith Sylla, Craig Taylor, Jon Thompson, and David Wong. Robert Yeager read Chapter 7, Charles Blyth read Chapter 8, and Susan Moller Okin read Chapter 9; Ralph Hanna III read the entire manuscript, as did Richard Firth Green and Peggy Knapp, the readers for the University of Pennsylvania Press. My attempts to respond to their valuable comments and suggestions made me happier with the book.

The late John Hazel Smith was energetically supportive in the early stages of this project. Not to be able to present the final result to him is saddening, as is being deprived of all the bracing talks we would have had along the way.

I wrote much of this book while I had a fellowship from the National Endowment for the Humanities, and I began revising while on a semester's leave from my department at North Carolina State University. In both cases I am deeply grateful to have had time to concentrate on the project—to read in circles, since things look different the next time around, to make false starts and reach deadends, and to get second winds. It was luxurious to be able to be wholly taken up by the subject.

I very much appreciate permission from the Master and Fellows of University College, Oxford, to reproduce the illumination in Figure 1, and from The New Yorker Magazine, Inc. to reproduce Donald Reilly's drawing in Figure 2.

The staff of North Carolina State University's D. H. Hill Library was helpful and generous, even indulgent, particularly the Circulation Department, led by Linda Fuller, and the Interlibrary Center, led by Ann Baker Ward.

David Baker's combination of meticulousness and intellectual engagement buoyed me during preparation of the manuscript. Mark Amos brought substance and fun to proofreading sessions. Mindy Brown, project editor at the Press, shepherded the book through production with great care. All three helped make the book more accurate.

While working on this book, I gave talks based on various parts of my research at the International Congress on Medieval Studies at the Medieval Institute of Western Michigan University (several times) and at the Modern Language Association Convention. The English departments at the University of North Carolina at Greensboro and the University of Colorado, as well as my own department at North Carolina State, all heard pieces of the book. Since nothing is as conducive to writing as thinking that someone wants to hear what you have to say, I am grateful for their lively responses.

Chapter 7 appeared in an earlier form in *Mediaevalia* 16 (1993), a special issue on Gower edited by Robert Yeager in honor of John Hurt Fisher. I appreciate permission to use the material here.

What acknowledgments acknowledge is the social aspect of the mostly solitary work of scholarship. Anyone attempting to historicize my work would have to note the local influence of Robert Lane, whose own enthusiastic study of the relationship between history and literature helped to hook me. Because he is a ready and inspiring interlocutor, a willing and astute reader, the social aspect of this project began at home. His support helped make this project both possible and a joy to work on.

I

Introduction

Therefore the lords came on the sixth day after Christmas to the
Guildhall of London where in the presence of the mayor and
community of the city they declared how and under what form
and wherefore they were doing these things and they rode there
with a great multitude. When they had done this they came to
the Tower of London with 500 men well armed, and seeing the
king seated in the room next to the chapel on his throne under a
canopy they made due obeisance, that is with a three-fold pros-
tration to the ground. Then the king nodded to them and they
modestly arose and started to converse with him.

— *Polychronicon* [1]

THE MONK OF WESTMINSTER'S account of the crisis of the English government in 1388 displays a surprising dissonance between the rebellious
lords' mission — to wrest control of the government of England from Richard II — and their obsequious behavior toward the king.[2] Few of the situations I discuss here produce such a radical contrast between deeds and
demeanor because the other actors, literary and historical, do not successfully seize power while leaving the ruler in place. Nevertheless, we will see
"due obeisance" mixed with prodding, pressure, and outright criticism.
The mixture of submission and aggression, flattery and resistance, is my
theme in this book.

To some, this mixture of respect and provocation may seem unlikely
in mirrors for princes.[3] First of all, the original writers of these treatises are

1. *Polychronicon Ranulphi Higden Monachi Cestrensis*, IX.114 (excerpted and translated by
A. R. Myers, *English Historical Documents*, vol. IV, no. 62, 155–56).

2. For a discussion of the continuation of the chronicle after the death of its original
writer, Ranulf Higden, see Gransden, *Historical Writing in England*, vol. ii, *c. 1307 to the Early
Sixteenth Century*, 157. The rebellious lords were later called the "Appellants" because they
appealed (accused) some of Richard's advisers of treason in parliament.

3. For a survey of the full range of works in the tradition of the mirrors for princes, see
W. Berges, *Die Fürstenspiegel des hohen und späten Mittelalters*. For more recent comments on

traditionally thought of as adopting the king's point of view.[4] Insofar as the treatises have political import, they ought not to be provocative. Furthermore, they are often seen as compilations of platitudes, clichés, and ancient stories so general, so distant in time and place, and so inert that they have no bearing on political concerns contemporary with their writers and translators. It makes a certain intuitive sense that works in the *Fürstenspiegel* tradition derived from the ninth-century pseudo-Aristotelian Arabic *Kitab sirr al-asrar* (*The Book of the Secret of Secrets*, often known in the West as the *Secretum Secretorum*), enthusiastically translated into Latin and the European vernaculars throughout the Middle Ages,[5] would have little to say to their specific contemporary contexts. Truisms such as "It is better to take good advice and avoid bad" seem timeless only because empty. They had authority because they were seen as Aristotle's advice to Alexander, but their popularity looks to some like evidence of the medieval English taste for "platitude" and "moral generality."[6]

On closer examination, their seeming emptiness is puzzling, since advice to the king was actually a matter of great importance in the late Middle Ages. The king's council was developing into an institution that had great power in the royal administration, especially when the king was incapable of ruling or incapacitated. Since Edward III was enfeebled by age in the last years of his reign, since Richard II came to the throne at the age of ten, since Henry IV was seriously ill several times during his reign, and since Henry VI came to the throne at the age of one year and as an adult suffered periods of insanity, there were long periods when the council was actually running the government. Since criticizing the king was sometimes dangerous, advisers on the council as well as those who were the king's personal friends and confidants were the foci of conflict and controversy, and criti-

---

the genre, see Jean-Philippe Genet's introduction to his *Four English Political Tracts of the Later Middle Ages*.

4. Q. Skinner, *The Foundations of Modern Political Thought*, vol. I, 216.

5. No Greek version is known, but the work first appears in the ninth century, when many important works of India, Persia, and Greece were being translated into Arabic (see the *Dictionary of the Middle Ages*, 12:128). The claim that it was translated from the Greek is therefore plausible, even if untrue. It was translated into Latin in the twelfth and thirteenth centuries, and there are 600 extant Latin manuscripts (C. B. Schmitt and D. Knox, comps., *Pseudo-Aristoteles Latinus*), 3; it was then translated into Dutch, English, French, German, Hebrew, Italian, Spanish (*Dictionary of the Middle Ages*, 8:37–38), Anglo-Norman (*Dictionary of the Middle Ages*, 1:264), Castilian, Catalan, Portuguese, Middle High German, Middle Low German, and Old Swedish (*Dictionary of the Middle Ages*, 8:435). There is even an early modern Russian translation (*Dictionary of the Middle Ages*, 8:38).

Dorothee Metlitzki gives a good account of how the Arabic work made its way to western Europe via Spain and Portugal in *The Matter of Araby in Medieval England*, 106–11.

6. A. B. Ferguson, *The Articulate Citizen and the English Renaissance*, 24 and 88.

cism was sometimes displaced onto them even when adult kings had control of their faculties and their governments. Furthermore, parliament was evolving, and relations among parliament, the council, the monarch and his personal advisers, the nobles, and the general populace were the subject of intense and sometimes contentious discussion. Often, those who wanted to reform the government attacked the council, so it became the focus of many struggles between the nobles and the king, with parliament maneuvering between them.[7] Given that the literary genre of advice manuals was so popular when advice to kings was such a visible issue, why should these works be so hard to connect to their social and political contexts?

The dangers of criticizing the king and his advisers encouraged a retreat to the safer territory of the advice manuals, which lessened the risks of contemporary politics. The constraints on discussion of political issues help explain the repetitive morality of the manuals and the literary works based on them. A writer or translator would be able to engage important contemporary issues without getting into trouble. As David Lawton says in a very suggestive article, the manuals' dullness is a disguise necessitated by the danger of writing frankly about contemporary political issues, but not a total avoidance of them.[8] The mirrors for princes are not only more topical than they appear to be but also more critical of the powerful than we might expect. Their deployment of the comfortingly familiar stories and maxims of the advice tradition is often strategic, and they display a combination of deference and challenge that is not as extreme as the one described in the *Polychronicon* but surely would have been recognizable to Richard's rebellious lords.

My goal in this book is to historicize a number of the important English mirrors for princes[9] — translations of the Latin versions of the *Secretum Secretorum*, two major works that draw heavily upon it (Book VII of Gower's *Confessio Amantis* and Hoccleve's *Regement of Princes*), and Chaucer's *Tale of Melibee*[10] — in order to show how they engage the political conflicts of their day using the time-tested (some would say time-worn)

7. J. F. Baldwin, *The King's Council in England During the Middle Ages*, 116–18; B. Lyon, *A Constitutional and Legal History of Medieval England*, 512.

8. D. Lawton, "Dullness and the Fifteenth Century."

9. For a fuller listing of the English heirs and analogues of the *Secretum Secretorum* and a discussion of their popularity in late medieval England, see R. F. Green, *Poets and Princepleasers*, chapter 5.

10. The *Melibee* is not directly related to the *Secretum Secretorum* but addresses some of the same themes. I include it here because it is an important mirror for princes very close in time to Gower's *Confessio Amantis* but demonstrating a very different relationship to the ruler it addresses.

elements of the *Fürstenspiegel* as camouflage for political commentary. Advice can become critique, and the audience for the work may include not only the prince to whom it is nominally addressed, but his subjects as well. This hypothesis raises two issues that will be my concern in the remainder of this chapter: the possibility of criticism of and ideological resistance to powerful governments, and the hermeneutics of reading camouflaged texts. They are closely related, since if the critique is disguised well enough to "fool" the government, there is no guarantee that it can be understood correctly by a wider audience, including us. The predicament of the writer facing restrictions on speech, as Robert Lane describes it, is that "strategies that would protect him also risked rendering unintelligible the sensitive material that required protection in the first place."[11]

The possibility of resistance—a term I will use to refer to many kinds of oppositional activity ranging from full-scale revolution to *sotto voce* grumbling—is currently an important topic in a number of academic disciplines and, in literary criticism, in Renaissance new historicism. Stephen Greenblatt's work—especially his essay "Invisible Bullets"—has been the most visible center of this discussion. New historicists and cultural materialists argue about Greenblatt's theory that much of what appears to be dissent is appropriated, contained, or actually generated by the power structure. Greenblatt says that "the subversiveness that is genuine and radical . . . is at the same time contained by the power it would appear to threaten. Indeed the subversiveness is the very product of that power and furthers its ends."[12] This conception is not a twentieth-century invention. Machiavelli mentions (without comment) the notion that a leader can increase his power by stirring resistance in order to crush it: "Accordingly, many people consider that a shrewd ruler should seize any opportunity to encourage hostile forces cunningly, so that when he crushes them his reputation and power will be greatly increased."[13]

There is a good bit of resistance to Greenblatt's nightmare of monolithic control in which ultimately only the government possesses political agency. Lee Patterson draws on Raymond Williams to claim that repressive governments cannot repress perfectly.[14] Carolyn Porter cites other theorists, including Bakhtin, whose notion of the multiplicity of voices denies

---

11. R. Lane, *Shepheards Devises*, 60.

12. S. Greenblatt, *Shakespearean Negotiations*, 30.

13. N. Machiavelli, *The Prince*, Q. Skinner, ed., chapter 20, 74.

14. L. Patterson, *Negotiating the Past*, 55. So does Frank Lentricchia in *Criticism and Social Change*, 15. See also J. Dollimore, "Introduction" to *Political Shakespeare*, 2–17, ed. J. Dollimore and A. Sinfield.

the unity of government itself (267–68).[15] David Norbrook points out that "a cultural theory ought not to lead to the logical deduction that the English Revolution cannot have happened" and describes other sources of agency in Renaissance England.[16] According to James Holstun, while some of those other sources, such as religious dissenters, often presented themselves as conservative, their posture was self-protective, not a sign that they aligned themselves with the government.[17] Many critics reject the static world that the theory produces or reject Greenblatt's dependence on or interpretation of Foucault's concept of power,[18] but the thesis is hard to falsify. The beauty and liability of a totalizing thesis of this kind is that almost no evidence of opposition besides a successful revolution seems to disprove it.

One of the reasons the argument about the possibility of opposition in the English Renaissance has captured so much attention is that it parallels larger arguments taking place in the social sciences. The most general one is the debate over the "dominant ideology thesis" in Marxism, a thesis drawing the same conclusions from Althusser that Greenblatt drew from Foucault: those who are in power also control the minds of those who are not.[19] Of course, the Marxists are in a different position from the new historicists: The Marxists are trying to explain why, in modern western Europe and America, a revolution hasn't happened while, as Norbrook points out, many Renaissance new historicists are ignoring one that did. Nevertheless, the similarity of the major issue they discuss — the possibility of opposition — is striking.[20]

Many smaller historical questions fit under the same general rubric. One medieval English example is the question of the nature and significance of the Rising of 1381. Was it a minor reaction to a temporary tax or part of a larger movement of resistance to authority? Barbara Hanawalt, who sees

15. C. Porter, "History and Literature."

16. D. Norbrook, "Life and Death of Renaissance Man," 108.

17. J. Holstun, "Ranting at the New Historicism," 198. Medieval reformers also were inclined to present themselves as conservatives. For instance, those responsible for the Rising in 1381 claimed to be protecting the king from bad advisers.

18. E.g., J. Howard, "The New Historicism in Renaissance Studies;" L. Patterson, *Negotiating the Past*, 63–72; and C. Porter, "History and Literature," 262–65. For a lucid exploration of the relationship between Marx and Foucault and between new historicism and Foucault, see Frank Lentricchia, *Ariel and the Police* (chapter 1, esp. 86–102).

19. See N. Abercrombie, S. Hill, and B. S. Turner for an account of and argument against the *Dominant Ideology Thesis*. They take their argument further in *Dominant Ideologies*.

20. Feminists wrestle with a similar issue when they recognize the ways in which women are created by patriarchy and thus prevented from opposing it. No one can speak as a woman in opposition to patriarchy because there are no women apart from it.

the rising as comprehensive protest against inequities in the system of land ownership, documents peasants pilfering and poaching and disputing taxes before and after the rising; she concludes that peasants were capable of self-conscious opposition to the ruling classes and thus that resistance was possible.[21]

An issue involving a higher class is the significance of the increasing power of the commons in parliament. Was it a sign of the increased importance of the gentry? Or were the members of commons actually controlled by the nobility? There has been a long debate about whether the nobility manipulated the elections to the commons and so dictated its agenda, or whether the commons thought of itself as independent and acted accordingly. Bishop Stubbs began the debate with his view of the growing role of the commons,[22] and other historians have subsequently undermined his point of view, especially H. G. Richardson[23] and G. O. Sayles.[24] Although Stubbs did call the growing power of the commons part of an English "constitution" when that term was perhaps premature, and although he was perhaps too teleological in his view of the relationship between medieval government and the later limited monarchy, he did understand the pressures that worked against the commons' independence (attempts to influence elections and royal influences of various kinds).[25] These are the pressures his critics later elaborated on.[26] The recent work on bastard feudalism continues the discussion of whether magnates could "pack" parliament with their supporters in order to procure parliamentary action in their favor.[27] These debates about the rising and the gentry in parliament entail the same larger question prominent in other disciplines: whether authentic, independent opposition to the ruling class is possible.

The work of James C. Scott is very helpful to those who want to argue that it is possible. Scott has documented the ways in which people who lack power — in many different places and historical periods — express their dissatisfaction with social structure and its inequities.[28] He is interested mostly

---

21. B. Hanawalt, "Peasant Resistance to Royal and Seigniorial Impositions."

22. Bishop W. Stubbs, *The Constitutional History of England in Its Origin and Development* (esp. vol. II).

23. H. G. Richardson, "The Commons and Medieval Politics."

24. G. O. Sayles, *The King's Parliament of England*, 122–26.

25. Bishop W. Stubbs, *The Constitutional History of England*, e.g., vol. II, 645, 649.

26. B. Guenée, *States and Rulers in Later Medieval Europe*, 226–30. On kings' struggles with the barons over the council, see B. Lyon, *A Constitutional and Legal History of Medieval England*, 504–12.

27. E.g., N. Saul, *Knights and Esquires*, chapters 3 and 4. See also Chapter 10 below.

28. J. C. Scott, *Weapons of the Weak: Everyday Forms of Peasant Resistance*; and *Domination and the Arts of Resistance: Hidden Transcripts*.

in people of a social stratum different from that of the writers I will be examining, but his work is germane because much of the behavior he discusses takes place while the master or overlord's back is turned or while the actor is outwardly smiling and assenting but secretly cursing and refusing. His work establishes that sometimes resistance is invisible but not nonexistent. One of the significant things about this research is that when the hidden transcript is successfully hidden, it is less easily assimilated into theories of a ruling class monopoly on ideology. The stories Scott compiles are about unacknowledged thoughts and actions, which are thus not likely to have been the result of upper-class manipulation. His work therefore strengthens theories of an oppositional culture.

Many kinds of expression are relevant to that culture. Although Scott himself is mostly interested in behavior that evades general view, he also describes behavior that occupies a middle ground between the compliant public face and the defiant private one and that is disguised or encoded just enough to escape punishment or repression. This is the territory of art, which can allow for, in Scott's phrase, "the smuggling of portions of the hidden transcript, suitably veiled, onto the public stage."[29] Sometimes medieval writers seek to escape punishment for exposing the hidden transcript by remaining anonymous.[30] In this book, however, I treat well-known authors and their methods for avoiding censure.

Since oppositional art sometimes calls forth not only censure but the censor, I want to return briefly to the subject of censorship, which gathers together a number of the topics I have addressed so far, including opposition, danger, disguise, and interpretation. According to Annabel Patterson, despite official censors and laws about the licensing of published material, during the English Renaissance censorship was remarkable not because of the way it worked but because of the way it did not. That is, the state apparatus did not prevent publication of all material that criticized or threatened the regime but, rather, ensured that political content was encoded or rendered ambiguous. But only somewhat. The intended audience of the offending work could still decipher its message. If the controversial message was not completely effaced, how can its passing through the censors' screen be explained? Although Patterson allows for the "fallibility or carelessness" of the censors, she believes that, in most cases, the censors understood the coded messages of the works they licensed. What mattered was that the

29. J. C. Scott, *Domination and the Arts of Resistance*, 157.
30. L. Kendrick, "Criticism of the Ruler, 1100–1400, in Provençal, Old French, and Middle English Verse," 427–96.

gestures of recognition of the censors' authority—the encoding of the material—had been made. Patterson believes that such gestures were enough, because the writers and the censors were playing by the same rules: "There were conventions that both sides accepted as to how far a writer could go in explicit address to the contentious issues of his day, how he could encode his opinions so that nobody would be *required* to make an example of him."[31]

The censors' motive for participating in this system was that the government wanted some control over what was published but was not willing to do what would have been necessary to gain total control. It was unwilling to appear to be that dictatorial or totalitarian. This is the cost that Patterson sees for the government when it refused to play the game with the writers. Indeed, the case of William Prynne, who was tried for treason in 1633 because his *Histriomastix* supposedly promoted insurrection,[32] is pivotal for Patterson's argument because Prynne's conviction and punishment (he was fined, stripped of his university degree, and imprisoned; half of each of his ears was cut off) shows the negative consequences for King Charles I's government of being heavy-handed about censorship: "By making Prynne a martyr, Charles took an irrevocable step toward civil war and a polarized culture. From that point, those who needed a symbol of his autocracy were not obliged, as Jonson had been [in *Sejanus*], to turn to Roman history, for Prynne's ears entered the territory of legend and symbol."[33] Better for the government to let writers point significantly at resonant but distant examples of tyranny than to become one itself. Knowing winks and nods were far preferable to open accusations. Censorship left its mark on literary works but did not obliterate their political content. It was a matter of deference, not capitulation, and once the deferential gesture was made, there was space for political discourse that challenged the regime. The mutual understanding according to which writers often claimed to be merely translating and turned to ancient and foreign examples and deliberate ambiguity as minimal disguises for political comment was thus less risky for both parties.[34]

It may seem unwarranted to read backward from Prynne's ears to the Middle Ages, a time during which there was no official censorship. But Noam Chomsky and Edward Herman have shown for our own period

31. A. Patterson, *Censorship and Interpretation*, 11.
32. A. Patterson, *Censorship and Interpretation*, 171.
33. A. Patterson, *Censorship and Interpretation*, 107.
34. On "functional ambiguity," see A. Patterson, *Censorship and Interpretation*, 11, 18, 48. On translating and "historical or other uninvented texts," see 57.

that it does not take an office of censorship to put limits on the media.[35] Whether or not the mechanisms of constraint in the Middle Ages, Renaissance, and modern world are comparable, there were medieval constraints on speech and writing, not officially instituted or announced but still effective. I discuss these constraints in Chapter 2. Some of the signs of constraint are visible in the works themselves — both in what appears to be intentional ambiguity[36] and in devotion to translation and historical examples — as we shall see in Chapters 6 through 8. The mixture of deference and challenge — to the rules of discourse and to the rulers who enforced them — provides a fruitful model for the medieval texts, and can be seen not only in writers who might be expected to be oppositional, but also in those who seem closest to the rulers they address.[37]

Patterson and Scott both invite us to think of the relationship between rulers and their subjects in something other than binary terms. The alternatives for political speech are not just entirely repressed or entirely free. There is something between either total containment or silent suffering and successful revolution. Although art often exists on this middle ground, whether and how art performs sociopolitical functions is often disputed. Does art reflect social structure? Create it? Expose contradictions in the ruling ideology?[38] Literary critics are becoming interested anew in literature's relationship to its social context just at the moment when historians are confronting the textuality of history,[39] a happy conjunction of disciplinary concerns that allows us to see that one of the things literature can do is to create a language in which to think and speak about social and political issues. One of my aims in this book is to show how the idioms of the literary works on advice and the idioms used by real actors in history intersect and influence each other.[40] In this way art becomes an actor in history. Another of

35. E. S. Herman and N. Chomsky, *Manufacturing Consent*; N. Chomsky, *Necessary Illusions*.

36. Post-structuralism has made us aware of the ambiguity of all language — its habit of saying and unsaying at the same time. It is difficult, if not impossible, to distinguish between intentional and unintentional ambiguity. Patterson has been criticized for not doing so (R. Helgerson, "Recent Studies in the English Renaissance"), but it cannot be done in the abstract. For her book, and for this one, close reading has to be the basis for arguments in each individual case.

37. For the effects of censorship on those often thought of as "court poets" in the Renaissance, see A. Patterson, *Censorship and Interpretation*, 57–58.

38. P. Macherey takes this tack in *A Theory of Literary Production*, 130–35. See also T. Eagleton, *Criticism and Ideology*, 89–97.

39. According to Lee Patterson, this trend reflects the influence of deconstruction. *Negotiating the Past*, 63.

40. For cogent discussions of this process, see J. G. A. Pocock's "Languages and Their Implications," and "Texts as Events."

my aims is to show how the literary works themselves participate in the social and political conflicts within which they occur and which, by providing an appropriate language for political discussion, they also enable.

There has been substantial work on the medieval English literature of political engagement. For instance, V. J. Scattergood in *Politics and Poetry in the Fifteenth Century*, Richard Firth Green in *Poets and Princepleasers: Literature and the English Court in the Late Middle Ages*, and Janet Coleman in *Medieval Readers and Writers: 1350–1400* have analyzed the ways in which medieval writers respond to and criticize social conditions in general and, in particular, the government and its policies. According to Coleman, the poems of complaint in the late fourteenth century "can be classified *thematically* as mirrors for princes."[41] They share with works that are more clearly derived from the *Secretum Secretorum* themes such as the inadequacies of young counsellors and the danger that flatterers will distort the king's perspective.[42] But perhaps because of the risks of retribution for pointed political critique, many of these poems are anonymous. For this reason the pressures on and motives of the individual writers cannot be analyzed. If the writer was known to his audience, especially if he was in a patron's employ or wished to be, he needed protection other than anonymity. As R. F. Green argues, the delicacy of the social positions of a number of the writers of advice whose names we know may account for the abstractions, generalities, and circumspection of their works.[43] It is the techniques for criticism used by writers in this sensitive position that I analyze and historicize in this study.

Historicizing literary works is always tricky, however, because it is difficult to define the context in which the work resonates: How large should it be temporally and geographically? Is the work responding to a local event, a major trend, or both? Sometimes no evidence of local events remains, and thus we are tempted to treat the work as a response to a long-term problem or change. But if the problem is a very large one, why would the writer have chosen one precise moment to address it? Critics have difficulty choosing the right time as well as time scale.

41. J. Coleman, "English Culture in the Fourteenth Century," 60. Also see chapter 3 ("The Literature of Social Unrest") in Coleman's *Medieval Readers and Writers* for more detailed readings of these works.

42. See, for instance, two poems from the Digby 102 manuscript, *Wyt and Wille* l. 27 (on young counsellors) and *Lerne to say wele, say litel or say noȝt* ll. 73–76 (on flatterers). The poems are edited by J. Kail in *Twenty-Six Political and Other Poems*, 14–24. J. Coleman discusses the poems of this manuscript in *Medieval Readers and Writers: 1350–1400*, 98–111.

43. R. F. Green, *Poets and Princepleasers*, 164–65.

The task is compounded by the impossibility of dating many medieval works precisely. The frequently uncertain dates of writing and publishing are often obstacles to the fine-tuning of historicist interpretations. We sometimes have to be satisfied with a range of dates between which a work might have been written.

Furthermore, as I suggested earlier when I mentioned the Rising of 1381 and the changing role of the commons in parliament, the history itself is often contested. In the course of working on this material, I have often found that one version of the past will illuminate a given work more than another. To historicize, one must pick one's historians.

And of course, the particular liability of analyzing discourse is that contemporaries cannot tell themselves the whole truth about the times they live in. But as Brian Stock says, "Accounting for what actually took place is recognized to be only a part of the story. The other part is the record of what individuals *thought* was taking place."[44] In general, I mean to be making claims about public discourse. I want to trace ways of talking about certain kinds of political problems.

Chapter 2 ("The Context for Literature: Public Discourse in the Late Middle Ages") describes the late medieval context for political speech, including the constraints on speech that existed even when an office of censorship or a procedure for licensing literature had yet to be established. The chapter also discusses the ways that various segments of society could put pressure on the government. In general, I am tracing upward and downward pressures,[45] both of which affect the paradoxical relations between advisers and rulers and leave their mark on literature.

Chapter 3 ("The *Secretum Secretorum* and the Governance of Kings") considers the English translations of the *Secretum Secretorum* as a group in order to outline their ideology of advice and the contradictions within it. These translations are all from the fifteenth century, but I discuss them early in the book because the *Secretum Secretorum* defines the tradition most of

---

44. B. Stock, *Listening for the Text*, 16; emphasis mine.
45. I am adapting Walter Ullmann's terms, the "ascending" and "descending" themes in government, from works like his *Individual and Society in the Middle Ages*. In "Celestial Hierarchies Revisted," Francis Oakley calls the terms "rich" and "original" but argues that they are not "valid keys to the understanding of medieval political thought," especially criticizing Ullmann's use of them to analyze medieval theorists like Bracton and to trace an overly stark binary opposition and overly steady progress between absolutism and constitutionalism in government. With the warning that the path between medieval and modern governments was not straight or smooth, the debate echoes that between Bishop Stubbs and his critics (see notes 22–25). Even taking Oakley's admonitions into account, the concepts are still quite useful for describing opposing—but sometimes simultaneous—forces in medieval culture.

the other works draw upon. I concentrate on what they have in common, rather than on their individual contributions, and on what they have in common with their Latin "originals," which would have been available to fourteenth-century writers.[46] They combine rhetoric that elevates the king with rhetoric that levels all ranks, as well as both deference to the king and the impulse to discipline him.[47] To rule well, the king must be ruled. In this chapter I examine the faultlines that rend the ideology of advice — the contradictory assertions of opposites and the stories that escape their morals.

Chapter 4 ("The *Secretum Secretorum* in Ireland") is the first of the chapters to historicize particular mirrors for princes. It is an attempt to observe the particular work that James Yonge's translation of the *Secretum Secretorum* was doing for him and for his patron, James Butler, the earl of Ormonde, in fifteenth-century Ireland. Yonge uses his translation to promote both himself and his patron and to criticize — mildly — both his patron and his patron's patron, the king.

In Chapter 5 ("Council, Counsel, and the Politics of Advice"), I examine the ways in which historical actors in particular fourteenth-century political confrontations used the tropes of advice the *Secretum Secretorum* developed. The contradiction between deference and challenge that the advice manuals cultivate develops in the historical arena. The whole tradition is deferential in that it directs criticism to the king's advisers and his choice of advisers, rather than to the king himself (this tactic carries its own risk, of course, since the advisers, too, are powerful). But in these political confrontations, we will see the blooming of the oppositional elements of the tropes of advice. These episodes in English history will reveal the confluence of the literary and political discourse of advice and thus illuminate the part that literature plays in the political life of late medieval England.

The next chapters (6 through 9) consider some literary works in roughly chronological order. In contrast to the powerful fourteenth-century politicians who used the tropes of advice to oppose a king, Chaucer uses one of the two tales he himself narrates in the *Canterbury Tales* to demonstrate the use of the tropes of advice to challenge a powerful group in order to support a king. Chapter 6 ("Chaucer's *Tale of Melibee*") tries to show how the two main approaches to the tale, historicism and an almost

46. The *Secretum Secretorum* was also available in French in fourteenth- and fifteenth-century England (N. Orme, *From Childhood to Chivalry*, 94).

47. Although he emphasizes the counsellors' need for resignation in the face of a willful monarch, W. Berges does affirm that sometimes the *Secretum Secretorum* seems to be addressed not to the king, but to the advisers themselves (*Die Fürstenspiegel des hohen und späten Mittelalters*, 112).

deconstructive formalism, which seem contradictory, are actually complementary and necessary to each other. As Lee Patterson says, because it attacks the idea of a timeless, transcendental logos by showing that it is "historically contingent and historically constructed," deconstruction itself is "nothing if not a historicism."[48] In Chapter 6 I historicize Chaucer's deconstruction of the tradition of the mirror for princes.[49]

Book VII of Gower's *Confessio Amantis*, though it is the first English work to be indebted to the *Secretum Secretorum*, demonstrates Gower's impatience with the tropes of advice and his dismissal of them in favor of a less-mediated relationship between a king and his people (Chapter 7, "O Political Gower"). Gower cloaks this message in old stories—classical and Biblical tales—but peppers them with more contemporary terms and idioms that bring their contemporary relevance into relief.

Hoccleve, deferential in order to beg money from his patron, the Prince of Wales, uses the tropes of advice both to challenge his hoped-for patron and to criticize the reigning king (Chapter 8, "A Mirror for the Prince of Wales"). In the process he comments on some of the most important and divisive issues facing the crown during the reign of Henry IV.

In "Machiavelli's *Prince*" (Chapter 9) I ask whether the most famous *Fürstenspiegel*—and the one reputed to revolutionize the genre—follows the pattern of praise and challenge found in the others. I therefore address the argument about whether the *Prince* is a typical medieval mirror for princes. My rereading of the medieval mirrors makes Machiavelli typical in unexpected ways. I connect his imitation and refusal to imitate his medieval sources with his own historical context and his ambitions for the work within that context.

Chapter 10 explores audiences for English mirrors for princes.

My aim in all that follows is to understand the functions the mirrors for princes were performing in the late Middle Ages. It may not be surprising that one of those functions was linguistic, the creation and refinement of a language for political actions. The "fictions of advice" in my title are both the literary works about advice and the ways in which historical actors talked about advice. In this book, I trace the intermixing of the literary and historical narratives of advice.[50]

48. "Making Identities in Fifteenth-Century England," 71, 70.

49. In *Chaucer and His Readers*, S. Lerer discusses how in the fifteenth century Chaucer acquired a reputation as a public poet based not on the *Melibee* but on some of the advisory lyric poems (17–18, chapter 4).

50. A recent book that traces this intermixing at a different social level is Steven Justice's *Writing and Rebellion*. By reading the six letters attributed to John Ball in the Rising of 1381

According to J. G. A. Pocock, when you are trying to define a set of idioms or tropes, a historical language,

the more authors you can show to have made use of it the better. If you can show them arguing with one another in it, so that it produces different results and grows and changes in the course of usage, better still; and if some Monsieur Jourdain should appear in your history who says "We seem to be talking in such and such an idiom, whose characteristics are such and such," and such as you have said they must have been, you get up and dance around the room. This does not happen very often.[51]

Thus tempted and thus warned, we begin.

---

against the background of village life — its agricultural and religious practices, its involvement with government and government documents — he is able to interpret the letters, often called enigmatic, and their participation in a process of "making a class" (192). Justice's project is very different from mine because the texts we each deal with inhabit such different worlds, but his admirable study is an exhilarating example of the historical contextualization of literature.

For another kind of intermixing, see G. Barnes's thematic treatment of *Counsel and Strategy in Middle English Romance*.

In *Romancing the Past: The Rise of Vernacular Prose Historiography in Thirteenth-Century France*, Gabrielle M. Spiegel reveals the surprising political valence of French chronicles — that they were not as royalist as many historians previously thought. She shows how they shape the relationship between the monarchy and their audience.

51. J. G. A. Pocock, "Texts as Events," 28, ed. K. Sharpe and S. N. Zwicker.

2

The Context for Literature: Public Discourse in the Late Middle Ages

[The effect of Magna Carta on the king]: Secque de libero ser-
vus effectus est. (And thus, a free man, he became a slave.)

— Henry Knighton, *Chronicon Henrici Knighton* [1]

Houme ne doit a roy retter talem pravitatem
Mes al maveis consiler per ferocitatem.
(One must not impute such wickedness to the king, but to his
evil counsellor in his savagery.)

— "Against the King's Taxes" [2]

IN THIS CHAPTER, I want to define late medieval England as a context for public literature.[3] I am particularly interested in the forging of England as a political community, especially those upward pressures that constrained the monarch and those downward pressures that constrained his subjects. Despite the lack of explicit codes of censorship defining acceptable discourse, both kinds of pressures affected what could be said and written on the subject of politics. One of the defining drives of medieval political theory and practice was to limit the ruler. The reaction to Magna Carta in *Chronicon Henrici Knighton*, the first epigraph to this chapter, overdrama-tizes the outcome of this particular round of the fight, making the stakes clear. The fight was continual because the rules were not settled. As Bernard Guenée notes, "Medieval monarchy was limited by theory but not con-trolled by institutions."[4] Much of the period I am concerned with here saw

---

1. J. R. Lumby, ed., vol. II, 189.
2. *Anglo-Norman Political Songs*, I. S. T. Aspin, ed., 110, 112. The translation is Aspin's. Also in T. Wright, ed., *Political Songs of England*, 182–87.
3. Because this book discusses some works of prose, I am adapting Anne Middleton's phrase from her article, "The Idea of Public Poetry in the Reign of Richard II."
4. B. Guenée, *States and Rulers in Later Medieval Europe*, 86.

the attempt—by a changing array of allies[5]—to create and refine institutions that limited monarchs and provided opportunities for others to participate in government. Various actors nudged each other, negotiated, and jockeyed for power. That the conflicts were often embodied in struggles over advice is reflected in my second epigraph.

I sketch out these conflicts in the sections below: "England as a Political Nation" and "News: Information Exchange and Political Dialogue" both trace the representation of the national community as a whole; "Limitations on the King" charts some of the attempts to control the king that constitute upward pressure; "Limitations on Speech in Parliament" and "Limitations on Nonparliamentary Speech" chart the crown's attempt to govern public discourse (i.e., downward pressure); and "The Poets Speak of Silence" shows how some poets registered such pressure.

England as a Political Nation

Magna Carta articulates not only the idea of limitations on the monarchy but also the idea that the people as a whole serve as the source of those limitations.[6] When the king accepted the charter, he accepted that his power could be constrained by "the community of the realm."[7] The community of the whole was acknowledged in several places in the first version, where the charter invoked "common counsel of the kingdom."[8] The charter required approval of the kingdom for the levying of taxes (paragraph 12, "scutage or aid") and provided for the summoning of advisers to obtain it (14). This provision and its striking phrase were deleted in subsequent versions of the charter, but the concept of consent to taxation survived, and taxation became a national matter, with parliament successfully asserting its right to be consulted.[9] Reference to the unified entity of the country remained. The king wanted "all these aforesaid customs and liberties . . . to

5. For instance, individual barons changed sides, and the parliament was sometimes on the king's side and sometimes not.

6. On the medieval idea that king was held responsible for and to his subjects by means of an oath by which his performance could be measured, see B. Guenée, *States and Rulers in Later Medieval Europe*, 171–72. The idea of a contractual relationship between king and people had many ramifications in the medieval period.

7. F. Thompson, *The First Century of Magna Carta*, 29.

8. C. Stephenson and F. G. Marcham, eds. and trans., *Sources of English Constitutional History* (no. 44, paragraphs 12 and 14), 117, 118.

9. B. Wilkinson, *Constitutional History*, vol. III, 243. Also see B. Guenée, *States and Rulers in Later Medieval Europe*, 180; B. Lyon, *A Constitutional and Legal History of Medieval England*, 548–52.

be observed in our kingdom toward our men, all men of our kingdom, both clergy and laity."[10] The concept of the constraints on the king imposed by the community of the realm also survived, becoming the basis for the English limited monarchy and for more democratic forms of government outside of England.[11]

Although Magna Carta was intended to improve life for all the king's subjects, when it was signed in 1215 the approval of the kingdom was to be vested in a small group of advisers; even the group of "all men" who were granted liberties was not universally inclusive. Women, villeins, and free men who owned no land had no standing. The kind of language found in the charter fits one of the definitions of ideology: the presentation of the interests of a small group as if they were the interests of the whole. But agreements to be limited by advice are dangerous to kings. Once the principle of limitation is established, adjustments can be made in the group that gives the advice. As Anthony Giddens points out, ideological language that presents the interests of some as the interest of all also creates leverage so that "all" can get into the act, or at least "more" can do so.[12] And, in time, the magnates gave way to the parliamentary commons as the representatives of the commonwealth.

An incident as small as Magna Carta is large reveals how deeply the barons' ideology of the community of the whole penetrated political consciousness. In 1265 the villagers of Peatling Magna attacked supporters of a royalist magnate. When called upon to account for their behavior, they justified the attack by saying that the supporters of the magnate were "contra utilitatem communitatis regni et contra barones" ("against the welfare of the community of the realm and against the barons").

There are a number of ways to read this incident. It could demonstrate Marxist false consciousness among the peasants who, by aligning themselves with the "barones," adopt the interests of a whole that in many ways excludes them. It might also be a shrewd use of aristocratic language at a strategic moment to manipulate the audience by deploying familiar, patriotic rhetoric. Or, it could exhibit the political consciousness that was a necessary precondition of a more representative government.[13] This last

10. Paragraph 60, 125; the Latin text is on 112 of F. Thompson's *The First Century of Magna Carta* ("omnes de regno nostro").

11. F. Thompson, *The First Century of Magna Carta*, 29–30.

12. A. Giddens, *Central Problems in Social Theory*, 193–94.

13. For a fuller narrative and interpretation of the incident, see H. Cam, "The Theory and Practice of Representation in Medieval England," 278, and *Law-Finders and Law-Makers in Medieval England*, 81–84.

possibility seems persuasive when we look at the the incident in the light of other nonaristocratic uses of the phrase "community of the realm." For instance, the Anglo-Norman poem "Against the King's Taxes," whose poet is clearly learned but has sympathy with the poor, advises the king not to go to war unless "la commune de sa terre velent consentire" ("the community of his realm consent to it").[14] D. A. Carpenter contextualizes the incident at Peatling Magna in a way that illuminates the peasants' stake in the conflict of the barons with the monarch. Peasants were not in the grip of false consciousness but "had reason to side with the baronial movement, since it had given them some redress against the oppressions of both their lords and the king. It had done so, at least in part, because the peasantry belonged to the community of the realm of thirteenth-century England, and were thus the concern of a movement publicly dedicated to that realm's reform."[15]

No matter which interpretation is correct, it is striking that such language about the realm as a whole was shared by the often-reaffirmed and resoundingly influential Magna Carta and the less-celebrated Peatling Magna villagers. This rhetoric was common currency for some very concrete reasons. Medieval England was remarkably unified — not in the sense that all its inhabitants across the spectrum of wealth, power, and status had similar material interests or agreed on issues, but in that they were aware of the country they lived in, their relations to the various parts of government, and the parts' relations to each other. Since Anglo-Saxon times there had been a concept of England and the English people, and after the Norman Conquest the sense that everyone had a stake in the workings of the central government grew. According to Bertie Wilkinson, "In England, the idea of liberty never became identified with local independence as it did in Germany or to a lesser extent in Italy and France." On the contrary, liberty had to be preserved precisely through contact with the national government.[16] For many reasons, including the various kinds of royal courts that connected people with the crown, the vitality of local governments did not lead to parochialism.[17] Instead, it increased national unity and the numbers of

14. *Anglo-Norman Political Songs*, ed. I. S. T. Aspin, 105–15. T. Wright, ed., *Political Songs of England*, 182–87.

15. D. A. Carpenter, "English Peasants in Politics 1258–1267," 4.

16. B. Wilkinson, *Constitutional History of Medieval England*, vol. III, 2.

17. For a discussion of how the county courts were the means by which many kinds of people (including villeins) had contact with the national government, see S. Justice's *Writing and Rebellion*, 55–59. In *The Governance of Norman and Angevin England 1086–1272*, W. L. Warren describes how government in the localities became a central government after the Norman Conquest.

people who had access to and interest in the political process. As Helen Cam notes, "It was the effective centralization of power under the Angevins that made possible the preservation and utilization of local institutions and local sentiment by the monarchy, which in its turn made possible the growth of the conception of the community of the realm."[18]

An additional reason that people from the shires, counties, towns, and boroughs looked to London and Westminster was the development of parliament, especially when it was used to funnel complaints and grievances from town and country to the capital. According to J. R. Maddicott, the presentation of petitions at regular parliaments in the late thirteenth century during the reign of Edward I "was a momentous innovation, for it meant that for the first time the voice of the aggrieved and of the socially insignificant could be heard at the centre of government."[19] Heard, at least in theory, by the king.[20] By the time of the Good Parliament in 1376, in which the commons took the lead in attacking the king's ministers, the "community of the realm" was represented not by the magnates, the great land-owning aristocrats, but by the parliamentary commons, minor land-owners who represented their localities.[21] The central government reached across geographical and class lines to help foster "the political nation."

The exchange of gentry for magnates might seem insignificant, especially from the point of view of a nonvoting freeman or peasant (let alone woman). But the participation in the courts of the shire that elected the members of the commons in parliament was quite broad: According to Helen Cam, "Though the knights or gentlemen will undoubtedly take the lead in county doings, they will be working with freemen of ungentle blood, yeomen, *valetti*, who may represent the shire at parliaments if knights are not available."[22] In addition, before the franchise was fully extended, the concept of representation provided a bridge from the gentry to the rest of the population. The members of the parliamentary commons were representatives who claimed to speak for the whole, and so claimed to

18. H. Cam, "The Theory and Practice of Representation in Medieval England," 277.

19. J. R. Maddicott, "Parliament and the Constituencies," 62. Also see G. O. Sayles, *The King's Parliament of England*, 76, 79.

20. In *Writing and Rebellion*, S. Justice says that this idea of the king as the audience of petitions in the shire courts helps to explain the rebels' allegiance to Richard II in 1381 (59).

21. J. R. Maddicott, "Parliament and the Constituencies," 61. B. Wilkinson agrees: "the early claim of the magnates to represent the interests of all the *regnum* became less and less acceptable, and indeed was less frequently advanced" (*Constitutional History of Medieval England, 1216–1399*, vol. III, 246).

22. H. Cam, "The Theory and Practice of Representation in Medieval England," 274.

be able to make promises that bound everyone in their localities. The power of attorney (*plena potestas* — literally "full power") that linked the people to their representatives did not depend on their having been elected by them. According to Philip Corrigan and Derek Sayer, "MPs represent all because they *speak* for all, not because they had been *chosen* by all."[23] What was important was that they did not speak only for themselves, which distinguished them from the lords in parliament. The *Modus Tenendi Parliamentum*, a fourteenth-century treatise on government, explains the predominance of the commons over the lords by saying that "each [of the magnates] is in Parliament for himself alone and for no one else." The source of a member of the commons' authority — the fact that their votes outweigh the lords' — is that he does not speak *per se*, but rather for "the whole *communitas* [community] of England."[24] Accordingly, in the *Modus Tenendi Parliamentum*, the name for the commons is *communitas*.

An important part of this history is a crucial change in the wording of the MPs' *plena potestas*, or power of attorney, the document that called the representatives of the localities to a session of parliament. In 1290, the summons of knights of the shire called them to appear "with full power for themselves and for all the community of the shire to counsel and consent, for themselves and for that community, *to those things which the earls, barons, and magnates aforesaid shall be led to agree on*" (emphasis mine).[25] By 1295, the formula had changed to require that the knights have "full and sufficient power for themselves and for the community of the aforesaid county . . . then and there for doing *what shall then be ordained by common counsel*" (emphasis mine).[26] In other words, at around the same time the parliament was becoming a conduit for petitions from the localities to the central government, the MPs were being freed from the will of the aristocrats and committed instead to the will of the nation as a whole.[27] In other words, "common counsel," the language about the community of the nation as a whole, was being used more frequently as the government was actually becoming more inclusive.

We have heard the language about the community as a whole uttered

23. P. Corrigan and D. Sayer, *The Great Arch: English State Formation as Cultural Revolution*, 29; emphasis mine.
24. Quoted by M. V. Clarke in *Medieval Representation and Consent*, 13.
25. B. Wilkinson, *Constitutional History of Medieval England*, vol. III, 307.
26. B. Wilkinson, *Constitutional History of Medieval England*, vol. III, 308.
27. The 1295 wording continued, with one minor addition, until 1872. For the importance of these changes in the wording of the summons, see J. G. Edwards, "The *Plena Potestas* of English Parliamentary Representatives," 146.

by kings, magnates, and villagers, each with different interests, casting it in different ways for different ends. Edward I, the king who invited the localities to address petitions to parliament, may have been soliciting complaints against his ministers and using public opinion against them.[28] In the process of refining the summons of the MPs to parliament, he and his legal counsellors were trying to ensure that decisions taken in parliament could be carried out, that his subjects, understanding their part in the decisions, would obey willingly. This was especially the case in matters of taxation. The evolution of the *plena potestas* was driven partly by the king's need for revenue: he increasingly described the parliament as the body that decided the interests of the realm as a whole, and the commons made it increasingly impossible to impose taxes without its approval.[29] He perhaps suffered this limitation on his power in the hope of obtaining ready compliance. It did not always work. For instance, the fact that the taxes imposed in the late 1370s and early 1380s were approved by the commons "for themselves and for the whole community of England"[30] did not prevent the Rising of 1381 that was motivated in large part by people's feeling that they were overtaxed. But the language of the *plena potestas* shows the crown trying to use the idea of the community of the whole for its own benefit.[31]

Different people and groups in different social strata were self-interestedly wielding the idea that everyone had some stake in the commonweal and thus some responsibility for protecting it. The idea was commandeered by those seeking to rule as well as those seeking to influence or resist their rulers. Its role in applying both descending and ascending political pressure indicates the importance it acquired in later political developments. It was important as well for providing a context in which writers could not only discuss the issue of commonweal but also address an audience that was attuned to it.

28. This hypothesis is controversial among historians. Maddicott defends it in "Parliament and the Constituencies," 64–68.

29. J. R. Lander, *The Limitations of English Monarchy in the Later Middle Ages*, 7. J. G. Edwards also argues for this link in "The *Plena Potestas* of English Parliamentary Representatives," 141.

30. This formulation is from the grant of a subsidy on certain commodities in 1379 (C. Stephenson and F. G. Marcham, eds. and trans., *Sources of English Constitutional History*, no. 63C, 236).

31. The language of the community as a whole appears, among other places, in the coronation oath of Edward II (1308, "the community of your realm") and the Statute of York (1322, "the whole community of the realm"), which restored Edward's power after it had been restricted by the Ordinances of 1311. C. Stephenson and F. G. Marcham, eds. and trans., *Sources of English Constitutional History*, no. 55, 192, and no. 58, 205.

News: Information Exchange and Political Dialogue

In order for people to feel connected to the community of the whole, they had to know what was going on in other parts of it, especially in London and Westminster. Politics stirred the appetite for news and depended on its flow. According to George Sayles, by the thirteenth century there was widespread interest in parliament and well-established channels for disseminating information about it. "There was no difficulty in acquiring information, for England was a much governed and busy country with a remarkable criss-cross of messengers, professional messengers, traveling regularly between London — or where the court, chancery, and the king's bench happened to be — and the local regions."[32] After the parliamentary petitions opened a channel of communications that carried information in both directions between the seat of government and the provinces, not only did the petitions travel from the localities to London, but announcements of parliamentary actions also traveled back.[33]

There is even more evidence of the information traffic in the fourteenth century.[34] Early in the reign of Edward III, MPs asked for written accounts of the deposition of Edward II to take back to their constituents, along with the reports of actions on petitions.[35] The fact that parliament had a role in the deposition made the hunger for news even more urgent.

As parliament gained more of a role in taxation, that, too, increased people's desire to know and the MPs' need to tell them to garner support for their actions. Since the *plena potestas* bound the constituents to their representatives' actions, the news of those actions mattered. Proclamation of parliamentary actions became habitual, especially during the war with France, begun in 1337, which required support through taxation. Royal proclamations, too, became an important propaganda tool, with the government ordering sheriffs to publish them in many places by reading them

32. G. Sayles, *The King's Parliament of England*, 72. See also B. Guenée, *States and Rulers in Later Medieval Europe*, 132–34.

33. According to B. Lyon, *A Constitutional and Legal History of Medieval England* (414), the bringing of news from the communities to the capital was one of the purposes of parliament.

34. H. Cam, *Liberties & Communities in Medieval England*, 223–35.

35. J. R. Maddicott, "Parliament and the Constituencies," 81, 84. Also, H. Cam, *Liberties & Communities in Medieval England*, 226. Requests for news to be "publicly read and declared to the people" were repeated after the deposition of Richard II. B. Wilkinson, *Constitutional History of Medieval England, 1216–1399*, II, 310.

on market days, posting them, and depositing them with justices of the peace.[36] For instance, a statute of 1361 begins, "These are the measures which our lord the king, the prelates, the lords, and the commons have ordained in this present parliament . . . , to be observed and publicly proclaimed throughout the kingdom."[37] The localities, thus informed, also became the sites of criticism and dissent, which was voiced in public meetings by participants of varying status.[38]

Because of the increase in literacy and the resurgence of English as the language of England, the publication of news, opinion, and propaganda through writing increased. According to Steven Justice, in the last quarter of the fourteenth century, broadsides began to be posted and circulated as part of public political conversations. Justice believes that the texts known as John Ball's letters were published as broadsides.[39] While they may have been a tool of organization for the rebels, they were also in themselves an act of rebellion. As Justice says, the rebels "sought command, command of their own collective lives and of the institutions that constrained them. And so they sought its medium: writing they could promulgate, could give effect in the political world."[40]

More elite "rebels" also used written documents in their struggle: as part of their campaign during their attack on Richard II's advisers, the Appellants wrote an open letter to the citizens of London defending their actions. They also announced their charges against the advisers and spread rumors about Richard's dealings with the king of France.[41] In the fifteenth century, there is even more evidence of the circulation of not only letters and broadsides (and letters as broadsides) but also newsletters, handbills, pamphlets, and political poems and prophecies. Some expressed opposition to the government, and some were the government's attempts to counter

36. J. R. Maddicott, "The County Community and the Making of Public Opinion in Fourteenth-Century England," 33–38.

37. C. Stephenson and F. G. Marcham, *Sources of English Constitutional History*, I, no. 62, 230. Sheriffs were often told to keep records of such public proclamations and return them to the chancery (J. R. Maddicott, "The County Community and the Making of Public Opinion in Fourteenth-Century England," 35). Undoubtedly they wanted to use the announcements to their advantage. Also, failure to record and publish laws was deemed a serious abuse of government (F. Thompson, *First Century of Magna Carta*, 32–33).

38. J. R. Maddicott, "The County Community and the Making of Public Opinion in Fourteenth-Century England," 39.

39. S. Justice, *Writing and Rebellion*, 29. See also 77.

40. S. Justice, *Writing and Rebellion*, 66.

41. R. H. Jones, *The Royal Policy of Richard II*, 45. The letter is reproduced in Henry Knighton, *Chronicon Henrici Knighton vel Cnitthon Monachi Leycestrensis*, ed. J. R. Lumby, vol. II, 246–47.

opposition.[42] News and interpretation of news therefore played an important role in the circuit established by efforts to influence the superior political authorities and the subordinate citizenry.

Colin Richmond draws together some of the themes I have been developing thus far:

> Not only are "central" and "local" meaningless terms within so small a country, which by the fifteenth century had been much and closely governed for five hundred years, the personnel at Westminster and in the localities overlapped, intermingled, interconnected. That is why and how information was conveyed to and fro so freely, so casually. Everyone, or almost everyone who was anyone, was in the know. This was open government.[43]

This ready circulation of news and opinion helped to create the political nation, foster political dialogue, and make England a fertile ground for the literature that is the subject of this book.[44]

Limitations on the King: Deposition and the Memory of Deposition

> A great part of the constitutional history of England in the medieval period might be said . . . to be a commentary, not upon *Magna Carta*, but upon the simple fact of the king's crying need for counsel and ever more counsel.[45]

Some of the limits on the king's power are implicit in the previous sections, especially in discussions of the development of parliament and the concept of the community as a whole. But in fact the origin of the limits on the king lie in an even earlier source, in the original Germanic conception of the king in feudal law. According to F. Kern, "The relationship between monarch and subject in all Germanic communities was expressed by the idea of mutual fealty, not by that of unilateral obedience. . . . Fealty was

42. J. R. Lander, *The Limitations of English Monarchy in the Later Middle Ages*, 45–47. See also C. Ross, "Rumour, Propaganda and Popular Opinion during the Wars of the Roses."
43. C. Richmond, "Hand and Mouth: Information Gathering and Use in England in the Later Middle Ages," 243.
44. See also J. Coleman, *Medieval Readers and Writers: 1350–1400*; P. R. Coss, "Aspects of Cultural Diffusion in Medieval England: The Early Romances, Local Society and Robin Hood;" R. F. Green, *Poets and Princepleasers*; and V. J. Scattergood, *Politics and Poetry in the Fifteenth Century*.
45. S. B. Chrimes, *English Constitutional Ideas in the Fifteenth Century*, 39.

binding upon the subject only so long as the monarch also fulfilled his duty."[46] This mutuality is the ancestor of the centuries-long conflict between the different parts of the realm that resulted when different groups sought to ensure, consolidate, or increase their power. In fact, a great deal of the history of English medieval government can be seen as the conflict between the king's search for more power, even to the extent of absolutism in some cases, and various subjects' search for the means to exercise their rights to participate in the political process and to resist what they saw as injustice.

I have already alluded to some of the manifestations of this conflict. In Magna Carta the magnates insisted on their right to advise the king, but the larger and more complex the government grew, the more the king tended to surround himself with experts and specialists. As we will see, these are the kinds of the stresses and strains that destroyed the rule of Richard II.[47] Although the council "was above all an instrument of the ruler,"[48] advice itself was used to constrain his actions. And parliament often had the opportunity to choose between alliance with the king and alliance with the magnates, triangulating in a way that has kept modern historians arguing about whether parliament's true role was oppositional or not (see the discussion of the parliamentary commons in Chapter 1).

The most extreme and violent examples of subjects' resistance to their monarch are the depositions of kings. According to William Huse Dunham, Jr. and Charles Wood, the five depositions in the last two centuries of the Middle Ages "created a doctrine of restraint upon the regal power that eventually became a part of England's constitutional or public law."[49] This *de facto* doctrine of the depositions had already been voiced in theory by political writers. In the middle of the twelfth century (1154–59), for instance, John of Salisbury justified the killing of tyrants by citing Biblical examples.[50] In the early fourteenth century (1324), Marsilius of Padua wrote that since the people are the true source of political authority, they must be the ones to elect, criticize, and, in some cases, remove the head of

46. F. Kern, *Kingship and the Law in the Middle Ages*, 135. In fact, some thought a wronged subject had a right, even a duty, to rebel. J. G. Bellamy, *The Law of Treason in England in the Later Middle Ages*, 10. Along with this conception of the king as feudal lord, there was also in England the idea that the king was the ruler of all the people. On the right to remove a tyrannical king, see B. Guenée, *States and Rulers in Later Medieval Europe*, 84–86.

47. B. Wilkinson, *Constitutional History of Medieval England*, vol. III, 27.

48. B. Wilkinson, *Constitutional History of Medieval England*, vol. III, 25.

49. W. H. Dunham, Jr. and C. Wood, "The Right to Rule in England: Depositions and the Kingdom's Authority, 1327–1485," 738.

50. John of Salisbury, *Policraticus*, VIII.20.

the government.[51] But the doctrine might have remained wholly theoretical if the actual depositions had never happened.

For my purposes in this book, the first deposition, that of Edward II in 1327, was the most important. The attempts to give it a parliamentary patina and the publication of the news to garner support for it made it a national event. The memory of it haunted — or I should say, was made to haunt — subsequent kings, including his son, Edward III, and his great-grandson, Richard II, who was himself deposed at the end of the century. The reign of Henry IV, who deposed Richard, was in turn haunted by his own demonstration of the possibility of removing a reigning monarch. As we will see in more detail in later chapters, both Edward III and Richard II were pointedly reminded of Edward II by critical magnates who were putting strong pressure on them. In both these crises, the threats of deposition were credible and the dissatisfactions of those who made them were widely known. The shadow of Edward II's deposition was long.[52]

As we will see later (Chapters 5 and 7), a number of these crises in governance not only were between the king and his advisers but were often said to be about the king's very choice of men to advise him. Behind S. B. Chrimes's rather mild statement that forms the epigraph to this section lies a good deal of political turmoil as kings and people struggled over sovereignty.

Limitations on Speech in Parliament

We have now seen a number of ways by which subjects pressured and tried to constrain their ruler — advice, propaganda, parliamentary opposition, and the threat of deposition. Kings also had an arsenal of weapons to try to control subjects, some of them honed in response to upward pressure from the subjects. According to J. G. Bellamy, English kings turned increasingly to Roman law (rather than the Germanic feudal law of mutual fealty) to bolster their position against assertive subjects.[53] Although none succeeded in becoming the absolute monarch of a theocratic state, one of the attempts

---

51. *Marsilius of Padua*, vol.II, *Defensor Pacis*, i.18.3, 87–88. See A. Gewirth's commentary, vol. I, 238. On medieval theories of deposition or tyrannicide in John of Salisbury, Thomas Aquinas, and John of Paris, see A. Monahan, *Consent, Coercion and Limit*, 68–69, 174–77, 197–200. Also see B. Guenée, *States and Rulers in Later Medieval Europe*, 84–88.

52. Perhaps Richard's campaign to have Edward II canonized (M. McKisack, *The Fourteenth Century*, 498) was an attempt to make it less threatening by making Edward a martyr.

53. J. G. Bellamy, *The Law of Treason in England in the Later Middle Ages*, 9–14.

to limit subjects' incursions on their power was the limitation on what MPs could say in parliament. Some of the cases were well enough known to have affected the general climate for political speech, which may in turn have affected literary writers who wanted to comment on the king and his actions.

The idea that members of parliament should be free to say what they pleased in commons was not stated explicitly until 1451.[54] Even then, when it had already been the subject of struggle in the parliament for at least a century and a half, it was not perfectly secure. We know about the struggle because there were times when members were punished for what they said in parliament—even in closed meetings. There was discussion of the need for discretion, though secrecy was compromised when the clerk of the commons was a chancery clerk who owed his first allegiance to the king. Not surprisingly, therefore, there were also pleas to the king not to listen to any except the commons' official spokesman.[55]

These requests are signs of uneasiness about speech in parliament, and though it is hard to know the impact of a few events on the daily conduct of business, the uneasiness was not entirely unfounded: In 1306, when his identity was finally revealed, Henry of Keighley was jailed for having put forward in 1301 a petition in commons that impugned the intentions of the king. He was not released until May 31, 1307.[56] Two cases later in the century also show what there was to fear from offended monarchs.

THE CASE OF PETER DE LA MARE

The case of Sir Peter de la Mare received a great deal of public attention and had long-standing effects. Its fascination lies in the fact that the account of it in the *Anonimalle Chronicle* gives us a picture of the creation of the position of "speaker of the commons" and testifies to popular interest in the case. This royal attempt to punish speech was known outside governmental circles. According to the chronicle, the people did not take the king's side, and de la Mare was lucky enough to live into a new reign and to be vindicated.

The commons took an active role in the Good Parliament of 1376,

54. J. E. Neale, "The Commons' Privilege of Free Speeech in Parliament," 154–55; H. G. Richardson, "The Commons and Medieval Politics," 45.

55. H. G. Richardson, "The Commons and Medieval Politics," 45.

56. For this case, see G. O. Sayles, *The King's Parliament of England*, 102.

perhaps even initiating the impeachments of Lord Latimer and Richard Lyons.[57] As the commons conferred, they designated Sir Peter to convey the results of their deliberations to the lords. They agreed that "what Sir Peter should speak by their direction all would approve and maintain."[58] John of Gaunt, the duke of Lancaster, seems to have understood the principle, asking,

Quel de vous avera la parlaunce et pronunciacion de ceo qe vous avez ordine parentre vous?

Which of you is the spokesman of what has been agreed among you?[59]

and later, simply "Qi parlera?" ("Who will speak?").[60] Since Lancaster was the powerful leader of the ruling party, which had had control of the council because of Edward III's age and weakness, even answering the question must have taken some courage. De la Mare not only answered, but delivered stinging indictments of several of the king's counsellors, who, along with the king's mistress Alice Perrers, were removed.[61]

The Good Parliament was a vivid demonstration of the commons' power, but its results were short-lived, and Sir Peter de la Mare was arrested and jailed for his prominent part in it, probably at the instigation of Alice Perrers and other targets of the Good Parliament.[62] He was released at the beginning of Richard II's reign, reelected to parliament, and again chosen as speaker. In the parliament of 1377, he began his speech to the king with a "protestation," a speech reminding the king that he spoke for the commons and not himself. Such protestations were often repeated by speakers in the following years.[63] Given that he had recently paid the penalty for being held particularly responsible for the commons' actions, it is small wonder that he claimed "that what he had to say was not said on his own personal account,

57. M. McKisack, *The Fourteenth Century*, 393.
58. "et ceo qe le dit sire Peirs dirroit par lour avyse toutz deverount assenter et ses dites mayntener." This is from the *Anonimalle Chronicle*, ed. V. H. Galbraith, 83. It is translated in A. R. Myers, ed., *English Historical Documents, 1327–1485*, no. 46, 119; and C. Stephenson and F. G. Marcham, eds., *Sources of English Constitutional History*, 611, 222. B. Wilkinson prints some of the story in *Constitutional History of Medieval England, 1216–1399*, II.221–23.
59. *Anonimalle Chronicle*, ed. V. H. Galbraith, 83; A. R. Myers, *English Historical Documents, 1327–1485*, 119.
60. *Anonimalle Chronicle*, ed. V. H. Galbraith, 85.
61. B. Lyon, *A Constitutional and Legal History of Medieval England*, 490, 560.
62. J. S. Roskell, *Parliament and Politics in Late Medieval England*, Vol. II, 8.
63. J .S. Roskell, *The Commons and Their Speakers in English Parliaments*, chapter 2.

but by the initiative, assent, and express will of all the commons there assembled."[64] The tradition of speaker's protestations, which de la Mare began in these very poignant circumstances, underlines the vulnerability of those who spoke *for* commons and perhaps of those who spoke *in* commons at a time when their rights to do so freely were by no means guaranteed.[65]

De la Mare's arrest was known outside of parliament and widely criticized, as we can see from the riot in 1377 during which Londoners defended their bishop against John of Gaunt when he came to defend his protégé John Wyclif. During the riot, which showed Gaunt's unpopularity after his actions against the Good Parliament of 1376, a priest who said de la Mare ought to have been hung was mauled; he later died. The crowd demanded that de la Mare be freed.[66] And according to the St. Albans chronicler, when de la Mare, newly released from captivity, returned to London to thank Richard II, he was greeted with acclaim like that given to Becket returning from exile in France.[67] The comparison to Becket is significant, since the troubles that led Becket to France in the first place were the result of his conflict with his king. De la Mare seems to have had popular support as he fought for the commons' right to speak frankly while trying to obtain good government.

THE CASE OF THOMAS HAXEY

The case of Thomas Haxey demonstrates Richard II's desire, late in his reign, to prevent criticism of his rule. In 1397, Haxey, a cleric representing an abbot, wrote a bill complaining about the size and extravagance of

64. *Rotuli Parliamentorum*, III, 5; E. Lodge and G. A. Thornton, eds., *English Constitutional Documents: 1307–1485*, 152. C. Stephenson and F. G. Marcham, eds., *Sources of English Constitutional History*, 63A, 232–33.

65. In 1378, the speaker asked to be excused of anything that appeared to be "esclaundre" or "vilanie de nostre seigneur le roi" (S. B. Chrimes and A. L. Brown, *Select Documents of English Constitutional History, 1307–1485*, no. 105, 118). These apologies look forward to restrictions on speech that we will examine in the next section, including slander laws and the Statute of Treasons. The speaker's need for such protestations does not mean that there were not occasionally plain speakers in parliament who were not tolerated and even valued. As A. L. Brown notes of the careers of Sir Arnold Savage, speaker in 1401 and 1404, and Sir John Tiptoft, speaker in 1406: "Loyal criticism was apparently acceptable, at least to Henry IV" ("Parliament, c. 1377–1422," 138). But speakers did not have the right to criticize with impunity.

66. In fact there were rumors that de la Mare had been sentenced to death. J. S. Roskell, *Parliament and Politics in Late Medieval England*, vol. II, 8–9.

67. J. S. Roskell, *Parliament and Politics in Late Medieval England*, vol. II, 8–9 and *The Commons and Their Speakers in English Parliaments, 1376–1523*, 122.

the king's household. The enraged Richard demanded that the speaker of the commons tell him who had presented the bill and that the lords try him. They did so, and convicted Haxey of treason for inciting the commons and anyone else against the household.[68] He was deprived of all his property and sentenced to death. Because of the protection of the Archbishop of Canterbury, he was not executed, and he lived until Richard was deposed. At parliament's request, he was exonerated by Henry IV in 1399.

Both the trial itself and the reversal of its results are vivid moments in the struggle over parliamentary speech. It is hard to forget the commons' obsequious apology to Richard for Haxey's criticisms and their affirmation of Richard's liberty:

Then, by the king's order, the commons came before the king in parliament; and there, with all the humility and obedience of which they were capable, they expressed deep grief, as appeared from their demeanour, that the king had formed such an opinion of them. And they humbly besought the king to hear and accept their apology: that it had never been their intention or will to express, present, or do anything which would offend or displease the king's royal majesty, *or would contravene his royal estate and liberty*, either in this matter concerning his own person and the government of his household, [in that] concerning the lords and ladies in his company, or in any other matter touching [the king] himself; for they well knew and understood that such matters pertained to them not at all, but solely to the king himself and to his [power of] ordinance.[69]

One version of Haxey's petition for exoneration in the first parliament of Henry IV's reign (there are two in the parliamentary roll) included as reasons for overturning the judgment the fact that it violated the "customs" of the commons and that overturning it would provide for "the salvation of the liberties of the said commons" ("salvation des Libertees de lez ditz communes").[70] Henry responded that the judgment against Haxey should be "utterly quashed, reversed, repealed, and annulled, and be held as of no force or effect," and that Haxey should be restored to his reputation and property. But despite the emphatic vindication of Haxey personally, Henry does not affirm the commons' rights to free speech.

68. M. McKisack, *The Fourteenth Century*, 477.

69. Emphasis mine; C. Stephenson and F. G. Marcham, *Sources of English Constitutional History*, 63H, 241; another translation of it appears in A. R. Myers, *English Historical Documents*, no. 69, 168. Parliament was in fact docile throughout the period of 1397–98 as Richard was acting on his desires for absolute rule. See J. S. Roskell's *The Commons and Their Speakers in English Parliaments, 1376–1523* (134) for examples in the second parliament of 1397 and the first of 1398.

70. *Rotuli Parliamentorum*, III. 434; C. Stephenson and F. G. Marcham, *Sources of English Constitutional History*, 66A, 257. Also printed in E. Lodge and G. A. Thornton, eds., *English Constitutional Documents, 1307–1485*, 159.

Historians disagree about the significance of these events. According to Bryce Lyon, the case affirmed "the right of freedom of debate" and of the commons' immunity; it was cited later as a precedent for the right of free speech.[71] But J. S. Roskell, concentrating on the case itself, not its later use, believes that the commons' objection to the conviction in 1399 was based on legal irregularities (e.g., retrospective application of a new definition of treason). Since Haxey was not a member of parliament at the time of his bill, he could not claim the limited immunity of members, which, in any case, did not apply in cases of treason.[72] Roskell notices King Henry's omission of any mention of the commons' liberties in his reply and concludes that the outcome of the case "cannot be regarded as even implying (how much less as containing) an official admission that the Commons were entitled to the privilege of free speech amongst themselves."[73]

This disagreement encapsulates the general debate among historians about the role of the commons, of which the underlying issue, as we saw in Chapter 1, is whether opposition to the king was possible in the Middle Ages. The lesson we can draw, and that contemporaries might have drawn from both parts of this drama, is just how dependent the commons' "liberties" during this period were on the personality of the king, his actual political situation, and his perception of it. This lesson is all the clearer when we remember that Richard II tried to punish Haxey at the end of his reign, although his advisers had allowed the vindication of Sir Peter de la Mare at the beginning of it. Those who were politically active had no clearly defined rights. They were thus subject to the uncertainties of royal whim, but royal power was uncertain, too. I doubt that the knowledge that the king occasionally could not or would not retaliate made speakers and writers any more secure. The shifting landscape of power made speaking and writing about politics a risky enterprise.

Limitations on Nonparliamentary Speech

After the Good Parliament, John of Gaunt was harrassed by angry citizens who implied that he was a traitor, a commoner, and not English. Gaunt enlisted help from the Bishop of Bangor, who threatened the citizens with

71. B. Lyon, *A Constitutional and Legal History of Medieval England*, 559.
72. E. Lodge and G. A. Thornton print the 1404 exemption, *English Constitutional Documents: 1307–1485*, 161.
73. J. S. Roskell, *The Commons and Their Speakers in English Parliaments*, 41.

excommunication, and from the king himself, who threatened them with death.[74] Negotiations produced some reparations (they included the deposition of the mayor of London), but the writers of anonymous lampoons spread around the city escaped punishment only because they were not apprehended.[75]

Prohibitions on speech were strengthened in the aftermath of the Good Parliament. Acting partly in response to John of Gaunt's feeling that he had been maligned, parliament in 1379 affirmed an old law from 1275 against the crime of *scandalum magnatum*. The statute makes speech critical of peers treasonous, even if it would not be so labeled if it concerned an ordinary person. When the chancellor introduced the statute to parliament, he explained that there were in the kingdom "bacbyters" who tell "fauxes, horribles, et perilouses mensonges des Seigneurs et autres" ("false, horrible, and dangerous lies about lords and others").[76] In presenting the bill the chancellor was acknowledging that speech could be dangerous and recognizing its power by labeling it treason. In one of the cases that invoked the statute, John Cavendish, a fishmonger, was fined 1,000 marks in 1384 for accusing Michael de la Pole, the chancellor, of bribery.[77] Although the statute was not used often in the Middle Ages, it was reaffirmed again in 1389 — after Richard had declared himself of age and reasserted control over the government — extending liability, if the originator of the defamation escaped detection, to those who disseminated it.[78]

Though *scandalum magnatum* was one of the few laws that could provide the grounds for defamation cases in the king's court, ecclesiastical and local courts offered places where people could sue each other over speech.[79] According to Carl Lindahl, slander, even in private places, was considered a social matter because everyone was deceived by untruths and because untruths might stir up social unrest not only between individuals but also between groups.[80] Lindahl finds that even when magnates and government officials were not involved, slander laws were used in London to enforce

74. V. J. Scattergood, *Politics and Poetry in the Fifteenth Century*, 21.

75. J. Barnie, *War in Medieval English Society*, 142–43. Barnie tells this story in a valuable appendix on "The Dangers of Political Comment in Fourteenth-Century England."

76. R. S. Roskell, *Parliament and Politics in Late Medieval England*, vol. I, Chapter IV, 47.

77. M. McKisack, *The Fourteenth Century*, 437; W. Holdsworth, *A History of English Law*, vol. III, 409; McKisack and Holdsworth each list a few other cases.

78. W. Holdsworth, *A History of English Law*, vol. III, 409.

79. W. Holdsworth, *A History of English Law*, vol. III, 410. R. H. Helmholz, ed., *Select Cases on Defamation to 1600*, lxvii–lxxii.

80. C. Lindahl, *Earnest Games: Folkloric Patterns in the Canterbury Tales*, 74–78.

hierarchy: "In 85 percent of the cases, social inferiors were punished for offending people of greater rank."[81] Even apart from *scandalum magnatum*, London was a place in which it was best to mind one's tongue.

Being on guard was especially prudent when one referred to the king, who had no need of scandal laws. There are a number of examples of the king's power to punish or at least threaten those who spoke against him. For instance, William Mildenhall was accused in chancery in 1391 of concealing the fact that his father had spoken disrespectfully of Richard. He was released on condition that he speak well of the king and report any who did not.[82] According to Adam of Usk, Richard imprisoned a monk for preaching about his follies,[83] and at his deposition Richard was accused of arresting another man who criticized him.[84] At the very height of his troubles with the Appellants, Richard issued a royal proclamation forbidding anyone to speak ill of the advisers whom the Appellants had attacked.[85]

After Richard's deposition, claiming to have seen him alive and acknowledging him as rightful king became treasonous offenses. A friar was executed in 1402 for doing so and for undermining Henry's claim to have rights to the throne based not only on "conquering," but also on inheritance and election.[86]

The king's ultimate weapon against his enemies was the 1352 Statute of Treasons, which prohibited speaking not about the life of the king, but about his death. Intended to clarify the definition of treason, it includes the expected prohibitions against making war on the king, aiding his enemies, counterfeiting the currency, or killing high government officials. But it also includes a curious clause saying that it will be considered treason

quant homme fait compasser ou ymaginer la mort nostre Seignur le Roi, ma dame sa compainge, ou de lour fitz primer et heir.

[i]f a man compasses or imagines the death of our lord the king, or our lady his consort, or of their eldest son and heir.[87]

81. C. Lindahl, *Earnest Games*, 78.
82. C. Barron, "The Quarrel of Richard II with London 1392–7," 179–80.
83. Adam of Usk, *Chronicon Adae de Usk*, ed. E. M. Thompson, 135.
84. J. G. Bellamy, *The Law of Treason in England in the Later Middle Ages*, 144–45.
85. *The Westminster Chronicle, 1381–1394*, 214–17.
86. V. S. Galbraith translates the supposed colloquy between Henry and the friar in *Kings and Chroniclers*, 234.
87. *Statutes of the Realm*, I, 319 f.; E. Lodge and G. A. Thornton, *English Constitutional Documents: 1307–1485*, 22; C. Stephenson and F. G. Marcham, *Sources of English Constitutional History*, 62F, 227.

This self-consuming artifact (upon hearing it, how can one help but imagine the death of the king?[88]) may be yet another echo of the deposition of Edward II. Like *scandalum magnatum*, the Statute of Treasons was little used but often reaffirmed.[89] Henry IV, insecure on the throne because of the way he acquired it and beset by rebellions, used the statute a number of times, as did later kings during the Wars of the Roses.[90] It hovered over the struggle between Richard II and the Appellants in the 1380s. The *Westminster Chronicle* reports that before they charged the royal favorites with treason, the Appellants declared before the whole parliament that they had never imagined the death of the king.[91] Richard does not seem to have been convinced, because in 1397 he had the parliament enact another treason bill, including the compassing clause, which he then used against the Appellants.[92]

There were only a few cases in which treasonous action did not accompany treasonous imagination, but in theory no action was necessary: Words were enough.[93] For this reason, the statute must have been one of the causes of the generally uninviting context for political speech in the later Middle Ages. Specific forms of political speech, especially political prophecies (1402), were also outlawed, and there were a number of celebrated cases that punished writers for criticizing leaders, including the king. The blinding of Lucas de la Barre in 1124, the humorous chastisement of Roger Baston in 1314, the Bishop's threats against the lampooners of John of Gaunt in 1377 (see above), and the grisly execution (by methods used against traitors) of John Holton in 1456 for writing "bills" criticizing the king, and of Wyllyam Collyngbourne in 1484 for writing a couplet derisive of the king and several advisers all lead V. J. Scattergood to conclude that the "writing of political verse was dangerous for those in any way critical of

88. On such prohibitions, see Michael Holquist, "Introduction. Corrupt Originals: The Paradox of Censorship," 14–15.

89. The United States has statutes and case law on the issue of threats to the president or "political hyperbole" that can be seen as threats, as we were reminded when Senator Jesse Helms said that if President Clinton were to visit a North Carolina military base, "He'd better have a bodyguard." Daniel Pollitt, "Courts have taken many 'threats' seriously," (Raleigh) *News and Observer*, December 2, 1994.

90. J. G. Bellamy, *The Law of Treason in England in the Middle Ages*, chapters 5 and 6; S. Rezneck, "Constructive Treason by Words in the Fifteenth Century."

91. The verbs are "consenserunt, cogitarunt aut ymaginarunt." *Westminster Chronicle*, ed. and trans. L. C. Hector and B. F. Harvey, 234–35.

92. J. G. Bellamy, *The Law of Treason in England in the Later Middle Ages*, 114.

93. J. G. Bellamy, *The Law of Treason in England in the Later Middle Ages*, 106, 116–18, 121–24, 161. See also S. Rezneck, "Constructive Treason by Words in the Fifteenth Century," 546.

the régime."[94] If anything, the sanctions increased in the fifteenth century. As the circulation of news and propaganda increased (see "News: Information Exchange and Political Dialogue," above), pursuit of poets and heretics became even more enthusiastic.[95] The more political writing there was, the more dangerous it seemed.

Writing was not a prerequisite for getting into trouble for political discourse. The day after John Ball was executed in St. Albans for his part in the Rising of 1381, John Shirle was arrested in Cambridge for holding forth in a tavern about the injustice of the sentence. According to the indictment against Shirle, he did a thorough job of offending officials of the government, many of whom had been targets of the rising itself: He claimed that "the stewards of the lord the king as well as the justices and many other officers and ministers of the king were more deserving to be drawn and hanged and to suffer other lawful pains and torments than John Balle."[96] One of the insights the case affords us is the speed with which the news of Ball's death traveled from one place to another,[97] uniting them into a single political community through communication of news (see above, "News").[98] Another is the change from labeling Shirle's talk "worthless" to saying it consists of "threats" which "redound to the prejudice of the crown of the lord the king and to the contempt and manifest disturbance of the people." Although, according to the report against him, Shirle seems to have carefully avoided accusing the king, the court, no doubt thinking of the rising, sees the danger posed to the king by social unrest stirred up against his government. According to Ralph Hanna III, the paradox is that, despite denigrating Shirle's "silly" speech, the court intensifies the voice of "*dis-turbing*" discontent by noticing the threat the speech contains.[99]

Considering these destabilizing kinds of speech, it is no wonder that medieval governments used sanctions against it to try to follow Aristotle's advice to Alexander in the *Secretum Secretorum*:

94. V. J. Scattergood, *Politics and Poetry in the Fifteenth Century*, 21. For an early Renaissance account of Collynbourne, his couplet, and his death as a traitor, see Robert Fabyan, *The New Chronicles of England and France in Two Parts*, ed. H. Ellis, 672.

95. On heretics, see H. G. Richardson, "Heresy and the Lay Power under Richard II"; and M. E. Aston, "Lollardy and Sedition, 1381–1431."

96. R. B. Dobson prints the indictment in the "Introduction to the Second Edition" of *The Peasants' Revolt of 1381*, xxviii–xxix.

97. R. B. Dobson, *The Peasants' Revolt of 1381*, xxix.

98. R. Hanna III, "Pilate's Voice/Shirley's Case," 797.

99. R. Hanna III, "Pilate's Voice/Shirley's Case," 799–800. Hanna disturbs the typography here to point out the connection between "disturb" and *turba*, a mob.

Contine te ergo ita ut nichil contra te possit dicere, et per hoc evitabis eorum facere.[100]

Strive to stop their tongues and thou shalt be safe from their actions. [101]

The Poets Speak of Silence:
The Trope of the Hidden Transcript

Writers themselves provide evidence of the dangers of critical speech. The rampant anonymity of medieval lyrics, including the poems of social protest, may testify to social critics' reluctance to be identified.[102] The so-called John of Bridlington explains his use of a pseudonym for his *Prophecies*: "I dare not set my name plainly in this letter, . . . firstly, because of the tongues of the envious, and secondly, because of the powers of the nobles; . . . for the envious malign an author, and the nobles, on account of anything detrimental written about them, hate him."[103] There are many warnings that critics are not welcomed, and that, as the anonymous poet of "On the Times" puts it, "Ho seythe truth he is schent."[104] Consequently, few can speak openly. Instead, oblique references to the hidden transcript — the fact that there is more that cannot be said — mark the lack of public debate.[105] For example, in *Piers Plowman*, Langland invites his audience to interpret the fable of the cat and the rats "for I ne dar" (Prologue.210). Although there are public issues to be discussed, poets often point to their inability to join in.

The result, significantly, is that the king lacks the information he needs to govern well: "The kyng knowyth not alle, / *non sunt qui vera loquuntur*" ("there are none who speak the truth").[106] This lament is the self-justifying but crippling theme of the anonymous poems *Richard the Redeless* and *Mum and the Sothsegger*, which are about events just after the deposition of

100. R. Steele and A. S. Fulton, eds., *Secretum Secretorum*, part I, chapter 15, 53 of Roger Bacon's Latin translation.

101. R. Steele and A. S. Fulton, eds., *Secretum Secretorum*, Fulton's English translation of the Arabic, discourse II, 188.

102. There are many interesting accounts of this poetry: e.g., R. H. Robbins, "Dissent in Middle English Literature"; and J. Coleman, *Medieval Readers and Writers: 1350–1400*.

103. T. Wright, ed., *Political Poems and Songs*, vol. I, 124. Quoted and translated in R. F. Green, *Poets and Princepleasers*, 164.

104. T. Wright, ed., *Political Poems and Songs*, vol. I, 271.

105. See the discussion of James C. Scott's *Domination and the Arts of Resistance: Hidden Transcripts* in Chapter 1.

106. T. Wright, ed., *Political Poems and Songs*, vol. I, 273.

Richard II and in the first ten years of the reign of Henry IV.[107] *Mum and the Sothsegger*, utterly convincing on the question of the king's need for information and the subject's duty to provide it, does not actually give the king much information because it is also utterly convincing on the dangers of doing so. It ends with the poet himself getting advice to write a book that will tell the king all the truths he needs to know to govern well by redressing the people's grievances.[108] It is hard to know whether the poet's adviser, the allegorical gardener, was urging him to write another book or whether the poem we have is, in fact, that very book. In any case, the poem is taken up more with the poet's unsuccessful search for a truth-teller than it is with abuses that need correcting, such as bribery. Along the way, he hears a great deal about the reasons to keep mum, since truth is so annoying it can bring bodily harm to its purveyor. As *Richard the Redeless* warns,

> . . . ho-so pleyned to the prince that pees shulde kepe,
> Of these mystirmen medlers of wrongis,
> He was lygh[t]liche ylaughte and y-luggyd of many,
> And y-mummyd on the mouthe and manaced to the deth.
> (Passus III.334–37)

> Whoever complained to the prince, who should keep the peace,
> By these men who are busy with wrong-doing
> He was quickly taken and baited by many
> And forcibly silenced and menaced with death.

In *Mum and the Sothsegger* too, the possibility that a frank speaker will "lose his life" or be "y-putte into prisone or y-pyned to deeth" (ll. 167–68) and Mum's warnings to the narrator to remain quiet "leste I soughte sorowe" (l. 581) and to "Be stille lest thou stumble" (l. 675) become even more vivid when the narrator sees a truth-teller who has been wounded (l. 847). No wonder that a truth-teller "Dyneth this day with Dreede" (l. 838).

The fact that the poem reads like a debate between Mum, who issues dire warnings of punishment, and the narrator and the gardener, who affirm the king's need for information about the realm and subjects' duty to

---

107. Helen Barr edits both in *The Piers Plowman Tradition*. M. Day and R. Steele edit them as fragments of a single work in *Mum and the Sothsegger*.

108. As we saw above (see "News: Information Exchange and Political Dialogue"), one of the functions of the knights of the shire was to bring such information to parliament. See B. Lyon, *A Constitutional and Legal History of Medieval England*, 414.

give it to him, may be part of the camouflage for the abuses the poem does reveal. The poem makes it clear that there is a need for camouflage since it is still risky to criticize the rule of Richard II even after he has been removed from the throne.

But, as we shall see, writers had their own ways to shield themselves from the risks of criticizing kings. One way to evade the crime of compassing was to turn to classical and Biblical stories: For instance, if one could not safely imagine the death of one's own king, one might turn to imagining the death of someone else's. The following chapters show how the mirrors for princes provide some of the camouflage materials, and how the writers and translators who were willing to use their names negotiated the dangerous terrain of public discourse in late medieval England.

3

The *Secretum Secretorum* and the Governance of Kings

By following [Aristotle's] good advice and obeying his commands, Alexander achieved his famous conquests of cities and countries, and ruled supreme in the regions of the earth far and wide, Arabs as well as Persians coming under his sway; nor did he ever oppose him in word or deed.

— "The Secret of Secrets" (176–77) [1]

These and manie other goodlie notable demonstraunces, admonishments, and doctrins, this victorius kinge shewed vnto this noble Prince and sonn, who w/t/h effect ensewed and followed . . . after the death of his Father, whereby he obtayned grace of our Lorde to obtaine to greate victories, and to manie glorious and incredible conquests through the helpe and succoure of our Lord, whereof he was never destitute.

— *The First English Life of King Henry the Fifth* (16) [2]

[An "Inconvience of Counsell"]: The Weakning of the Authority of Princes, as if they were lesse of Themselves.

— Sir Francis Bacon, *The Essayes or Counsells* (65)

THE FIRST TWO EPIGRAPHS for this chapter highlight the historical scope of the rhetoric of advice that shapes the relationship between Aristotle and Alexander in the ninth-century Arabic *Kitab sirr al-asrar* and that between Henry IV and his son, the future Henry V, in a sixteenth-century English royal biography. The two widely separated texts show surprising consonance in their claim for advice: If he follows the right advice, a ruler will rule successfully. By surrendering to the right adviser, a ruler will conquer

---

1. "The Translation from the Arabic: The Secret of Secrets," ed. A. S. Fulton. In *Opera hactenus inedita Rogeri Baconi . . . Secretum Secretorum . . . [and] Versio Anglicana ex Arabico*, ed. R. Steele and A. S. Fulton. Henceforth, the translation from the Arabic will be listed as "The Secret of Secrets," edited by A. S. Fulton.
2. Ed. C. L. Kingsford.

others. This is the paradox of advice that makes "the governance of princes" into a pun that permeates the *Fürstenspiegel* tradition. On the one hand, it is widely agreed that the mirrors for princes take the ruler's point of view because the writer is subordinate to and wants favor from the ruler.[3] He consequently humbles himself, flatters the ruler, and promotes the appropriately hierarchical view of society in which rulers exercise power and subjects obey. But on the other hand, the contrary premise is equally and more subversively fundamental to the genre: To rule well, the king must be ruled.[4]

There is another source of interference with the simple ideology of hierarchy and subjects' obedience: The genre is embedded with numerous smaller contradictions and paradoxes. The mirrors for princes are encyclopedic in nature and widely distributed geographically and temporally, and since many translators and editors added and subtracted material as they pleased, the works gathered contradictory accretions. In addition, the hierarchical model that the manuals seem to support is too simple to describe the actual relations between kings and advisers. For all these reasons, the advice manuals give conflicting advice and tell stories that slip away from their supposed morals. This chapter will examine the ideology of advice that the manuals claim to support and examine these two characteristics that allow for the ideology to be undermined — the need for the king to obey, and the works' tendency to deconstruct themselves. It will examine a number of versions of the *Secretum Secretorum*,[5] laying the foundation for the later chapters' more thorough readings of individual mirrors for princes.

The King Governing

The *Secretum Secretorum* seems to have been presented to rulers of various kinds, and its adoption of the ruler's point of view is often evident in the

3. On the Renaissance humanists' advice manuals "from the ruler's point of view," see Q. Skinner, *The Foundations of Modern Political Thought*, vol. I, 216.

4. One English translation of the *Secretum Secretorum* is called "The Governance of Lordschipes" (R. Steele, ed.); the same pun is in Hoccleve's title for his contribution to the genre, *The Regement of Princes*.

5. There are twelve published English translations of the *Secretum Secretorum*, two Latin translations, and an English translation of an Arabic version. In this chapter I will refer to any of these when they are relevant, while concentrating on "The Governance of Lordschipes" from MS. Lambeth 501 because it may be the earliest ("Soon after 1400") of the full-length English translations (R. Steele, *Three Prose Versions of the Secretum Secretorum*). I will usually label quotations from this translation with page numbers in parentheses in the text, and otherwise use the notes for references. I will defer most of my comments on James Yonge's translation for James Butler, earl of Ormonde, until the next chapter.

language of presentation. The "Governance of Lordschipes" (MS. Lambeth 501) is a translation of the Latin version of the *Secretum Secretorum* made for Guy de Vere of Valence, Bishop of Tripoli. In his dedicatory epistle, the man who translates the work from Arabic into Latin is humble and complimentary, as might be expected at such a moment. He styles himself "þe lest of [Guy's] clerks."[6] Guy, on the other hand, is a paragon of perspicacity:

As mikel as þe mone ys more shinynge þan þe oþer sterrys, and as þe bem of þe sonne ys moor bryght þan þe light of the mone, As mekyl þe clernesse of ȝoure wyt & þe depnesse of ȝoure conynge passys all men þat now er on any syde þe see, as wel Barbarys as Latyns yn litterure.

What is more, Guy possesses

þe clennesse of Noe, þe strenth of abraham, þe faith of ysaak, þe longe lastynge of Iacob, þe sofferynge of Moyse, þe stabilnesse of Iosue, þe deuocioun of hely, þe perfeccioun of helise, þe Benignite of dauid, þe wit of Salamon. . . . (41)

The list goes on. Embarrassingly. Guy is the culmination of Western civilization. This dedication is perhaps extreme, but valuable because it highlights the mirror for princes' partisanship. They are typically on the princes' side.

This partisanship shapes the work. For instance, the treatise discusses the risks of trust. There is no anxiety about whether or not advisers are being critical enough of rulers' pet projects. There is a great deal of anxiety about whether they have the rulers' welfare at heart or are just out for their own gain. Consequently, the treatise offers a test for avarice that will help sort out good counsellors from bad. The ruler is to fake a financial crisis to see whether the candidate for counsellor suggests using money from the treasury or extracting it from the subjects, or whether instead he proves his virtue by offering to contribute his own.[7]

In addition, the treatise lists people and things not to be trusted, including women, doctors (one should always seek a second opinion—in fact, many opinions), and poison. This colorful list culminates in Aristotle's reminiscences about how he saved Alexander from a poisonous woman by

6. He also asks that the reader believe, if there is something in the text he does not like, that it is due to the translator's "vnconynge & vnwyt," not "malyce" (R. Steele, ed., *Three Prose Versions*, 42). This wish is strikingly like Chaucer's Retraction at the end of the *Canterbury Tales*.

7. R. Steele and A. S. Fulton, 140 (Latin), and 236 (Arabic). For a version of this test in MS Lambeth 501, see R. Steele, *Three Prose Versions*, 102.

warning him: "the hete of fleschly kennynge with here" would have killed him.[8] The import of the story is that Aristotle's knowledge can rescue Alexander from the dangers offered by the world and his own instincts.

Aristotle also offers a story about a Magus and a Jew — one of the few extended narratives in most versions of the treatise — demonstrating the inadvisability of trusting someone of a different religion. It shows once again that Aristotle adopts Alexander's point of view, wishing to guard and protect him. This is also the purpose of the information on physiognomy that is supposed to help Alexander take the measure of others — their propensity toward laziness, lustfulness, greed, and so forth — by interpreting their outward appearances.

The Arabic version climaxes with recipes for a series of talismans that promise various forms of mastery. One subjugates nature: "the kingdom of the world will be thine."[9] Another is "a mighty secret"[10] that acquires "both the higher and the lower powers."[11] Another is so great that it replaces all others; Alexander needs "no other charm except this one alone."[12] However, the one Aristotle presents first is "the greatest secret."[13] Alexander is to make it from "the substance of Saturn, Jupiter, Mars, Venus, Mercury, and the moon" and turn it into a signet ring inlaid with a ruby engraved with the picture of a lion ridden by a crowned black man with wings. This miraculous icon is responsible for love and hate, it wards off evil, and it frightens one's enemies. But its most impressive property is that it guarantees the hierarchical social organization on which monarchy is based: "It secures the submission and obedience of the people."[14] The obedience of the people is the essence of the book. The talisman is the secret of secrets, and *The Secret of Secrets* in another form.

When it is not supplied by magic, it must be achieved by virtue, especially justice. The virtue is connected to natural order and presented in terms of its near-cosmic benefits:

It is through justice that the heavens stand over the earth. . . . And justice is the form of the reason which God gives to those most beloved of Him. It is with justice that

8. MS Lambeth 501, cap. 30. R. Steele, *Three Prose Versions*, 64. R. Steele and A. S. Fulton, eds., *Opera hactenus inedita . . . Secretum Secretorum*, 60 (Latin) and 191 (English translation of the Arabic text).

9. A. S. Fulton, "The Secret of Secrets," 259.

10. A. S. Fulton, 261.

11. A. S. Fulton, 262.

12. A. S. Fulton, 259.

13. A. S. Fulton, 258.

14. A. S. Fulton, 257.

the earth is populated, kingdoms are established, people become obedient, savages are tamed and the wild ones are civilized, distant ones are drawn near, souls become safe from destruction, and rulers become immune from all sorts of evils.[15]

Justice is like the talisman in that it is integral to the natural and supernatural hierarchy and gives rulers power that protects them.[16] But what the talisman provides in a supernatural, mystical, and permanent way, justice requires a ruler to earn over and over again.

In MS Lambeth 501, the only magic that procures obedience is the use of the seed of a special plant, and it must be fed to subjects individually. The general obedience of the people must be earned socially, not magically. But the treatment of justice, like that of the talisman, is presented from the point of view of the king. Justice, Aristotle tells Alexander in Royal 18 A.vii, is good for you:

Rightwisnes is forme and vndirstonding, whiche god made and sent to his creaturis. and bi rightwisnes was þe erthe bildid, and kyngis made to mayntene it, for it makith sugestis obeyshaunte, and prowde men meke, and savith the persones from harme, and therfore seyne men of ynde that Iustice of a good lord is bettir to þe pepille than the habundaunce of goodis of the erthe, and bettir than the reyne that fallith from hevene . . . ffor alle kyngis were made to mayntene Iustice and rightwisnes, for it is the helthe of sugetis.[17]

Righteousness makes subjects obedient and keeps "persones" safe. And not only is righteousness necessary to kings, kings are necessary for righteousness.[18] Aristotle's exhortations on behalf of justice and righteousness might in fact have been good for subjects. The behavior Aristotle recommends in the chapter of the Lambeth manuscript titled "Of obedyence" (how kings should earn subjects' obedience) might have made subjects' lives better (59). Most of the listings of the fifteen virtues of a good counsellor include various skills that a good counsellor has for restoring justice to the oppressed.[19] What I wish to emphasize here is that the argument is put very baldly in terms of the ruler's self-interest.

15. A. S. Fulton, 224. The Latin translation of this passage is on 123.

16. For instance, in MS Lambeth 501, the chapter on "right," or justice, appears between chapters on magic stones and the power of trees and those on the order of the universe and the heavenly spheres (R. Steele, ed., *Three Prose Versions*, 87–95).

17. MS Reg. 18 A. vij. B.M. (R. Steele, *Three Prose Versions*, cap. 58, 33).

18. R. Steele, cap. 58, 33.

19. In the Arabic, the relevant virtues are listed eleventh and fifteenth. A. S. Fulton, "The Secret of Secrets," 237–38. The Latin is on 142–43. A Middle English example of the list is in cap. 102 of MS Lambeth 501 (R. Steele, *Three Prose Versions*), 103–4.

Governing the King

But that presentation cannot disguise the fact that virtues are different from amulets in requiring something of the king. Except for the occasional promise that the amulets can confer virtue as well as power,[20] the virtue is more rigorous, demanding that the king act, sometimes in opposition to his own inclinations. Virtues are disciplines.

In fact, the very existence of the book is predicated on the fact that the king can't always get what he wants. Alexander, in the midst of a campaign against the Persians, summons Aristotle to his side for advice. Aristotle refuses to come, offering excuses, especially the feebleness of old age (MS Lambeth 501, 47). He sends the book instead, as a substitute for his presence. In other words, the book is born not only out of absence, like much writing, but out of disobedience. Alexander begins by being frustrated.

Furthermore, most translations start with effusive praise of Aristotle, whose position is analogous to that of the translator, and who therefore basks in the glory reflected by the glorious clerk. Aristotle also functions as a screen behind whom the translator can hide his criticisms of his patron. The elevation of Aristotle thus is an important initiating move in the treatises, many of which start with his brilliance and virtues and the angel who came to him to say "I sall name þe bettir Angel þan man" (47). What follows is the claim, as in the first epigraph at the start of this chapter, that Alexander was a successful ruler *because* he took Aristotle's advice:

Als longe als he leuyd was Alexander valiant by kepynge of his [Aristotle's] hale counseil, folowand his biddyngys; and for þat he conquerd Citee3, and hadde victory of all kyngdomes, and of all þe world he oon hadde chefe gouernaunce. . . . (47)

This principle is demonstrated by the story of the Persians. Because they are so reasonable that they can rule on their own, Alexander wants to kill them. After Aristotle's "biddyngys" to treat them with "debonertee" because it will result in their doing Alexander's "biddynges," Alexander acquiesces, and the Persians become the most "obeissaunt to hym of alle Naciuns" (48). The repetition of the word "biddings" outlines the paradoxical dynamic between the two men. In the mid-fifteenth-century Ashmole manuscript, the formulation is even starker because the repeated words are "comaundement/comaundementis."[21] But in both versions, the

20. In MS Lambeth 501, the stone makes virtue possible (R. Steele, *Three Prose Versions*, 88).
21. MS Ashmole 396 (M. A. Manzalaoui, ed., *Secretum Secretorum*, 28–29).

paradox of advice is clear: Alexander conquered the world because he was conquered by Aristotle.

This paradox is contained in the very advice to take advice, which makes a subject of the king: "[I]t is needfull that in alle thy werkys and needes, that thou haue good counseill. . . . And . . . trust nat so miche in thyne owne witte and in the height [of] thyn estate, but that thou take awise and counseill of othir."[22] The slightly condescending tone of this counsel may account for its being voiced by a king to his son. It therefore comes to the reader of the treatise filtered by both the angelic Aristotle and an ancient king, but it still diminishes not only the king's own intelligence but also the power of his office.

A large percentage of the Arabic version of the *Secretum Secretorum* and most of the translations are taken up by equally condescending advice about the conduct of ordinary life, including eating, sleeping, bathing, and dressing. It includes hygiene matters as small as when to clean one's teeth and comb one's hair. Since much of this material is an attempt to moderate the king's desires and schedule his activities, it constitutes a discipline of the kind Foucault describes as the regimen of prisoners in *Discipline and Punish: The Birth of the Prison*.[23] In the section on advice in the Arabic original, Aristotle even goes so far as to suggest that Alexander accept the advice that "is opposite to thine own desire."[24] Furthermore, many of the virtues recommended to Alexander, including mercy and pity, involve restraint of one kind or another. The closest thing to an exception to this disciplinary policy is the news that the season for sexual excess is spring, but even though excess is countenanced, it is regulated by limiting its duration. Furthermore, this hedged invitation to abandon moderation is present only in the Arabic. It is muted in the Latin and disappears entirely from the Middle English translations.[25] The Lambeth translator describes the natural beauties of spring in language suitable for lyric, but for the king he offers only suggestions on diet and medicine appropriate for the season. He notes the "stirynge of þy body" in spring, but only to suggest blood-letting and the use of purgatives (73).

Another attack on the "height" of the king's estate comes with some specific advice about how he should choose his counsellors. The story of

22. University College, Oxford MS. 85, M.A. Manzalaoui, ed., 368.

23. M. Foucault, *Discipline and Punish*, 6–7.

24. A. S. Fulton, ed., "The Secret of Secrets," 232.

25. The Arabic passage is in A. S. Fulton's translation, "The Secret of Secrets," 200. The Latin translation Steele offers in *Opera hactanus inedita Rogeri Baconi . . . Secretum Secretorum* promises sexual success in spring, but not excess (77).

the weaver's son who grew up to advise kings demonstrates that plane-
tary influence (i.e., individual nature) is more important than class origins.
Though his parents wanted to teach him "som craft of here wyrkynges,"
not even beatings could persuade him to take up weaving. Instead, he "put
him to folk of disceplyne, and he gat sciences, & knew cours and tyme vpon
heuenly þinges, & maners and gouernaill of kynges, and after bycome a
greet conseyller" (100). Another story tells of a king's son who could not
learn the art of ruling but insisted instead on becoming a blacksmith (100).
These two reciprocal stories have the effect of lowering the king's status by
putting him on the same level as the lower classes.

This egalitarian principle is stated more boldly in the list of the fifteen
virtues of a good counsellor. Among other things, a good counsellor keeps
an open court and receives people to hear their complaints and redress their
grievances. He treats all people alike because they are created equal, removing all injustice and

nullam penitus faciens differenciam in personis et gradibus hominum quos Deus
creavit eqaules.[26]

making no difference at all between persons and ranks of men whom God created
equal.

This claim might even seem to be an oxymoron.[27] How can there be ranks
if God created all men equal? The passage could possibly be saying that
distinctions should be made only between ranks, not within them, since
men of one rank are equal. The grammatical difference in modern English
between restrictive and nonrestrictive clauses might have helped if it had
been available: "One should not distinguish between those *particular* persons and ranks that God made equal" versus "one should not distinguish
between *any* persons or ranks because God made *all* of them equal." But
this grammatical rule does not help us interpret the phrase, since it was not
used in Latin, and comma placement in Middle English was not systematic.
Latin methods of distinguishing between different kinds of relative clauses
(such as those of fact and those of characteristic) do not help here. Some of

26. R. Steele and A. S. Fulton, *Opera hactenus inedita Rogeri Baconi . . . Secretum Secreto-rum.*, 142.
27. It does not appear in the Arabic original. See A. S. Fulton, ed., "The Secret of Se-crets," 236–37.

the Middle English versions retain the ambiguity, as when a good adviser is defined by the Lambeth translator as someone who makes

no difference in þe persones, no in þe degreeȝ of men þat god hauys maad euen. (103)

But other translations are less equivocating and more egalitarian. Good counsellors treat all equally,

makyng no difference in persones [and] grees of men, for God created them all egally.[28]

Johannes de Caritate's translation also states the principle unequivocally, "God hath formyd alle men equalle."[29] I am not sure whether these are bold interpretations of the Latin or just clarifications of what the Latin was generally understood to mean, but at least in this form, it offers an abstract statement of the moral demonstrated by the story of the weavers' son and the prince-become-blacksmith. Social divisions are artificial, not divinely ordained, an idea that puts pressure on the hierarchical organization of society that differentiates between kings and peasants, between Guy de Vere and the "least clerk" who translates for him. Although we must be careful not to interpret this idea anachronistically, it is clear that the counsellor must not use status as a filter with which to discriminate. The ideal held out for the good counsellor is that at times the humanly created distinctions between people should be ignored.

Thus, despite the rhetoric of the address of the servant to the patron that often elevates the patron in the dedicatory letters at the beginning of the advice manuals, there is something inherently leveling about advice. In Johannes de Caritate's Middle English translation, when Hermes is asked why the adviser's idea is always better than the king's, he answers that "þe dome of hym þat sekyth counsel is robbyd or drawn owte of wylle."[30] That metaphor is telling. The king must ask advice, but when he does so, he is weakened—as Sir Francis Bacon says in the third epigraph for this chapter—or diminished. The illumination from the University College, Oxford Manuscript 85 of the *Secretum Secretorum* images the relationship well (see

28. The Ashmole manuscript (mid-fifteenth century), M. A. Manzalaoui, ed., *Secretum Secretorum*, 80.
29. M. A. Manzalaoui, ed., *Secretum Secretorum*, 189.
30. M. A. Manzalaoui, ed., *Secretum Secretorum*, 185.

Figure 1. University College, Oxford, MS. 85, p. 70. Permission granted by the
Masters and Fellows of University College, Oxford.

Figure 1).[31] It differs from many pictures of writers presenting books to patrons in which the writer kneels before the king. Instead, the king (presumably Alexander) sits on his throne on a dais, while the adviser (probably Aristotle) stands before him enumerating his suggestions, counting them off on his fingers. Although the throne usually elevates the king and symbolizes his superior status,[32] the two men's heads are almost at the same height, and their eyes, which are on the same level, meet.[33]

Deconstructing the Ideology of Advice

The king must ask advice, but to do so lowers him. The governance of princes results in the king's paradoxical dependence on those he rules. But even if the advice-taking king had not turned out to be surprisingly vulnerable, the ideology of advice in the *Secretum Secretorum* would not be simple or straightforward.

We have already seen the book's origin in Aristotle's disobedience — his refusal to join Alexander on his military campaign. There is a further difficulty in the very title *Secret of Secrets*. As Aristotle agrees to write Alexander a book that would substitute for his presence, he raises the question that since what Alexander wants to know can hardly be contained and understood by "mannys brest," how can it be painted or written "in dedly skyns" (49)?[34] Furthermore, since the secrets should not fall into the wrong hands, Aristotle will write "in parcell openly" but "in parcell . . . couertly." He will write "by fygurs" (49).[35] There is some indication that he will not write down everything he knows. And in several versions there is a suggestion that Aristotle could not write it "fully" because of "croked age and bodely vanyté."[36] So there are a number of reasons, having to do with Aristotle's will and physical capacities, and with human nature in general, that either the book is not really the secret of secrets, or it is unreadable.

31. M. A. Manzalaoui uses it for the frontispiece of his edition of nine Middle English translations.

32. On the meaning of the throne, see W. Ullmann, *The Individual and Society in the Middle Ages*, 28–30.

33. In *Chaucer and His Readers*, S. Lerer reproduces and discusses an image of Lydgate presenting *The Fall of Princes* to Duke Humphrey in which, since both men are seated, their heads are on the same level. Lerer interprets this image as showing the poet "as an equal to his master" (40–41, 44).

34. Also Ashmole, M. A. Manzalaoui, ed., *Secretum Secretorum*, 30; English translation of the Arabic, A. S. Fulton, ed., "The Secret of Secrets," 178.

35. Also Ashmole, M. A. Manzalaoui, ed., 40.

36. Ashmole, M. A. Manzalaoui, ed., 19.

With this familiar trope of the hiddenness of truth, Aristotle proclaims the great value of the material in the book and simultaneously makes it unavailable. In several versions, he addresses the problem:

Yf thou hede it wele, rede it wele, and vndrestande it wele, thou shalt fully fynde it. And I wene ther shall be none obstakell betwix the and it, or it and [the]. For God hath yeve the so grete an vnderstandyng, a swyftnesse of engyne, and knowlchyng of literature and science, and specially by my precedent doctryne that Y gaf you before this, that by thy-self thow shalt reprove and fyguratyfly vndrestande all that thou desirest. . . . For the desire of thy fervent wille shall open to the the way to the accomplysshyng of thy purpose to brynge it to the ende desired, oure Lorde grauntyng.[37]

As his assurances go on, the obstacle he claims will not exist between the book and Alexander looms larger ("If you read it well . . . ," "If God grants"). It gets even larger for other readers, for instance those of us who have not been privately tutored by Aristotle and whose understanding and swiftness of engine he has not certified in advance. Understanding is either circular or impossible.

These signs that the work is both secret and not secret and both useful and not useful as advice should keep us from being surprised at other fissures. For instance, there is an unacknowledged conflict between the advice always to take advice and the warnings against trusting anyone. A king should always get advice because he is only one man.[38] As support for this idea, Aristotle claims that advice can never hurt the king: If he doesn't like the advice he gets, he can just not take it (101).[39] If this were really sufficient safeguard against bad advice, why would a king need to be suspicious that his counsellors were out to take advantage of him, and why test them by inventing a financial crisis and watching their responses to be sure of their loyalty? If the king were really sure of his own judgment, he would be able to choose unerringly between good advice and bad advice. But of course if he were sure of his own judgment, he might not need advice at all. The problem is compounded by the admonition that the king should take the advice that most goes against his own inclination.[40] Therefore, his own inclination will consistently mislead him when he chooses among counsellors. In other words, simultaneously he must trust others, not trust others,

37. MS Ashmole, M. A. Manzalaoui, ed., 30; MS Lambeth 501, R. Steele, ed., *Three Prose Versions,* 49.
38. A. S. Fulton, ed., "The Secret of Secrets," 235. MS Reg.18 A, R. Steele, ed., *Three Prose Versions,* 34.
39. A. S. Fulton, ed., "The Secret of Secrets," 235.
40. A. S. Fulton, ed., 232.

rely on his own judgment, and not rely on his own judgment. The interpretive problems associated with advice mean that no king is immune from errors in judgment, his own and others'. Caution and subterfuge are natural responses, but they are likely to be insufficient to prevent trouble, and may actually cause it.

Another safeguard against bad and even malicious advice is to multiply it. According to Proverbs 24.6, "there shall be safety where there are many counsels." In the Arabic text, the safeguard against medical malice is to multiply opinions, for "a single man is liable to be seduced." Alexander is to summon ten physicians and take only those medicines they prescribe unanimously.[41] Perhaps in response to such advice, in many versions a king calls an international conference of physicians to have them create one medicine "so nobil and profitable" that it will obviate the need for any others. These are the results of the consultation:

The Grekis seiden that who so euyr dranke euery morowe twies his mouth fulle of hoot watir þat it shulde make a man hoole, and þat him shulde nede noon othir medicyne. The phisiciens of ynde seiden that who so ete the graynes of whijt mylle fastyng with watir cresses it profitith moche, or who so ete eche morowe of alibi Amei 7 dragmes [drams], and of swete grapis and Reysynes, he shalle haue no dowte of flewme, and he shalle haue the bettir vndirstondyng, and he shalle haue no quarteyne, and who so etith notes or ffygis with leves of Rewe, that day him thar drede of no venyme.[42]

The Greek doctors try to live up to their assignment, but the Indian doctors fail at the assignment because they present two alternative medicines (connected by "or") and a third (connected to the list by "and") that seems a compulsory complement to the others. But no matter what the proper combination, no consensus is reached, and the alternatives do not amount to one medicine that replaces the rest of the pharmacy. Since most translations then slide into Aristotle's personal recommendations, there is no resolution to Alexander's request for a panacea.[43] The diversity of opinion that is supposed to be a safeguard against treachery turns out to be fruitless. If the unsuccessful conference is any indication, there is no hope of trying to find safety in groups of doctors who agree. The conference is futile, and the text's aim for easily digestible advice is defeated.

I have already mentioned another of the places in which the *Secretum*

41. A. S. Fulton, ed., 191.
42. MS Reg. 18 A. vij. B.M., R. Steele, ed., *Three Prose Versions*, 32.
43. Other translations distribute the prescriptions differently among the doctors, but in none is there agreement. E.g., the Ashmole version, M. A. Manzalaoui, ed., 61–62.

Secretorum advocates suspicion—the narrative about the inadvisability of trusting someone of a different religion. This story—about a prosperous Magus and a poor Jew—also demonstrates the difficulty of giving advice that is coherent. The story preaches on a chauvinistic command: " . . . neuer haue trist yn man þat trowys noght þy lawe, þat it fall noght to þe as it fille to twoo men" (104). The two men travel together and exchange information on their creeds. The Magus believes in a God who acts justly in the world. His creed would be called by moral philosophers "universal love"—care for everyone—and the Jew's would be called "love with distinction"—care only for those who are related in some way. The Jew calls upon the Magus to live up to the law he espouses by lending him the mule he rides on, and then proceeds to take advantage of the Magus's good will by stealing the mule and all the Magus's supplies and leaving him stranded in the desert. The Magus prays to God for help, and their positions are reversed again: The Magus finds the Jew thrown down and severely beaten by the mule. Then the Jew once again prompts the Magus to be generous according to his law. He argues, "repreue me noght of þing passyd, ffor y shewyd þat þat was my lawe & my fayth," and he appeals once more to the Magus's creed (106). The Magus forgives him, carries him home on the mule, and sees to his care. The Jew dies anyway.

So far the story illustrates its counsel fairly well as a negative example: "Don't trust those not of your law." But the relationship between the moral and the story is disrupted because the introduction says the story is about what happened to *two* men. The story might be better labeled "what happened to the Magus when he trusted a Jew," but at the end of the story, the Magus is restored to his property and his home, and the Jew is dead. The fact that the introduction insists that the story is about both men highlights the Jew's experience: His "trust" in the Magus's law doesn't cure his poverty and costs him his life. It is somewhat disturbing to realize that trusting the trustworthy Magus was more dangerous than trusting the untrustworthy Jew.

The story's relationship to its moral gets more tenuous because it refuses to end there. It goes on to tell how the king of the city, impressed with the goodness of the Magus's law and the integrity with which he lives up to it, appoints the Magus his counsellor. So the Magus is rewarded for doing exactly what Aristotle advises Alexander against—trusting someone not of his creed—and his reward for violating this advice is to become an adviser to a king! The end of the fable subverts its beginning.

One way to explain the fable's self-destruction is "interference" from several sources. The Christian context in which the work finds itself may hijack the fable and deflect it from its moral. The Magus aiding the kicked and injured Jew looks a great deal like the good Samaritan, who set the wounded man "upon his own beast, brought him to an inn, and took care of him" (Luke 10.34). How could this be a negative model for behavior? His almost typological similarity to the rescuer in Jesus' parable makes the Magus look more admirable than foolish. Universal love converts paranoid pragmatism.

Another source of interference may be Jesus' criteria for separating the saved from the damned in Matthew 25.40: Those who clothed, fed, and sheltered "one of these my least brethren," Jesus tells the saved, "did it to me." In a Christian context, the story cannot make its point. The religious ideology abrogates distinctions among persons.

But the story's point is blunted even without Christianity by its context in the book itself. Aristotle has been providing criteria for choosing counsellors. Just before this story, he has detailed the fifteen virtues of a good adviser and, as we have already seen, suggested testing candidates' reactions to a phony financial crisis (102). The list of the fifteen virtues includes not being interested in accumulating wealth and being willing to "make no difference in persones, no in þe degrees of men þat god hauys maad even" (103), a precept we have already examined. The story of the Magus and the Jew neatly demonstrates the worth of the Magus in just these terms. If he is to live up to the ideal definition, an adviser must always act toward the Jew as the Magus does in the story. And though the story presents the Magus as a negative example, someone not to imitate, he is rewarded with position and power.

So the story slips from its intended moral and demonstrates another instead. But the meta-moral is the moral of the slippage. The story wriggles out from under the rule that justified telling it. Narrative eludes maxim.

All of the contradictions I have been examining in this section elaborate in an interesting way the central paradox of advice because they all have to do with the issue of trust. On the one hand, advice can never harm the ruler because he can reject "bad" advice. On the other hand, he must test his counsellors, multiply his doctors, and treat people from other cultures with suspicion. In other words, advice makes him vulnerable, and he must take advice about how to counteract it. Advice against advice is self-contradictory because if one does not take the advice to be suspicious, he takes the suspect advice. But if he avoids the suspect advice, he is taking the advice to be suspicious. Therefore, he is logically trapped into taking *some* kind of advice, and the suspicion is futile.[44] Presumably Aristotle would say that *his* advice is privileged, while only the advice of others deserves a skeptical reading, but since he must send his intentions in writing, which can never transmit those intentions perfectly, and since he writes in figures, even his text demands interpretation. The reader is alone and vulnerable to bad advice, misinterpretation, and the indeterminacy of meaning.

What is the political import of these cracks and fissures in the smooth ideology of advice? This chapter has ranged through a number of versions of the *Secretum Secretorum* covering a large span of history and geography. We cannot historicize without looking at a single version anchored in a specific time and place. But we can see in general terms its appeal to the groups of people who translated it and who were its intended readers. The work's obvious attempts to adopt the point of view of the ruler made some rulers willing to receive it as a gift, sometimes even requesting it. Perhaps the prestige of Aristotle helped. But the work veers just enough from the ruler's point of view, confounding the platitudes of advice and submitting the ruler to its discipline, that some writers did not mind giving it to them. It may be that there was just enough ambiguity in the work to allow its mix of deference and challenge to be used to address particular situations. As Annabel Patterson contends, it may not have taken much deference to cover over the challenges that would have been unacceptable if they were less ambiguous and more readable. But the deference had to be there.[45] The challenges were there, too: in the suggestion that to rule peacefully over an obedient populace, the ruler must embrace justice, with the concomitant threat that the result of injustice might be disobedience (93); in the leveling suggestion that good counsellors can be found among the lower classes because all men are equal; and in the overarching paradox that to rule well, a king must be ruled.

Aristotle provides the necessary clue to the popularity of the work with both rulers and subjects when he announces that its meaning is "the secret of secrets" and that its readers will have to interpret it according to what they already know. Its contradictions and ambiguity allow its rhetoric of submission to camouflage its agenda of subversion. The hermeneutics of secrecy is sometimes the hermeneutics of covert political challenge. In Chapters 4, 6, 7, 8, and 9, we will look at the play of deference and challenge in particular mirrors for princes in particular times and places.

44. For this paradox in Chaucer's *Tale of Melibee*, see J. Ferster, *Chaucer on Interpretation*, 19–21, and Chapter 6 below.
45. A. Patterson, *Censorship and Interpretation*, e.g., 11–15.

4

The *Secretum Secretorum* in Ireland

IN 1422 THE ANGLO-IRISH WRITER James Yonge translated the *Secretum Secretorum* for his employer, James Butler, earl of Ormonde, Henry V's lieutenant in Ireland. Not coincidentally, this translation is more "personable" than some others. While tailoring the treatise to the man for whom he served as secretary[1] with references to Irish history and contemporary Irish events, Yonge creates the impression of an individual voice speaking to an audience he knows well. That he is doing so in a very specific context allows us some insight into the function his translation might have been expected to perform, both for him and for his patron.

Deference and Challenge: Yonge and Ormonde

Yonge's translation shares with the others the double rhetoric of deference and challenge (see Chapter 3) that is encapsulated in the title, "The Gouernaunce of Prynces." The deference appears right at the start when, in the prologue,[2] Yonge recommends himself as a "pouer Seruant" to Ormonde's "hey lordshipp" (121).[3] He goes on in a conventional vein: He wants to further "yowre honoure and profite of body and Sowle," and Ormonde deserves the translation because of his "gracious kyndly gentilnesse" and "Souerayne nobilnes" (121–22). Through his diction, Yonge makes Ormonde sound just like Alexander: Aristotle praises Alexander because "the heynys of thyn Engyn lyghtly may Parcew the depnys of Sotilte" (127),

---

1. E. Curtis, *A History of Medieval Ireland from 1086 to 1513*, 294.
2. Some of the Middle English versions include the dedication of the Latin translation to Guy de Vere of Valence, Bishop of Tripoli. They don't usually write their own prologues with references to the contemporary scene.
3. I will label quotations in parentheses by page number. The edition is that of Robert Steele, ed., *Three Prose Versions of the Secreta Secretorum*.

while Yonge praises Ormonde for "the Sotilte of youre witte, and the clernys of youre engyn" (122).

Yonge's arrangement of the prefatory material, including Aristotle's letter about the interpretation of the *Secretum Secretorum*, is another deferential move. In the previous chapter, we saw Aristotle's confidence that Alexander could interpret the difficult, secretive work because he had had such a good education. Yonge's Aristotle more reverentially assures Alexander that with "this epystle . . . thow mayste thy Selfe consaille, lyke as y wer wyth the" (127). This is a strange formulation. On the one hand, it simply claims that the book will stand in for Aristotle's presence. But on the other, it admits that even when Aristotle was present, Alexander advised himself. Alexander is as well off with a text as he was with a live tutor, because the presence of the tutor never made all that much difference anyway. This is reminiscent of a common trope of advice: The ruler is so wise that he really does not need it. Alexander is his own best adviser. Insofar as Aristotle and Alexander are figures for Yonge and Ormonde, this is a gesture in which the narrator backs away from presuming to guide the reader.

Toward the end of the "Gouernaunce of Prynces," Yonge is explicit about this hesitation to preempt his reader's judgment. After a section on physiognomy, which teaches how to judge the characters of others by their appearance, he presents another guide to physiognomy: "Now gracious lorde, wylle I translate the scyence of Physnomy to you in a shortyr manere, for Sum bokys of arystotiles makynge haue that scyence shortyr than othyr: And so may ye chese wych ye beste Plesyth" (232). By refusing to choose between the two available versions of the treatise, he hands over control to Ormonde. It is as if even "advising" Ormonde by selecting one version of the treatise for "The Gouernaunce of Prynces" is too presumptuous.

Since the other side of the equation between Ormonde and Alexander is an equation between Yonge and Aristotle, the deference to Ormonde also begins to turn into a challenge. If the earl is almost the equal of the conqueror, the translator is almost the equal of the philosopher. Using the trope of *sapientia et fortitudo*, Yonge recommends Aristotle and his book because they teach the "witte" and "wysdome of vndyrstondynge" that are necessary for the proper, chivalric wielding of "Strynth and Powere" (121). Promoting the work as a civilizer, a preventer of "outrage and wodnys," Yonge puts himself in the line of "the moste wyse clerkes and Maysteris of renoune that haue beyn afor vs in al tymys" (121). Thus, while praising Ormonde as a lord already so genteel as not to need teaching, Yonge also notes that translating the work makes him progeny of Aristotle and "Tully the grette clerke" (122). Although this is certainly true within the terms of the tradition,[4] it could have gone without saying. But Yonge advances himself and the necessity, if a budding conqueror wants to win battles, of studying "clergeable bokys" (122). It seems perfectly appropriate, then, that when Alexander saw the usefulness of the stories of his "welbelowid clerke," he made him "his maystyr and chyfe counsailloure of his royalme" (122). Not only was Aristotle nobly born and learned, and as in other texts, worthy to be called more angel than man (122),[5] but he was also a prophet. Furthermore, the reason Aristotle does not obey Alexander's summons is more assertive than in other versions: It is not that he is too old and feeble, but that he is too busy teaching other students (127). In promoting his source, Yonge promotes himself, and for his source, the sky's the limit. By the end of the prologue, the "pouer Seruant" is not so poor. Yonge's deference goes hand in hand with his self-confidence, which gives him standing not only to advise but, as we shall see, to admonish his patron.

This self-confidence is evident in Yonge's sense of competitiveness with "rhymers," to whom he condescends because they praise for pay. Princes should desire good fame, a commodity which Yonge himself is conferring, but should avoid "Rymoris whyche Praysythe Hym Beste that most Ham yewyth" (176; also see 157). Yonge is performing a similar social function, but seems to consider himself superior to poets.[6]

Yonge also promotes himself by calling attention to his activity not only as translator (122) but also as author: He promises to add material to the book, including "olde ensamplis and new" (123). He is not a mere passive medium, but a shaper of the text. I want to examine the "entremedelid" (123) material to see how it fits into both what I have called the double rhetoric of deference and challenge and the work's fifteenth-century Irish context.

Two matters that come under the category of "challenge" are related: death and equality. Concern with the death of the king is not foreign to mirrors for princes, but it is unusual to use Alexander himself as an example. Alexander contemplates his own mortality when he is wounded: "This wounde shewyth wel that I is not god, but a dedly man, for hit

---

4. Yonge emphasizes the point later by listing other great rulers who had great philosophers and writers as their teachers (150). He is not afraid to include Nero — as a negative example, of course — who killed his master Seneca (151–52).

5. Arabic, ed. A. S. Fulton, 176. Also, ed. M. A. Manzalaoui, *Secretum Secretorum*, 28; ed. R. Steele, *Three Prose Versions*, 3.

6. In *Poets and Princepleasers*, R. F. Green mentions the competition in Ireland between "court writers and local bards" (199).

grewyth me sore" (177). More astonishing, when one considers that much of the work is addressed to Alexander in the second person singular, is the fact that Yonge reports Alexander's death and the philosopher's reflections on it (151). When the "you" to whom much of the work is addressed dies, the rhetorical relationship between writer and reader is compromised.[7]

To the subject of the death of the king, Yonge adds the *ubi sunt* trope from elegaic poetry to convey the power of death:

And therfor sholde no mane hym Pryde of heynysse, or of richesse, of Empire, of roialte, of lordshupp, ne of erthely honoure, for abyde thay may not endure, but Sone shall Passe, and as flouris shall fade . . . Wher ben thay that helde the grete festes and grete mangries [banquets] makid? Where been thay that noryssheth the grete horsyn of pryce? Where ben tho that ladd the grete hostes? Where ben the Weldy [mighty] Werriours, the Dukes and the tyrauntes? (153–54)

The answer to these questions prompts the observation that death destroys differences: "Al thay byth into Powdyr. . . . Be-holde hare graues! deme yf thou cannyst, who was serwaunt, who was lorde, who was riches and who was Pouer. Discerene yf thou canyste the Persone of the kynge fro the Person of the knawe, the strange fro the febill, the fayre fro the fowle" (154). Included in this list of collapsed oppositions are words Yonge used in his dedication about himself and Ormonde: "seruant," "pouer," and "lordshipp" (121). The implication is that the hierarchical relationship, too, will be leveled.

Given this attention to democracy in death, it is not surprising that Yonge's version of what in many translations is a somewhat equivocal statement of egalitarian principle (see Chapter 3) is not equivocal at all. A good counsellor should "yeue euche man hesyn [what's his], helpe tho that nede haue, and whan he shall Iustificacion done, he sholde noone dyuersite of Persones make; for-why, god made al men y-lyke" (211). Furthermore, Yonge includes the stories of the weaver's son who grew up to advise kings and the Indian prince who grew up to be a blacksmith, but shifts their position in the work. Rather than demonstrating that kings should search as widely as possible for good counsellors, they are moved to the section on physiognomy (216–17), where they can more easily make their general

---

7. Yonge does not seem concerned with inconsistencies of rhetorical address. Some of the work is addressed to the earl of Ormonde in the second person singular, so that it switches between the fiction of Aristotle advising Alexander and the contemporary fact of Yonge's work of translating for his patron. And in one place, Yonge narrates one of Ormonde's deeds in the third person (203–4).

point that individual nature and abilities (helped along by education) some-times outweigh the social class of one's parents.[8]

Of course Yonge is not thoroughly egalitarian, and he does not sup-press material that reinforces hierarchy and class division. For instance, he says that a king should obey God and his people will obey him (136); that sovereigns should obey God and correct their subjects (159); that par-ents should chastise their children and rulers their subjects (160, 167); that nobles love chivalry because of their "hey Parage" [rank]; and that churls love money because of their "lowe hertis and lytill" (172). But although he is not a democrat, his inclusion of material that levels distinctions is part of the rhetoric of challenge, which is connected to his sense of his own au-thority. That we know his name, that he is enough of Aristotle's peer to add his own material to the text, that he self-consciously shapes it, that he can remind his patron of the death of rulers and its equalizing power, and that he affirms univeral equality—these are all assertions of power vis-à-vis Ormonde.

His power is the power of learning. I have already said that he elevates himself by elevating the tradition he identifies with and continues. One way he does this is by expanding on the treatise's praise of education in Greece. For instance, like the Lambeth translator, Yonge advocates education for all children and prizes for the best; he gives, among his reasons, the quite pragmatic one that since kings need good press, they might as well train people to glorify their deeds in writing. But in the Lambeth version, the writers are called "studiantȝ;"[9] in contrast, Yonge calls them clerks (144). As we have seen, this is also his designation for Aristotle, Seneca, and other classical luminaries. And himself. His justification for fostering clerks is slightly more idealized than the Lambeth translator's: "by wrytynge of bokis, the whyche makyth clerkys to be Studiers, thyngis that Passyd byth men may cun ayeyne, and in bokis a man may See ham oppynly" (144). And shortly afterward, he quotes St. Bernard to advise that laws be com-mitted to writing and that illiterate rulers follow "the consaill of letterid men"; he also quotes Deuteronomy to say that kings (presumably literate ones, too) should "'take ensampill of the law of Prestis,' that is to sey, of letterid men" (149).

All of this is consonant with what we have seen from the very start

8. Yonge also announces the moral—"Many a pore man shewyth wysdome and reysone, And many a Prynce grete foly wythout reysone"—without telling the stories in the section on prudence (158).

9. R. Steele, ed., *Three Prose Versions*, 63.

of the work, that Yonge's sense of his weight and importance derives from his learning. Two things are crucial here: One is the fact that he is deploying the traditions he commands — the mirror for princes, the Bible, classical history — on behalf of and at the request of his patron. The translation is a learned display but also, as Yonge tells and then reminds us, an act of obedience (122, 248). In addition, since the earl of Ormonde himself had the reputation of being something of a scholar and antiquarian,[10] Yonge's enhancement of the praise of learning in the *Secretum Secretorum* was likely to have been well-received. In praising men with classical learning, he was praising not only himself but also Ormonde. It was not that Yonge made himself Ormonde's equal. Rather, they were in some sense colleagues. Yonge claimed a certain standing because of his learning, which made him in this regard Ormonde's peer.

It may be that his relationship with Ormonde gave Yonge a sense of entitlement — not necessarily to wealth or privilege, but instead to discourse. This is what we are seeing when Yonge tells a story about Ormonde. It tells of victory in a long military campaign against the Irish, referring to Ormonde in the third person even though some of the book has been addressed to him in the second. It appears under the rubric "Of dyuers ryght good and necessary nobilteis of the vertu of orison" (203) and demonstrates, accordingly, the power of prayer against enemies. But instead of merely celebrating his patron's success, Yonge warns him against vainglory for reasons that include the fact that the glory and honor do not belong to him in the first place; they belong to God (204).

Yonge is not chastising Ormonde, who does not seem to have done anything wrong yet. Yonge is merely warning him: "this nobill erle shold nat vaynglory haue . . ." (204). Perhaps the rhetoric is meant to magnify the deed. The implication is that this triumph was so great (despite its consisting, like many of the battles in this work, of burning and destroying towns and agricultural lands) that the temptation to vainglory would be very strong. The solution, like the cause of the triumph in the first place, is prayer (205). Thus, the contemporary event gets folded into discussion of morality, and provides Yonge with an opportunity both to glorify Ormonde and to assume the posture of his counsellor. Just as Aristotle counseled Alexander, the current danger allows him to advise his patron in his own right, not merely as a translator of Aristotle.

10. C. L. Kingsford, *English Historical Literature in the Fifteenth Century*, 5; *The First English Life of King Henry the Fifth . . .* , xviii; E. Curtis, *A History of Medieval Ireland*, 294.

Ireland "Entremedelid": The Writer, the Patron, and the Patron's Patron

Some of the interpolated stories of Ireland fit the pattern of this story of Ormonde's military prowess: They are made to demonstrate a moral point. For example, like other translators of the *Secretum Secretorum*, Yonge discusses the proper balance of thriftiness and largess for a king. Unlike the others, he uses Sir Stephen Scrope's stinginess toward the Irish to demonstrate that leaders guilty of "extorcionys" make enemies and lose the good will of their people. When Scrope reformed—because his wife threatened to leave him[11]—he was rewarded with military success against rebellious Irish subjects.[12] Ormonde's grandfather was rewarded even more gloriously: During his battle at the Red Moor of Athy, the sun stood still so that his troops could complete their slaughter. The cause of this miracle was his hatred of lechery (129).[13]

One of the most interesting Irish interpolations—a story about how Arthur McMirgh violated a truce with Ormonde's father—occurs just after the story of the Magus and the Jew (166). Perhaps to accommodate this story, the rubric for the Magus and the Jew is changed from the usual "Don't trust those who don't believe in your law" to "a prynce sholde not truste to his enemy" (164). The new rubric fits the story rather badly (as does the traditional one, of course—see Chapter 3), but I think that Yonge was willing to sacrifice some precision to make this mirror for princes into a mirror for his particular "prince." Since the stories I have mentioned so far feature Ormonde and his father and grandfather, the work reflects the glory of the earl and his family.

But I believe that there was another intended audience for the added Irish material—King Henry V. In 1422 Ormonde was nearing the end of his two-year term as lieutenant of Ireland. He wanted the king to reappoint him for a second term, but had a rival in his enemy John Talbot, who had been his predecessor in the job and wanted it back. The competition was heated. In 1421, the Irish parliament had sent messengers to Henry with articles condemning the abuses of Talbot's administration.[14] One of

---

11. Women figure in several of the contemporary stories as causes of men's behavior, good or bad.

12. Yonge says Scrope was able to kill Walter Burke, an Irish rebel, but Burke seems to have outlived Scrope. See A. J. Otway-Ruthven, *A History of Medieval Ireland*, 346, 357.

13. According to Curtis, this remarkable event was reported to have occurred in 1420 in a battle fought by the earl himself, not his grandfather (*A History of Medieval Ireland*, 297).

14. A. J. Otway-Ruthven, *A History of Medieval Ireland*, 359–60.

the messengers was Sir Christopher Preston, whom Talbot had had arrested three years earlier for a conspiracy that was allegedly connected to Ormonde's faction.[15] Then in 1422, Talbot accused Ormonde of treason in a great council in England before Henry.[16] With such accusations flying back and forth, the atmosphere surrounding the choice of the new lieutenant of Ireland was highly charged. We can gauge the intensity of the controversy by the reaction of John, duke of Bedford, when he reviewed it as Regent of England: he recoiled from the "dissensions, commotions, lawsuits, scandals, and intolerable evils."[17]

Adherents of both candidates lobbied the king. In March, Ormonde solicited testimonials from several counties about his administration, as well as endorsements from a number of bishops, sheriffs, counties, and towns. Limerick county, for example, commended his successes in wars against "the Irish enemy and the English rebels of our lord the king."[18] This appeal supported Ormonde's candidacy by making Ormonde's enemies Henry's enemies, thereby giving Henry a stake in Ormonde's successes.

This is precisely what "The Gouernaunce of Prynces" does. The story about Ormonde's victory through prayer is introduced by a long list of antagonists. They are all, according to Yonge, using a phrase very reminiscent of that used in Limerick's testimony on Ormonde's behalf, "Irish enemys and rebell[s]." And the clergy who performed the prayers that were responsible for Ormonde's success asked God "for the good esplaite [success] of the forsayden oure kynge henry, than beynge in Fraunce, and for the forsayd Erle his lyeutenaunt of Irland . . ." (203). The careful linking of Ormonde with Henry is part of Ormonde's request to have his tenure as lieutenant extended.

Two of the Irish additions are flattering to Henry. One, the story of how the Irish came under English rule in the first place, justifies England's title to Ireland. The main argument is that the Irish submitted to English rule during the reign of Henry II. But it is preceded by a geographical fantasy in which the Irish people came originally from Bayonne, Spain, which was ruled by a king who also ruled England. The connection to Henry V is that he deserves to rule the Irish because he, too, is lord of Bayonne (184).

The other story that flatters Henry may have been included to confirm

15. A. J. Otway-Ruthven, *A History of Medieval Ireland*, 353–54. When arrested, Preston had in his possession a copy of the coronation oath and the treatise on parliament, *Modus Tenendi Parliamentum* (see Chapter 2).

16. A. J. Otway-Ruthven, *A History of Medieval Ireland*, 361.

17. Quoted by E. Curtis, *A History of Medieval Ireland from 1086 to 1513*, 296.

18. Quoted by A. J. Otway-Ruthven, *A History of Medieval Ireland*, 361.

his right to rule England itself: It justifies the deposition of Richard II (136–37). Yonge's rendition of the deposition is interesting because it accuses Richard of living a life of "avoutry and lechurie" after he married the underage French princess; of having Thomas of Woodstock and Richard, earl of Arundel, murdered; and—the clincher—of being unsuccessful in Ireland on his last trip there. Thousands gathered to help Henry of Lancaster depose him.

This was a campaign that Ormonde did not win. Henry died at the end of August, and in October Talbot's brother was appointed justiciar and another member of his faction was appointed chancellor. But the failure of Ormande's political campaign notwithstanding, "The Gouernaunce of Prynces" reads like a part of his dossier.[19]

I have proposed that the "Gouernaunce of Prynces" had two social functions: (1) to define Yonge's relationship with Ormonde to show that Yonge is not only an obedient servant but also a prestigious counsellor; and (2) to present Ormonde as the proper choice for lieutenant of Ireland. These functions might seem to interfere with each other. If Yonge can elevate his own status enough to warn his employer of the sins he is susceptible to, does Ormonde then appear to lack the power and rectitude needed by lieutenants of Ireland? Does Yonge's promotion of himself undermine his promotion of his candidate?

I do not think so. The warning to Ormonde is warning of a potential sin, and as such is hypothetical, not an immediate threat to Ormonde's righteousness. And Yonge's advocacy of Ormonde as lieutenant does no harm to and may even enhance his own prestige, which in turn strengthens his ability to advise Henry about whom to appoint for the job.

Several examples will further illustrate the subtleties of the various upward and downward pressures in the relationship between Yonge and a monarch. In Chapter 1, I said that criticism of a king's advisers was often a way to criticize a king without insulting him too directly. The trope was often used against Richard II. But despite discussing advice and the evils of flattery, when Yonge comes to tell the story of Richard II (136–37), the preeminent story of his generation about the effects of bad counsel from flattering partisans, he does not mention either one. The reason for this change from the late fourteenth-century accounts may be that once Richard is dead, there is no need for the veil. Yonge seems to be quite comfortable

---

19. Ormonde became lieutenant of Ireland again at a later date, and his feud with Talbot's supporters, who were entrenched in the administration, continued to be a major source of turmoil in Ireland until the middle of the century (A. J. Otway-Ruthven, 371–76).

in presenting specific justifications for Richard's deposition. They all post-date the great 1386–89 crisis over counsel, and they include accusations of personal sin and the political murder of magnates. Unlike those who tell the story in the midst of the crisis of the eighties, Yonge has no need of the code of counsel. Insofar as there was a Lancastrian audience for his work, they would presumably have been happy to hear specific accusations against Richard.

But Yonge is less direct in criticizing the present king. Most versions of the *Secretum Secretorum* tell the ruler to test counsellors by pretending to be in the midst of a financial crisis and asking for the candidates' advice. The one who offers his own funds wins (210; see Chapter 3 for further discussion of this ruse). The discussion of this device would seem to be a wonderful place for expansion on the theme of Ormonde's virtue. Since Ormonde had paid some of the expenses of his army out of his own pocket, and had apparently promised to spend more of his own money,[20] this passage would seem to have a felicitous place for praise of his commitment to the welfare of his people. But Yonge resists.

The possibility of a Henrican audience for the translation might explain why Yonge did not take this opportunity for an Irish insertion that might have seemed very natural. But many commanders had done the same thing, and in the context of his feud with Talbot and their rivalry for Henry's favor, this strategy would not have been clever: Not only did Talbot do the same thing during his six-year term before Ormonde's, but Henry had also done it at least once as Prince of Wales.[21] Furthermore, to point out the constant impoverishment of Irish government (which, according to some historians, was a chief source of corruption and political trouble) was to point out that England habitually did not meet its obligations there. Henry, his energy directed toward France, might not have been happy to be reminded of the results of his neglect of Ireland.

But Yonge does not bypass the subject entirely. Other translations mention the king's power to spend public money[22] and the wisdom of keeping one's hands off other men's possessions.[23] But Yonge is unequivocal on the point that what the king has the power to spend is his own wealth. Yonge's Aristotle is very clear that he means to discuss money that

20. A. J. Otway-Ruthven, *A History of Medieval Ireland*, 360.
21. C. Allmand, *Henry V*, 28–29. See Chapter 8 below.
22. E.g., R. Steele, ed., *Three Prose Versions*, 7. Manzalaoui, ed., *Secretum Secretorum*, 32, 127, 282.
23. E.g., R. Steele and A. S. Fulton, eds., *Opus Hactenus inedita Rogeri Baconi*, 44.

belongs to the king. He announces the topic as being "how moche thou mayste despende of thyn owyn propyr" ("private property," 130). He then goes on to say that "frely aftyr thy Power thow mayste yeue of thyne owyn. For yf thow Spendyst or yeveste othyr men goodes, thow Passyste Frauncesse, and out of Fredome thow walkyst" (130–31). Perhaps this minor clarification of Yonge's is too suble to have gotten him into much trouble, but it might have reminded those in the know of Ormonde's sacrifice. It is impossible to say whether Henry might have felt comradeship with Ormonde since he did the same thing, or whether he would have been annoyed to be confronted with the administration's impoverishment. If Yonge reproduces Aristotle's financial wisdom with the written equivalent of a wink or a slightly emphatic inflection, then he is not taking a large risk. He may be doing exactly enough to avoid making Henry angry while reminding him of Ormonde's commitment to the good of Ireland. But in any case, Yonge does not leave this touchy subject completely alone.

Yonge is more direct in his criticism of Henry as he narrates Ormonde's military victory that I discussed earlier. As he warns Ormonde against vainglory, he lists four reasons to avoid it. The fourth is a little puzzling. It is:

the lytill thanke that he had of ham that hym shuldyn beste haue rewardid and commendid. And ther-for this nobill erle may Sey that, that the appostill Sayde vnto thymothe, "know thou," he Seyth, "that in the latyste dayes ther shullyn be Perillous tymes, And men Shullyn be lowynge ham-Selfe, couetous, Prowte, heygh, claundrynge, inobedyente, and vnkynde with-all." Of vnkyndnes spekyth Seneca, and Sayth, "He is an onkynde man that denyeth hym to haue recevid a good dede. . . . And He is moste vnkynde of all that foryetyth Benefactes." (205)

He goes on a little longer in this vein, and ends with the observation that whether or not one is rewarded, he should do all the good he can. This is not exactly the moral that arises most naturally from the sulky observation that Ormonde has received little thanks for his efforts. Anything that prevents vainglory ought to be positive, not a liability that needs to be overcome. The lack of thanks coming to Ormonde must register as a criticism of Henry, Ormonde's superior and commander at Agincourt and the logical source of rewards for success on behalf of the empire.

Thus, the dance of deference and challenge involves not only the patron but also the king. The social work that the translation could do was finely tuned. When Yonge promotes himself as a fit colleague for Ormonde, he also makes himself a worthy counsellor, someone worthy to recommend

Ormonde to the king. What he offers to both men, as in other versions of the *Secretum Secretorum*, is the knowledge of how to procure their people's docility,[24] but that does not require his own. He feels free to broach topics that might have made both his superiors uncomfortable. Thus, Yonge's moves may have been subtle enough to flatter himself, flatter Ormonde, and flatter Henry, all at the same time and without sacrificing his freedom to carp. His power derived partly from the fact that the book was a translation of prestigious sources, and partly from the fact that Yonge adapted it in a very active and sometimes assertive way. As we saw in Chapter 3, the *Secretum Secretorum* was never a monolithic whole that presented a single ideology. By supplementing it, Yonge shaped it to perform complicated social functions in a complicated political context.

24. E.g., the story of Alexander and the Persians that we examined in Chapter 3 offers the ruler the secret to an obedient populace (R. Steele, ed., *Three Prose Versions*, 3; M. A. Manzalaoui, ed., *Secretum Secretorum*, 28).

5

Council, Counsel, and the
Politics of Advice

However, it is pious to believe that such acts [simony and usury
in the court of Rome], perpetrated on the advice of the wicked,
ought not to be set down to the pope's decision.

—*Matthew Paris's English History*, III, 88

[Although a fraud was perpetrated on him,] I do not excuse him
in that matter; for a pope ought to be such a man as not to deceive or be deceived.

—*Matthew Paris's English History*, III, 102

MY PURPOSE IN THIS CHAPTER is to explore fourteenth-century uses of
language about advice to the king in political conflicts. I am interested in
the historical events—what actually happened, as far as modern historians
can tell [1]—and how people talked about them. In order to talk about them,
medieval writers often had recourse to the literary tradition of the mirrors
for princes. My first epigraph for this chapter explains some of the obsessive
talk about advice. Piety, respect for authority, and regard for his own safety
might move a writer to take refuge in the tropes of advice. Better to attribute the ruler's crimes and misdemeanors to his advisers than to blame the
ruler himself. Matthew Paris is candid about how the turn to the rhetoric
of advice is a matter of will and decorum. It is sometimes also a matter of
self-protection. The poet of the Anglo-Norman poem known as "Against
the King's Taxes" is equally clear about the prohibition against criticism
of the king:

Houme ne doit a roy retter talem pravitatem
Mes al maveis consiler per ferocitatem.

1. Modern historians test the chronicles by comparing them to nonexpository sources,
but also by comparing them to each other.

One must not impute such wickedness to the king, but to his evil counsellor in his savagery.[2]

Implicit in the use of the language of advice is what cannot be said at all.

The connection between advice and prohibitions on speech reveals that the tropes of advice are deployed in the medieval power struggles between rulers and the ruled. The tropes of advice are often part of the attempt to limit the king. This is sometimes but not always true of the mirrors for princes themselves, because they are often written for rulers of one sort or another and sometimes adopt or pretend to adopt rulers' points of view. But as we saw in Chapters 2, 3, and 4, always implicit in the genre of advice to the king was the idea of the control of the king. It is therefore not surprising that those Englishmen who strove to contain their kings often seized on the *topoi* of advice as tools in their struggles. I hope to show in this chapter that the historical and literary modes of discussion about advice were intertwined, even dependent on each other.

Still Harping on Advice

There are several reasons for the ubiquitousness of advice in fourteenth-century discussions of government. For one thing, the fourteenth century saw the development of the council as an administrative body that helped to run the government of England. Its importance increased because neither parliament nor the royal household could handle all the requests and petitions they received and because the country went through several periods during which the king was too senile or too juvenile to rule on his own.[3] The council became a crucial part of the bureaucracy that did the work of the government.[4]

The household, however, including the king's personal advisers, did not disappear. Both the official council and the private counsellors were visible parts of the regime. At various times the choice of members of one or both of these groups was publicly contested and therefore highly contro-

---

2. I. S. T. Aspin, ed., *Anglo-Norman Political Songs*, 110, 112.

3. These include the dotage of Edward III and the minorities of Richard II and Henry VI. In addition, Henry IV was occasionally too ill to govern.

4. See J. F. Baldwin, *The King's Council in England During the Middle Ages*; B. Lyon, *A Constitutional and Legal History of Medieval England*, 504–11; A. L. Brown, *The Governance of Late Medieval England, 1272–1461*, chapter 2; and C. Given-Wilson, *The Royal Household and the King's Affinity*, 183–84.

versial. Richard II provides a gauge of the importance of the choice of the king's council and his personal counsel. When parliament asked him in 1386 to remove the chancellor and treasurer from his administration, he replied that to oblige them he would not remove so much as a kitchen scullion.[5] And when in 1389, after his long minority, he declared himself of age and able to take full control of the government, he defined his majority by announcing that he would appoint whom he liked to the council.[6]

The significance of these battles has been very controversial among modern historians. Some treat the battles as attempts by the magnates, the great land-owning peers, to limit the monarch.[7] Others, for instance Richard H. Jones, treat it as a struggle over patronage.[8] In the former case, what is at stake is the power to influence the king's policy decisions. In the latter, what is at stake is the peers' access to the wealth he distributed. According to Jones, talk about advice is a cover for writers' real interests.[9]

Some of the particular purposes of the hereditary peers might have been to make sure that the king's friends, those he chose to help him govern, did not stand between them and the rewards of patronage. For instance, Piers Gaveston, the unpopular favorite of Edward II, not only received patronage, but also influenced the king's distribution of it to others.[10] According to the *Annales Paulini*, Edward allowed Gaveston so much control over decisions about requests and petitions that he was regarded as a second king.[11] Despite being "from no great family" and a Gascon (that is, an outsider), he directed the flow of patronage. This was certainly one reason for aristocratic resentment against him.[12]

Constitutionalism and patronage are not mutually exclusive possibilities. The conflicts probably arose because the increasingly bureaucratized

5. Henry Knighton, *Chronicon Henrici Knighton vel Cnitthon: Monachi Leycestrensis*, ed. J. R. Lumby, II, 215.

6. " . . . quos voluero ad Consilium advocabo. . . ." Thomas Walsingham, *Chronica Monasterii S. Albani, Historia Anglicana*, II, 181. This passage from Walsingham's chronicle is translated as document no. 66 in vol. 4 of *English Historical Documents*, ed. A. R. Myers, 164–65.

7. According to B. Wilkinson, the deposition of Edward II established the modern importance of parliament, and "the history of the modern limited monarchy may also be said to have begun at this moment." *Constitutional History of Medieval England, 1216–1399*, vol. II: *Politics and the Constitution 1307–1399*, 26–27. For critiques of this idea, see Chapter 1, notes 23 to 25, and below, note 72.

8. See below, note 49.

9. R. H. Jones, *The Royal Policy of Richard II: Absolutism in the Later Middle Ages*, 122–23.

10. J. S. Hamilton, *Piers Gaveston: Earl of Cornwall, 1307–1312*, 15.

11. W. Stubbs, ed., *Chronicles of the Reigns of Edward I and Edward II*, 259 (excerpted and translated in B. Wilkinson, *Constitutional History of Medieval England 1216–1399*, vol. II: 108).

12. N. Fryde, *The Tyranny and Fall of Edward II*, 14–15.

and centralized government encroached on the prerogatives and income of the feudal aristocracy. When the lords felt edged out of the inner circle, they sought to reclaim their influence on the king in order to promote their interests and to put themselves in the way of his largesse. Their talk of their *rights* to advise the king was an indirect reference to their considerable financial and military resources. They probably did not mean to enhance the parliament's authority when they used it in support of their own aims, but in effect they did. And they may not have meant to demonstrate a theory of limited monarchy or establish a precedent that could be followed by others, but in effect they did. Even if their revolutions were conservative ones to recoup feudal power, they used language and tactics that could be adapted and adopted by others.

Edward II

I begin with the deposition of Edward II because, although it took place a half century before the start of the period on which I concentrate in this book, as I said in Chapter 2, it cast its shadow over the rest of the century. It lurked in the background during Edward III's and Richard II's reigns even before Richard was deposed. It was repeated because it was remembered. And, like other struggles in Edward's reign, it was cast in terms of advice.

In the document that justifies the deposition of Edward II, four out of six reasons mention advice. In two of them, bad advice is the explanation for his unwise actions that damaged the public interest: He attacked the church and nobility through "evil counsel" and failed to fulfill his coronation oath, especially the provision to "do justice to all," because of "evil councillors." But the first two provisions are about advice itself. The king's son will be crowned in his stead[13] for these reasons:

First, because the king is incompetent to govern in person. Throughout his reign he has been controlled and governed by others who have given him evil counsel, to his own dishonour and to the destruction of holy church and of all his people, without his being willing to see or understand what is good or evil or to make amendment, or his being willing to do as was required by the great and wise men of his realm, or to allow amendment to be made.

And throughout his reign he has not been willing to listen to good counsel, or to

13. With a tact that qualifies as what modern media critics call "double speak," the action is described as the choice of the son rather than the setting aside of the father.

adopt it, or to give himself to the good government of his realm; but he has always given himself up to unseemly works and occupations, neglecting to satisfy the needs of his realm.[14]

As we have seen, these twin accusations exactly mirror exhortations in the *Fürstenspiegel* tradition: "Accept good advice; reject bad." The *Secretum Secretorum* argues that rulers should solicit advice because it can never hurt them; they can pick and choose, adopting only the best.[15] As training for leadership, such counsel is not terribly helpful because it is so vague. It offers no help in the crucial matter of distinguishing the good from the bad.

But as an accusation against a monarch, the generalities work better. Edward's lack of judgment, his inability to "understand what is good or evil" is precisely what's being attacked. As Matthew Paris indicates in the second epigraph at the start of this chapter, the ruler's exemption from blame finally runs out.

It perhaps serves the magnates' purposes to be vague so as to avoid arguments over specific charges. Edward's alliances with unpopular counsellors like the Despensers and, earlier in the reign, Piers Gaveston, must have been known well enough (and, in the case of accusations of a sexual relationship with Gaveston, scandalous enough) not to demand elaboration. The charges against Edward end on just such a note, referring to his character flaws, which "are so notorious that they cannot be denied." Some of what cannot be denied can also go without saying.

It does not even seem to matter that the two first accusations contain a contradiction: The king is blamed for needing help in governing; yet if he had taken no advice at all, they would have criticized him for that, since they also blame him for not taking help from good counsellors.[16]

Some of this advice talk was a cover for noble self-interest. Edward was not really being removed from the throne for being dependent, but

14. B. Wilkinson prints a translation of the document in *Constitutional History of Medieval England, 1216–1399*, vol. II: *Politics and the Constitution, 1307–1399*, 170–71.

15. For instance, the Arabic *Secretum Secretorum* says, "Always take counsel. . . . For if [others'] counsel is better than thine own, thou mayest accept it, and if it is weaker than thine own, thou canst do without it." A. S. Fulton, ed., "The Secret of Secrets," 235. Bacon translates this passage on 137 of the same volume. See also 134 of the Hürnheim edition for another Latin translation. An example of this sentiment in Middle English is "Noone harme may cvm of consaill . . ." (R. Steele and A. S. Fulton, eds., 209). Also see 34.

16. When serving as Prime Minister, Margaret Thatcher expressed frustration over a similar bind: "At one time I am accused of being isolated and not consulting anyone; at another time, I am accused of taking consultations with those who have something interesting to say. People have to make up their mind which they are criticizing." This comment was broadcast as part of a segment called "British Anti-German Sentiment" on National Public Radio's "All Things Considered," July 17, 1990.

for being dependent on the wrong people. The issue was the king's alienation of too many of the powerful lords of his realm. Like Gaveston, the earlier favorite, the Despensers profited from their relationship with the king in ways that made other magnates see them as rivals. But the Despensers also instilled fear: Their greed led them to manipulate vulnerable people — sometimes by emotional and sometimes by physical intimidation — in order to acquire valuable property. They did not mind breaking the law themselves, and they often had the assistance of royal officials, and sometimes even the king's connivance. Whereas Gaveston might scoop up for himself or his friends property that the king was ready to distribute, the Despensers went after property they fancied, whether or not it was "available." According to Natalie Fryde, "there was not a landowner in England who could feel his possessions safe from their avarice or have any assurance that he was likely to be able to hand on his property to a young and defenceless heir without danger." [17]

But it is striking that the deposition of Edward II deploys the language not so much of property rights as of the advice manuals. If one thinks that the *Fürstenspiegel* sides with the ruler, then it is striking in a paradoxical way that political actors wrench the language of advice out of the royalist context in order to oppose the king. If one thinks, as I do, that the mirrors for princes take many opportunities to criticize the ruler, it is a less paradoxical move from literary work to political action. It is easier to see how the literary works provide the terms in which deposition of the king can be spoken in public.

Edward III

The deposition of Edward II was invoked as a threat to Edward III in the crisis of 1340–41. The conflict between Archbishop of Canterbury John Stratford, formerly the chancellor, and Edward III had to do, as many of the century's struggles did, with war against France and the need to raise money for it from a reluctant church and a grudging populace. Edward had been successful in battle at Sluys in June of 1340 and had hopes of success with the siege of Tournai, but found himself hampered by the lack of supplies the government could not afford and pressed by creditors. In September he was forced to accept a truce at Esplechin. In late November he

17. N. Fryde, *The Tyranny and Fall of Edward II*, 106. See also 107–18.

made a surprise visit to England to attack the financial administrators, imprisoning officials from several parts of the government, and to make the collection of taxes more strict. His targets included Stratford, no longer chancellor but blamed for tax collection and expenditures during his tenure. Stratford had to defend himself, as well as imprisoned officials, especially clerics, against the charges, and to defend the church in general against the pressure of taxes. He refused a summons to London, insisting on a hearing in parliament, and began issuing statements in what became an extended verbal battle with the king. The documents of the battle afford a rare and valuable glimpse of mid-fourteenth-century political rhetoric.[18]

On December 29, 1340, Archbishop Stratford preached a sermon — in English, so that all could understand — on the text from Ecclesiastes, "In his time he did not fear the prince." The text was appropriate for the occasion, which was both a commemoration of the anniversary of the martyrdom of Thomas Becket during his struggle with Henry II and a strategic move in Stratford's struggle with his own king. He was using history to shore up his own authority in his challenge to the king while implying that he was ready for martyrdom.[19] Stratford's complicated performance included not only tears and self-blame, but also a claim that Magna Carta had been violated. He then pronounced sentences of greater excommunication against six categories of the king's advisers, including those who had violated Magna Carta by imprisoning clerics. The features of the sermon that are consonant with the tradition of the mirrors for princes are Stratford's avoidance of the names of individuals whom he blamed as unworthy counsellors, and explicit exemption of the king from the excommunication.[20] Stratford used the conventions of the political tradition to try to protect himself with a preemptive strike — tacitly acknowledging that it is dangerous to speak so openly to the king.

Stratford's next salvo was a widely circulated letter to Edward on January 1 of the new year. The letter contains very few specific charges about what the king was doing wrong. Instead, it is about advice:

18. For fuller accounts of the events of the crisis, see M. McKisack, *The Fourteenth Century*, chapter VI, esp. 163–81; R. M. Haines, *Archbishop John Stratford*, 278–327; W. M. Ormrod, *The Reign of Edward III*, 11–15, 84–86.

19. According to one chronicler, when Edward was blocking Stratford's entrance into parliament in late April, Stratford had a conversation with one of the king's supporters about whether he was worthy of martyrdom (R. M. Haines, *Archbishop John Stratford*, 315–16). The explicitness of the discussion reveals the political valence of the model of Becket and the concept of martyrdom.

20. R. M. Haines, *Archbishop John Stratford*, 287.

Tresdouce seignur, vous please assavoir qe la plus soveraigne chose qe tiengt lez rois et lez princes en due et en covenable estat si est bon et sage counsail. Et purceo dit li sages: "En ses motz de counsails, ceo est assavoir bons, il y aad sauvete." . . . plusours rois de Israel et dez aultres terres ount este mys a meschief par malveis counsail. Et, sire, qil ne vous desplease, vous le poetz remembrer de vostre temps: qar par la malveis counsail qe nostre sire voz pieeres, qe Dieux assoile, avoit, il fist prendre, countre la ley de sa terre et le graunt chartre, lez peres et aultres gentz de la terre, et mist ascuns a vilain mort, dascuns fist prendre lour biens et ceo qils en avoient, et ascuns mist a raunzon; et qest avunutz de lui par cele cause vous, sire, le savetz.

Most gentle lord, please you to know that the most sovereign thing that holdeth kings and princes in due and fitting estate is good and wise counsel. And therefore saith the wise man: "In multitude of counsellors there is safety." . . . [And] have many kings of Israel and of other lands been brought to trouble by evil counsel. And, sire, let it displease you not, you may remember it in your own time: for by the evil counsel which our lord your father, whom God assoil, had, he made seize, against the law of his land and the great charter, the peers and other people, and put some to shameful death, and of others he made seize their goods and what they possessed, and some he put to ransom; and what happened to him for that cause, you, sire, do know.[21]

The advisability of plural advisers seems to come straight out of the *Fürstenspiegel* tradition. According to the *Secretum Secretorum*, it is always better to have more than one.[22]

But, as in the case of Edward II, the king is eventually held responsible for the actions of his government, advice or no advice. Edward II was done in by bad advice "that he had" because of what he himself did. The list of misdeeds makes clear that they are *his* misdeeds. Stratford then uses the specific indictment of the father for a vaguely worded but unmistakable threat to the son. And since Stratford was active in the movement to replace Edward II with Edward III, he had excellent credentials as a deposer of kings.

With this introduction, Stratford goes on to the problems of the current reign, including three that exactly repeat the accusations against Edward II at his deposition: violation of the coronation oath, violation of

---

21. Robertus de Avesbury, *De Gestis Mirabilibus Regis Edwardi Tertii*, ed. E. M. Thompson. The letter and an English translation of it are on 324–29. For the full reference, see *Adae Murimuth* . . . in the Works Cited list. Thompson's translation is also printed, along with several other documents and accounts of the crisis, in B. Wilkinson's *Constitutional History of Medieval England, 1216–1399*, vol. II: *Politics and the Constitution, 1307–1399*, 190–93. A. R. Myers also translates the letter in *English Historical Documents: 1327–1485*, no. 23, 72–73.

22. The English translation of the Arabic text gives this advice on 235 of the volume edited by R. Steele and A. S. Fulton. Bacon's translation is on 139. James Yonge's Middle English version of this is on 209 of R. Steele's edition.

Magna Carta, and taking bad advice ("malveis consail"). Stratford does not identify the bad counsellors, but describes them in the traditional way as those who seek their own gain ("lour profit") rather than the king's honor or the good of the country ("vostre honur od salvacion de la terre").[23]

The concern over self-interested counsellors is consonant with the mirrors for princes, which worry about the damage that can be done by greedy advisers. In some versions of the *Secretum Secretorum*, indifference to money is one of the fifteen virtues of a good counsellor. As we saw in Chapters 3 and 4, a number of versions offer tests for avarice that will allow a ruler to avoid greedy counsellors.[24] Edward has failed the test of testing and discarding money-loving counsellors.

When it comes to the corollary complaint — that he did not take good advice — Stratford is not shy, and not constrained by the *Fürstenspiegel* assumption that good advice can be found at any rank in society. He is definitive about the source of good advice: the magnates, clerical and lay. Edward's past successes, which won him "les coers de vostre people" ("the hearts of your people"), were attained "par bone avisement des prelatz, piers, grauntz et sage du counsail de la terre" ("by good avisement of the prelates, peers, the great men and wise of the council of the land"). Although Edward was not imitating his father, who ignored the counsel of the "great and wise men of his realm,"[25] Stratford accuses him of exactly that, following the pattern established by the deposition of Edward II and repeated later in the nobles' struggles with Richard II. Stratford shapes the *Fürstenspiegel* counsel about advice to his own ends.

Stratford asserts his willingness to face an inquiry by parliament[26] into the kingdom's finances, and ends with an apology for speaking "si grossement la verite" ("so largely the truth") and an affirmation of his affection for the king.[27] Despite the generalities of his accusations, Stratford apologizes for being brutally frank, as if the tropes of advice are not quite enough protection on their own and their protective power must be reinforced.

23. Robertus de Avesbury, *De Gestis Mirabilibus Regis Edwardi Tertii*, 325, 328.

24. Kings are advised to fake a financial crisis and reject as adviser anyone who recommends that they use their subjects' money, and choose anyone who offers his own. The English translation of the Arabic is on 236 of R. Steele and A. S. Fulton, eds. Bacon's Latin translation is on 140 of the same volume. In Hürnheim's edition, the passage is on 136. There are Middle English versions in R. Steele's edition, 35, 101–2, and 210.

25. B. Wilkinson, *Constitutional History of Medieval England, 1216–1399*, vol. II: *Politics and the Constitution, 1307–1399*, 170. In *The Fourteenth Century*, M. McKisack says that the changes in Edward's government that so annoyed Stratford were motivated by his special administrative needs while Edward was trying to finance the war with France (158–61).

26. Robertus de Avesbury, *De Gestis Mirabilibus Regis Edwardi Tertii*, 326, 329.

27. Robertus de Avesbury, *De Gestis Mirabilibus Regis Edwardi Tertii*, 327, 329.

The conflict was eventually resolved with a reconciliation between king and archbishop, though the archbishop never again held high office in Edward's administration. Both of them were probably to blame for the clash. Edward had jumped into the war while finances were uncertain and against the advice of his counsellors. Although Stratford probably did not deserve the king's accusations of financial profligacy, corruption, and even treasonous encouragement of resistance to taxes, his threat to excommunicate members of the administration was a serious attack on royal policy, and the council probably could have managed the taxes more efficiently and maximized the returns.[28]

Among the questions over which these two strong personalities collided were who had the authority to levy taxes, whether or not lay courts could discipline clerks, and whether magnates really could demand, as Magna Carta promised, trials by juries of their peers.[29] The other important question was who should advise the king. One of the contentions of Stratford and his supporters was that parliament should have the right to appoint and dismiss the king's advisers. They prevailed on this point when the king accepted a version of it in a statute.[30]

This concern is related to the claim that the magnates, clerical and lay, have the right to advise the king. This claim harks back to the magnates' fear, during the previous reign, of being displaced either by less noble upstarts (Gaveston) or by a small, unscrupulous, greedy aristocratic faction (the Despensers). It was most in evidence when the king was on the continent surrounded by *familiares* and relatively isolated from the council at home.[31] This matter is easily expressed by the tropes of advice and allows Stratford to sound like a *Fürstenspiegel* in his letter to Edward as he complains about the king's taking bad advice. But it is important to note that Stratford's historical position makes him take exception to the mirrors for princes by demanding that counsellors come from among the "great men" of the realm. As we have seen, many translations of the *Secretum Secretorum* promote the widest possible search for good counsellors.[32] The ruler is encouraged not to rule out the young, the poor, or the humbly born — or

28. W. M. Ormrod, *The Reign of Edward III*, 85.

29. R. M. Haines, *Archbishop John Stratford*, 325. For another discussion of possible interpretations of these events, see B. Wilkinson, *Constitutional History of Medieval England, 1216–1399*, vol. II: *Politics and the Constitution, 1307–1399*, 176–87.

30. W. M. Ormrod, *The Reign of Edward III*, 85.

31. A. Tuck, *Crown and Nobility, 1272–1461*, 124.

32. See Chapter 3 above.

even the short in stature[33] — as possible sources of wisdom. Archbishop Stratford's aims are less catholic. His brief is for the magnates as the king's rightful counsellors.[34] He uses whatever platitudes of the advice tradition are appropriate to his struggle, along with the events of recent history that enhance his stature and authority.[35] He provides the interesting spectacle of an adviser using the tropes of advice to defend himself against the accusations of the king he advised.

At the end of Edward III's reign another struggle about advice sounded some similar themes in different circumstances. Since Edward was becoming senile, it was really a struggle over who should run the government. Edward's son, John of Gaunt, had dominated the council for several years in the hope of pursuing foreign wars more vigorously than his father could. The commons' restiveness about war, taxes, and corruption among the king's advisers came to a head in the parliament of 1376 ("The Good Parliament"; see Chapter 2, "Limitations on Speech in Parliament") with their demands for a new council and their impeachment of the king's chamberlain, Lord William Latimer, who controlled a great deal of royal patronage, and Richard Lyons, a very influential merchant in the court.[36] Their success was brief,[37] but marked an important moment in the development of the relations among court, council, and parliament,[38] showing very clearly that when a king was weak, control of the government necessitated control of the council.

33. The rather puzzling defense of short men in the translations may be the result of an ambiguity in the Arabic, which uses a word that can mean either "small" or "humble." Roger Bacon's Latin translation gives the literal, rather than the figurative meaning — as do many of the Middle English versions — and translates the Arabic word as "parvam staturam" (R. Steele and A. S. Fulton, eds., 137, 234). Other translations, perhaps led by the same exemplar, follow suit.

34. With a reference to Rehoboam, he specifically excludes young counsellors. See Chapter 7 on Gower's use of Rehoboam.

35. In *The Tyranny and Fall of Edward II*, N. Fryde suggests that when he dismissed Stratford as chancellor in 1340, and Stratford's brother, who took his place for a time, Edward III "wiped away some of the last connections with his father's disastrous reign" (227) — and also the connections with that disastrous reign's disastrous end, of which Stratford continued to remind him. See also Fryde's "Edward III's Removal of His Ministers and Judges, 1340–41."

36. For a good account of the court and the place of Latimer and Lyons within it, see C. Given-Wilson, *The Royal Household and the King's Affinity*, 146–54.

37. After the death of his brother, the Black Prince, who was believed to have favored the commons' cause, Gaunt successfully restored his partisans to court. As we saw in Chapter 2, Peter de la Mare was imprisoned for his role as speaker of the commons.

38. It was the first impeachment of counsellors by parliament. B. Lyon, *A Constitutional and Legal History of Medieval England*, 509.

As in Edward's conflict with Archbishop Stratford, the tropes of advice were a prominent part of the Good Parliament. One premise of the proceedings was that any misbehavior by counsellors was done without the king's knowledge. Whatever the parliament did not approve of was done "en desceit le roy" ("in deceit of the king").[39] The commons was adopting Mathew of Paris's "pious" attitude in the first epigraph at the start of this chapter. Nothing is the king's fault because no one around him will tell him the truth ("ne nulle ne ad entour le roy qe luy voet dire la veritee"[40]).

Another related premise was that whatever action the parliament took was for the benefit of the king and kingdom ("pur profit del roy et roialme"[41]). As is often (but not always) the case in the mirrors for princes, the king is not to blame and the critics are on his side.

In contrast, the bad counsellors are out for their own gain. None of them

ne loialment ne *profitablement* voet conseilere, mes toutz iours de iapery et mokery et procurere lour *profite* demesne; par qay nous vous dioms qe nous ne dirroms pluis tanqe toutz ceux qe sount entour le roy qe sount fautours et male conselours soient remowez et voidez de nostre seignur le roy et qe le chaunceller et tresorer qe ore sount, soient aleges de lour offices, qare ils ne sount pas *profit* a blez. (Emphasis mine)[42]

will . . . give him loyal and profitable counsel, but always they mock and scoff and work for their own profit. Wherefore we declare to you that we will say nothing further until those who are about the king, who are traitors and evil counsellors, be removed and ejected from his presence, and until the present chancellor and treasurer be removed from their offices, for they are not worth a straw.[43]

This passage uses the trope of the self-interested adviser so important in the *Secretum Secretorum*. The fault of these men is exploitation of their positions of power to enhance their personal fortunes. The three uses of "profit" accentuate the difference between what they do — make profits — and what

39. *The Anonimalle Chronicle*, ed. V. H. Galbraith, 91. According to B. Wilkinson, the writer of this chronicle "clearly had access to first-hand information about the Good Parliament" (*Constitutional History of Medieval England, 1216–1399*, vol. II: *Politics and the Constitution, 1307–1399*, 210).

40. *Anonimalle Chronicle*, 90. This theme appeared again later in *Mum and the Sothsegger*. See Chapter 2 ("The Poets Speak of Silence").

41. *Anonimalle Chronicle*, 81.

42. *Anonimalle Chronicle*, 90–91.

43. B. Wilkinson, *Constitutional History of Medieval England, 1216–1399*, vol. II: *Politics and the Constitution, 1307–1399*, 222.

they ought to do — provide the king with advice that has value and actually *be*, in themselves, valuable. But "ils ne sount pas profit a blez."[44]

May McKisack is not convinced that the impeached officials were guilty of all charges made against them. She says that Latimer's defense was plausible, that some of Lyons's defenses against financial wrongdoing are confirmed by the records, and that there were extenuating circumstances for some of the misdeeds of other men accused by the commons.[45] If she is right, her view highlights the degree to which the tropes of advice shape the events of 1376. The commons puts its grievances in terms provided by the mirrors for princes.

Richard II

A combination of historical reference and *Fürstenspiegel* language was mobilized in the conflict of 1386–89 between Richard II and the Appellant lords. The tropes of advice were used differently than in the earlier crises, partly because the circumstances were different, and partly because the earlier crises had already happened and could serve as precedents.

In response to the Rising of 1381, which had been caused by the taxes levied to support the war with France, Richard II had been attempting to make peace. The lords who came to be known as Appellants after they appealed (accused) some of Richard's advisers of treason in parliament had profited from the war and wanted it to continue.[46] The traditional feudal function of the great lords of the land was military. Insofar as Richard turned away from the war, he lessened his dependence on the feudal aristocracy and frustrated their interests in war-making.[47] Insofar as he turned

44. It is undoubtedly coincidence, but an interesting one, that when distinguishing between useful and uselesss advice, the early fifteenth-century Reg. 18 A manuscript of the *Secretum Secretorum* translates the Latin "utile" and "inutile" (R. Steele and A. S. Fulton, eds., 139) as "profitable" and "nought profytable" (R. Steele, ed., *Three Prose Versions*, 101). The mid-fifteenth-century Ashmole version uses "profit" with the other meaning: Bad counsellors may endanger the kingdom if they pay too much attention to "their owne profites" (M. A. Manzalaoui, ed., 78).

45. M. McKisack, *The Fourteenth Century*, 391–92.

46. The five Appellants were Thomas of Woodstock, duke of Gloucester; Henry of Bolingbroke, earl of Derby; Richard Arundel, earl of Arundel; Thomas Beauchamp, earl of Warwick; and Thomas Mowbray, earl of Nottingham. For information about them, their activities, and their resources, see A. Goodman, *The Loyal Conspiracy*.

47. In *War, Justice, and Public Order*, R. W. Kaueper discusses the current of conflict between medieval states and kings, on the one hand, and, on the other, the militaristic chivalric classes (184–99).

to others for the running of the government, the magnates were less often the recipients of the king's patronage, just at the time when they were not reaping the profits of the war.[48] They found this erosion of their sources of wealth intolerable.[49] They turned to the tropes of advice to try to regain some of their advantage.

Like Edward II's favorite Piers Gaveston, Robert de Vere became a symbol of what the magnates thought of as misplaced patronage. Their intense antagonism toward him, which lasted beyond his banishment and death, can be partially explained by his position between the magnates and the king. He inherited the title of earl of Oxford. Richard elevated him first to marquis of Dublin (1385) and then to duke of Ireland (1386) and bestowed on him gifts of castles and land. When, during the Merciless Parliament of 1388, de Vere was appealed of treason along with Michael de la Pole, Robert Tresilian, Nicholas Brembre, and the archbishop of York,[50] the Appellants installed themselves and their partisans on the council, reasserting what they took to be their rightful place in the king's government.

The appeals of treason are explicit about the Appellants' concern with the king's distribution of patronage. According to the *Westminster Chronicle*, the accused

caused our lord the king to give sundry manors, lands, rents, offices, and bailiwicks to sundry other persons of their affinity and to other persons from whom they have taken great gifts and bribes . . . [and] great gifts of gold and silver as well of his own goods and jewels, as of the goods and treasure of the realm. . . . [Also they] caused

48. For detailed information about Richard's household, see C. Given-Wilson, *The Royal Household and the King's Affinity*. For the dilution of aristocratic influence on Richard in the period before the Appellants' initiatives in parliament, see A. Tuck, *Richard II and the English Nobility*, chapters 3 and 4.

49. On the importance of patronage to the crisis, see R. H. Jones, *The Royal Policy of Richard II*, 122; A. Tuck, *Richard II and the English Nobility*, e.g., 86, 102, 127; A. Tuck, *Crown and Nobility, 1272–1461*, 196. C. Given-Wilson says that the issue of government corruption was more important than patronage in the Appellants' resentment of Richard, and that patronage was not important; Richard had little to give away (*The Royal Household and the King's Affinity*, 200–201, 132–33). But Given-Wilson admits that though many of Richard's courtiers did not benefit from his patronage, "they were thought to be doing so" (188), and the gifts Richard could bestow were given "to a rather narrow circle of favourites" (132). Though Given-Wilson is persuasive that not all of Richard's choices were unreasonable, Richard occasionally acquired them improperly in the first place (133). And since the scarcity of resources does not usually encourage the self-interested to guard their prerogatives any less jealously, Given-Wilson himself, Jones, and Tuck provide enough evidence for us to believe that patronage was a part of the Appellants' case against Richard.

50. He had already been effectively removed from the council and the household. When his army was defeated by the Appellants at Radcot Bridge in December of 1387, he had fled to the Continent.

sundry insufficient and unsuitable persons to have the guard and sovereignty of sundry lordships, castles, and theatres of war.[51]

The Appellants were *not* explicit about their own stake in this "misdirection" of royal gifts. Probably to avoid looking self-interested, they used the familiar trope from the mirrors for princes so that their complaint was not "He didn't give me enough," but "He gave too much to the undeserving." As the MS Reg. 18 A of the *Secretum Secretorum* warns, "ffor he that yevith his good to suche as be not worthi . . . is but lost."[52]

The appeals were also explicit about the issue of the lords' access to the king but, again, without specifically mentioning themselves. The accused and their traitorous circle

seeing the tenderness of the age of our lord the king and the innocence of his royal person, caused him to apprehend as truth so many false things (entendre com pur verite tantz de faux choses) . . . against loyalty and good faith imagined and contrived that they entirely engrossed in all things his love and firm faith and belief and caused him to hate his loyal lords and subjects by whom of right he ought rather to have been governed (par queux il duist de droit pluis avoir este governe). And moreover, accroaching to themselves royal power, by disfranchising our said lord the king of his sovereignty and impairing and diminishing his royal prerogative and regality they made him so far obey them that he was sworn to be governed, counselled, and guided by them (destre governe, conseille et demesne par eux).

[They] would not suffer the great men of the realm or the good counsellors of the king to speak to or approach the king to give him wholesome advice nor the king to speak to them except in [their] presence and hearing.[53]

As in the Good Parliament, the king is blameless, and there is concern for his access to truth. This is related to the concern for their own access to him ("If he won't see me, he will not know the truth"). These are familiar issues from the *Fürstenspiegel* tradition. The Appellants also adopt the trope that makes the king a subject. It seems to be a given that he must be governed (at least in part because of his youth, but as we have seen, this language is used about mature monarchs as well). What is at issue is merely who will do it. This language is appropriate to the parliamentary action, which is directed not against the king, but against his advisers, and it attributes to

51. L. C. Hector and B. F. Harvey, eds. The French, which I have not quoted, is on pages 244–46, the English on pages 245 and 247.
52. R. Steele, ed., *Three Prose Versions*, 7.
53. *Westminster Chronicle*. The French is on 240 and 242, and the English on 241 and 243. Not surprisingly, if one considers the proximity of Abbey to parliament, the chronicle writer had access to a number of parliamentary documents about the Merciless Parliament. See B. F. Harvey's introduction, xlv.

him very little volition. The accused "made" the king commit the disapproved acts, and they are the ones who will suffer.

Most of the thirty-nine accusations, involving everything from the pardoning of "horrible felonies and treasons" to the creation of a council without the consultation of the lords and the pursuit of a truce with France, are couched in terms of advice. Even though most of the accusations show the Appellants' disapproval of actions taken by the king himself, most are blamed on the counsel of the "mesfesours et traitours" ("misfeasors and traitors"), who, "par faux ymaginacions, covynes et accrochementz" ("by their false contrivances, conspiracies, and accroachments"), misled him.[54]

It may seem remarkable that the Appellants use the language of advice at all, let alone so deferentially, meticulously avoiding public blame of Richard for the executive misdeeds of his reign. The comments of two historians will help explain their use of deferential tropes of advice. According to Anthony Tuck, the medieval king was so strong, and the mechanisms for mediating disputes so inadequate, that the only aristocratic solution for disputes was to depose him.[55] According to Chris Given-Wilson, if, at a particular moment of conflict, they decided not to depose him, their only alternative was advice.[56]

This narrowing of options occurred during the events of the late 1380s. The lords seem to have threatened to depose Richard twice, once in 1386 before the impeachment of the chancellor, Michael de la Pole, and once in late 1387 before the appeals of treason against five of Richard's favorites and the purge of the royal household.[57] There is some reason to believe that the Appellants actually did depose him for three days in December of 1387.[58] But whether or not the deposition happened, the rumors of it lead Dunham and Wood to conclude that "some of Richard II's subjects thought of Edward II's deposition as a precedent and that circumstances might again rise that would remove the stigma of sacrilege from a king's dethronement."[59] As Given-Wilson says, when they decided not to depose

---

54. *Westminster Chronicle*, French, 254; English, 255.

55. A. Tuck, *Richard II and the English Nobility*, 225.

56. C. Given-Wilson, *The Royal Household and the King's Affinity*, 187.

57. In A. Tuck, *Richard II and the English Nobility*, A. Tuck discusses why they decided not to (119).

58. The manuscript that relates the deposition and "recrowning" of Richard II (the chronicle of the abbey of Whalley, Lancashire) is printed in M. V. Clarke's *Fourteenth-Century Studies* (91–95). The section on the deposition is reprinted in Chrimes and Brown, eds., *Select Documents* (no. 127, 145).

59. W. H. Dunham, Jr. and C. T. Wood, "The Right to Rule in England: Depositions and the Kingdom's Authority, 1327–1485," 744.

him or not to depose him permanently, they were thrown back on the language of advice.

In 1386, as in the crisis of 1340–41, some history—the memory of the deposition of Edward II—was combined with the tropes of advice. According to Henry Knighton's chronicle, when the parliament began the impeachment of the chancellor and treasurer, Richard II stayed away from parliament. When the Appellants asked him "with most humble subjection" to attend so that parliament could proceed, he replied by talking about their rebellion ("our people and commons resist and rise up against us") and the possibility of his asking help from France. The lords denounced that idea ("That is no sane plan") and raised the subject of deposition:

There remains one thing more for us to show to you on behalf of your people. It is permitted by another ancient law—and one put into practice not long ago, unfortunately—that if the king by malignant counsel or foolish contumacy or contempt or wanton will or for any other improper reason, should alienate himself from his people, and should be unwilling to be governed and guided by the laws and statutes and laudable ordinances with the wholesome counsel of the lords and magnates of the realm, but rashly in his insane counsels exercise his own peculiar desire, then it is lawful for them, with the common consent of the people of the realm to pluck down the king from his royal throne, and to raise to the throne in his stead some very near kinsman of the royal house.[60]

The elements of this account, which seems to favor the Appellants, should be quite familiar by now. They include the idea that the king must be governed, following the advice of the magnates rather than following the advice of others (by definition, "malignant counsel") or his own idiosyncratic whim, that the magnates represent the people and the public interest, that the people's consent would justify deposition, and that the deposition of Edward II was a model for future action. According to the chronicler, at the reference to the deposition of Edward, "the king was recalled entirely from anger."

Thus the tradition of advice and the memories of deposition are intertwined. Both are parts of what Dunham and Wood call the "doctrine of restraint" on the monarch. As we saw in the chapters on the *Secretum Secretorum*, the writers of advice manuals can criticize the rulers to whom they are addressed, or at least adopt a superior attitude from which they can subject the ruler to their strictures. They can at times take advantage of one

---

60. *Chronicon Henrici Knighton*, II, excerpted and translated in A. R. Myers, ed., *English Historical Documents: 1327–1485*, no. 60, 151.

of the premises on which they are based, that the king needs to be ruled. This idea is explicit in the *Polychronicon*'s account of the Appellants' threat to depose Richard in 1387:

But finally they asserted that it was necessary for him to correct these errors and to submit himself to the rule of the lords. But if he refused to do this, he must know that his heir was undoubtedly of full age, and wished freely for the good of the realm and its salvation to obey them and to be governed under their rule. The king was stupefied and said that he wished to submit himself to them as was fitting in lawful things and to be governed by their wise counsel, saving his crown and royal dignity, and he affirmed this on his own oath.[61]

Richard, faced with the image of an heir ready to enact—"freely"—the trope of the government of the king, instantly follows suit. The terms used in *The Westminster Chronicle* to describe this incident are very similar. They include phrases such as "subicere se regimini dominorum" ("submit himself to the control of the lords"), "sub eorum regimine gubernari" ("to be governed under their rule"), and "eorum salubri consilio gubernari" ("to be governed by their wholesome advice"). The sins of the treasonous counsellors include forcing the king to be governed by them ("destre governe").[62] But there is no question that the king must be governed. The only question is by whom. In both accounts, the lords win the day with a mixture of threat, history lesson, and rhetoric from the *Fürstenspiegel* tradition. In a sense, in the midst of their conflict with Richard, the disgruntled lords allow the tropes of advice to reach their full potential for antagonism toward the ruler.[63]

Perhaps encouraged by this political mobilization of the tropes of advice, other writers could nurture their potential for such antagonism. As we will see in Chapter 7, Gower included in Book VII of the *Confessio Amantis* a number of stories of the removal and death of kings. And after he was deposed for good, Richard himself became a story for the mirrors for princes. Shortly after 1400, MS Reg. 18 A.vii of the *Secretum Secretorum*

61. *Polychronicon*, excerpted and translated in A. R. Myers, ed., *English Historical Documents, 1327–1485*, no. 62, 156.

62. L. C. Hector and B. F. Harvey, trans. and eds., *The Westminster Chronicle*, 228–29, 240–41. I have made changes in their translations.

63. A curious statute of 1386 reflects the importance of advice in governing the king. After the impeachments and the appointment of commissioners to reform the government, a law was enacted against giving to the king openly or in secret: "Counsel, Exhortation, or Motion, whereby the King should repeal their Power. . . ." This statute against advice attempts to maintain control of the king by controlling what advisers said to him. *Statutes of the Realm*, II, 42.

turns a story about prodigal kings into the story of "þe distruccion of þe kyngdom of Ingelond." In the Latin text, the example is the kings of Syria; the principle is that kings should not give away so much of their own wealth that they have to steal their subjects'. The punishment is that "insurrexit populus contra eos, et nomina eorum de terra penitus deleverunt."[64] No names are mentioned in the English manuscript—neither Richard's nor Henry's. Responsibility for the end of the reign is attributed to "þe poeple," who cried to God,[65] but the story is undoubtedly connected to accusations during the Merciless Parliament that Richard gave too many gifts to the "unsuitable."

As we saw in Chapter 4, James Yonge was much franker about Richard's deposition in "Gouernaunce of Prynces" in 1422, not integrating the story into a traditional exemplum, not masking the name of the king, but identifying him, probably in order to flatter Henry V. Thus, the historical actors adopt literary terms and in turn become part of literature.

The intertwining of the genres—determined by the Appellants' paucity of political options and perhaps helped along by the chronicle writers—shaped the story of Richard by using the terms from the advice manuals. By focusing on Richard's choice of counsellors during the conflict of the late 1380s, the lords and their historians told the story of a Richard II who was impressionable, a bad judge of character, and prone to accept advice from selfish, grasping men.

Henry IV

When Richard was finally deposed in earnest, the tropes of advice figured differently. By the time the parliament published "the record and process of the renunciation by King Richard, and . . . of the deposition of the same King Richard," the deposition was a *fait accompli* and there was no need to hide criticism of him behind the facade of advice. Through the deposition, parliament refused merely to blame the advisers and to wrest control of the council away from the king, as the Appellants had done in 1386–88. Appropriately, reasons for the deposition were stated in terms of the king's own actions, not his acceptance of bad advice. There was no need for the convention that others bewitched him. On the contrary, there was a need to blame him in order to justify the drastic upheaval of a deposition. There-

64. R. Steele and A. S. Fulton, eds., *Secretum Secretorum*, 44.
65. R. Steele, ed., *Three Prose Versions*, 52.

fore, according to parliament, he squandered his own patrimony and seized lands and violated laws himself.[66] Between 1388 and 1399, Richard's sins had been transmuted from the acceptance of unwise advice from the wrong advisers to the refusal to take advice at all. His counsellors were mentioned, but were portrayed as being helpless victims of his arbitrary whim. He was accused of resisting their advice by declaring that "his laws were in his own mouth or, occasionally, in his own breast."[67] He prevented his counsellors from doing their jobs:

Also, in many great councils of the king, the Lords of the kingdom and the justices and others were charged that they would faithfully counsel the monarch in matters touching his estate and that of the kingdom. But the same Lords, justices and others were frequently so suddenly and fiercely upbraided and reproved by the king, for giving counsel according to their discretion, that they dared not tell the truth.[68]

In terms of the mirrors for princes, his sin of counsel was in rejecting it.

The mirrors for princes were also present when parliament blamed Richard because he "gave the greater part of his said patrimony to unworthy persons," and consequently had to impose taxes that "outrageously oppressed his people, to the impoverishment of his kingdom."[69] As we have seen, this accusation comes directly from the *Secretum Secretorum*.

Advice also appeared when Thomas Arundel, Archbishop of Canterbury, compared Richard's refusal to take advice with Henry's intentions. He announced that "it is the will of the king to be counselled and governed by the honourable, wise and discreet persons of his realm and to do the best for the government of himself and of his realm by their common counsel and assent. He does not wish to be governed by his own will, nor by his willful purpose or singular opinion, but by common advice, counsel, and assent."[70] In willing not to will, Henry was surely contrasting him-

66. The account of the deposition is in *Rotuli Parliamentorum*, III, 415–34 (excerpted and translated by C. Stephenson and F. G. Marcham, eds., *Sources of English Constitutional History*, vol. I, no. 66, 250–57). The parliamentary charges are also excerpted and translated in B. Wilkinson, *Constitutional History of Medieval England, 1216–1399*, vol. II: *Politics and the Constitution, 1307–1399*, 309–18.

67. *Sources of English Constitutional History*, C. Stephenson and F. G. Marcham, eds. and trans., no. 66A, 252.

68. B. Wilkinson, *Constitutional History of Medieval England, 1216–1399*, vol. II: *Politics and the Constitution, 1307–1399*, 314.

69. *Sources of English Constitutional History*, C. Stephenson and F. G. Marcham, eds. and trans., no. 66A, 252. Also B. Wilkinson, *Constitutional History of Medieval England*, vol. II: *Politics and the Constitution, 1307–1399*, 313.

70. B. Wilkinson, *Constitutional History of England in the Fifteenth Century (1399–1485) with Illustrative Documents*, 43. See also 297–98. For the French text, see S. B. Chrimes and A. L. Brown, eds., *Select Documents of English Constitutional History: 1307–1485*, no. 167, 194.

self with the willful Richard. Henry promised not to rule by his own will, and the possibility of his being advised by the wrong people or the wrong sort of people (as were Richard and Edward II) is not mentioned. After Edward II's deposition, Edward III promised to rule with the advice of the magnates.[71] Henry's promise is significantly different. Although he wants his advisers to be "wise," there is no suggestion that they must be "great." The language implies much more inclusiveness. What is invited is "common counsel" and "common advice" for the good of the realm. As we saw in Chapter 3, according to the *Secretum Secretorum*, the search for good advisers should be wide. English politicians did not generally match its inclusiveness. Arundel's rhetoric seems to open the search a little, moving Henry a little closer to the position that the *Secretum Secretorum* had taken for centuries.

Henry did not mean that he wished to preside over a democratic revolution, or even a continuing aristocratic one.[72] But deposition of Richard was part of the process that lessened the importance of the great feudal lords in England in the late Middle Ages. In 1399, Richard had the support of most of the magnates, but succumbed to the revolution because he did not have the support of the gentry.[73] Henry, because his support among the magnates was shaky, depended on the gentry. According to Bertie Wilkinson, the deposition of Richard bound king and people together to the exclusion of the magnates. England came to be defined less by a feudal hierarchy and more by "the 'national' order of the early modern state."[74] As we saw in Chapter 2, language about the community as a whole contributed to that sense of a national order with citizens who participated in it. As we will see in Chapter 7, Gower believed that the king's relationship with his advisers was less important than his relationship with his people. Although change in this direction was neither steady nor inevitable, in the long sweep of history, he was right.

71. B. Wilkinson, *Constitutional History of Medieval England vol. II: Politics and the Constitution, 1307–1399*, 159.

72. As we saw in Chapter 1 (notes 22–25), twentieth-century historians have spent much energy evaluating Bishop Stubbs's idea that in the Lancastrian period England experimented with a constitutionalism in which parliament had more power than it was to have again for centuries until the creation of a true constitutional monarchy (*The Constitutional History of England*, III, 5). Few modern historians go as far as Stubbs. A. L. Brown's "The Commons and the Council in the Reign of Henry IV" exemplifies modern objections, but Brown does not deny that "the Commons were capable of sustained criticism on matters which affected them directly, and that Henry IV by force of circumstances and probably by nature also was conciliatory in dealing with the Commons" (28–29).

73. C. Given-Wilson, *The Royal Household and the King's Affinity*, 267.

74. B. Wilkinson, *The Later Middle Ages in England, 1216–1485*, 236.

In this chapter we have seen political actors choosing among the tropes of advice that the culture — including the mirrors for princes — made available. Richard H. Jones points to this interdependency when he characterizes the late fourteenth-century view of Richard II: "The frivolous spendthrift king, the youthful irresponsible council, the sycophantic agents of despotism and the constitutional party of opposition in the commons have only slowly and partially been recognized as the literary creations of Richard's contemporary enemies or of later authors whose particular purposes they served."[75] By "literary creations," Jones may mean "untruths." But his complaint also highlights the ways in which historical actors — all of those I discuss in this chapter, not just the enemies of Richard II — borrow their vocabulary from the mirror for princes tradition. The authors of the mirrors for princes provided nuanced models of relationships between rulers and subjects that were dances of deference and delicate challenge. Magnates and kings, accepting some of the literary terms and rejecting others, performed these dances on a grander scale involving life and death and the fate of the nation.

75. R. H. Jones, *The Royal Policy of Richard II: Absolutism in the Later Middle Ages*, 123.

6

Chaucer's *Tale of Melibee*: Advice to the King and Advice to the King's Advisers

> Nothing is more necessary in arduous deliberations, and nothing, on the other hand more dangerous, than asking advice.
>
> — Guicciardini, *Storia d'Italia* (1:16)[1]

ALTHOUGH CHAUCER'S *TALE OF MELIBEE* is a *Fürstenspiegel*, unlike the other works I consider in this book, it is not a direct descendant of the *Secretum Secretorum*.[2] It is therefore interesting to see that, like pseudo-Aristotle's mirror for princes, the *Melibee* registers profound ambivalences about the project of educating the ruler. The *Secretum Secretorum* moves between supporting the ruler by providing him with all the knowledge he needs to win others' obedience and doubting whether that knowledge can or should be communicated. It also slides between supporting the ruler in his quest to subjugate others and its own quest to subjugate him. The *Melibee* displays both kinds of ambivalence — the hermeneutical ambivalence about whether the educational project can succeed leads to the subjugation of the ruler: When it becomes clear that Melibee either cannot or will not understand or implement the policy Prudence recommends, she takes over and does it herself. The dilemma that this poses for interpreters of the tale is that on the one hand the ambivalence seems to shut down the genre, rendering it useless as a guide either to abstract issues of advice or to concrete historical events. And yet, this self-consuming artifact invites historicizing because its discussion of war and peace seems undeniably topical. If

1. Quoted in Albert Cook, *History/Writing*, 103.
2. Chaucer's source was a French translation of Albertano of Brescia's *Liber Consolationis et Consilii*. On the *Melibee*'s genre, see L. Patterson, "'What Man Artow?'" 139–40.

we assume that the tale was written in the late 1380s (1386–90),[3] it seems to address issues about military policy and the revolt of the Appellant lords against Richard II. It appears that the story of Melibeus was brought to Chaucer's mind by events just prior to the time of its composition. The *Melibee* therefore offers us another opportunity to decipher the way the paradoxes and contradictions of advice function in a particular historical context.

The tale makes a good case study because of its two very distinct interpretive traditions, divided between those who take it seriously — that is, think it has some topical relevance — and those who think its irony and contradictions preclude its having a political message. Either the tale is a pointed comment on some contemporary issue, or it implodes before it can reach its mark. Although these two groups — for shorthand I'll call them "the historicists" and "the formalists" — have not engaged each other directly, I believe that both approaches must be part of an interpretation of the tale. I will attempt to reconcile these aspects of the tale — that it presents itself as a serious contribution to moral and political discourse, and that it seems to trip over its own seriousness.

This conflict is heightened for the *Melibee*, as opposed to other *Canterbury Tales*, because along with its companion, *Sir Thopas*, it is told by the Chaucerian narrator. It is tempting to look there for a key to Chaucer's understanding of himself and his role as a writer in late fourteenth-century England. In this chapter, I will consider the *Melibee* and its critics, the political scene in England in the middle and late 1380s, and Chaucer's position during that time, in order to ascertain what kind of social work the tale might be doing. I will then put this reading into the context of recent historicist approaches to Chaucer.

---

3. *The Riverside Chaucer*, 923. In *The Development and Chronology of Chaucer's Works*, J. S. P. Tatlock provides evidence for the several different dates (194–95), including the middle eighties and also an "early" date (195). At one point he offers 1388 as the "earliest" date (194). Some critics accept an earlier date, for example, D. Palomo, "What Chaucer Really Did to *Le Livre de Melibee*," 313–14; R. F. Green, *Poets and Princepleasers*, 143; L. J. Matthews, "The Date of Chaucer's *Melibee* and the Stages of the Tale's Incorporation in the *Canterbury Tales*"; L. Patterson, "'What Man Artow?'" 139–40. H. Cooper supports a later date on the basis of the mention of the "wilde hert" (l. 1325) in association with a king (Richard adopted the badge of the white hart in 1390) and the fact that the tale seems addressed to "the wayward king of the early 1390s rather than the child" (*Oxford Guides to Chaucer: The Canterbury Tales*, 312). The determination of the date is often part of a hermeneutical circle. That is, one's judgment about the date is influenced by one's interpretation of the meaning of the tale and its relationship to contemporary events and vice versa.

The *Melibee*

I begin with a prior question that will reveal some of the difficulties of the enterprise: What difference does it make that Chaucer's version of this story is a very close translation of his early fourteenth-century French source by Renaud de Louens, which is itself a translation of the thirteenth-century *Liber consolationis et consilii* by Albertano of Brescia?[4] Deconstruction is prepared to answer this question according to its own attack on the prestige of origins, as Daniel Kempton does with "a statement of principle: Geoffrey Chaucer's source, his literary antecedent, is not an origin and arbiter of the tale's meaning but merely another version of the text, which is heard in the background as a counterpoint or dissonance."[5]

This principle is not far from the pragmatic conclusion we must come to if we look at the historicists' interpretations of Albertano of Brescia's treatise. According to Gardiner Stillwell, it criticized "the lawlessness of feudal nobles in northern Italy, men who were unwilling to submit the settlement of their feuds to legal institutions set up by the *bourgeoisie* of the Lombard communes."[6] But Paul Olson sees it as a reply to Frederick II of Hohenstaufen's theory of theocratic absolutist rule.[7] If the original can be read as an answer to both anarchy and absolutism, Kempton is right that the meaning of the ancestor does not dictate the meaning of the heir. The source will not function as an independent variable that fixes the meaning of subsequent versions. All the versions are subject to interpretation. So the historicists' need to historicize the source as well as its progeny is matched by the deconstructionist's refusal to be cowed by origins. Neither school of critics will, by itself, resolve the contradictions of the *Melibee*.

Various historicists have attempted to connect Chaucer's version to specific events in Chaucer's time. They all notice the extraordinary coincidences between the story of Melibee and fourteenth-century events, especially arguments about war versus peace, about who should advise the

---

4. According to T. Sundby, ed., Albertano of Brescia wrote the *Liber Consolationis et Consilii* in 1246 (VI). According to J. Burke Severs, Renaud de Louens translated it as *Le Livre de Mellibee et Prudence* sometime after 1336 (W. F. Bryan and G. Dempster, eds., *Sources and Analogues of Chaucer's Canterbury Tales*, 560).

5. D. Kempton, "Chaucer's Tale of Melibee," 275, n. 7.

6. G. Stillwell, "The Political Meaning of Chaucer's *Tale of Melibee*," 434. In *War in Medieval English Society*, J. Barnie seems to follow Stillwell (132). Both follow Sundby (XVI).

7. P. Olson, *The "Canterbury Tales" and the Good Society*, 120.

king, and about mediation of disputes, especially by women. The different historical events to which the historicist critics want to connect the tale are all plausible referents for the allegory because there was a common thread of war and peace and counsel among the events of the late fourteenth century and because the allegory is vague.[8] There was a good deal of war, and there were enough sentiments for peace that Chaucer might well have wanted to contribute to the discussion. And it is likely that anyone who wanted to do so would see the wisdom of doing so in an oblique manner. But the multiple candidates for the war and peace in the tale—for instance, the French war,[9] Gaunt's war with Castile,[10] the peace agreement with Flanders[11]—explain why many of the critics mention the importance of advice in the fourteenth century. If the tale is merely saying that advice is advisable, there is less need to pin down exactly what its particular advice was about.[12]

But the questions still remain: What in his own time made Chaucer think of the previous generation's French translation of the even older Italian story of Melibeus? And for what purpose did he mean to use it? Why did he want to insert it into the contemporary scene? How many, if any, relevant historical events did he mean to be drawing in? How current were they? For instance, did he mean readers of a story about a woman who convinces a man to make peace with his enemies to think of the end of Edward III's reign when Alice Perrers was accused of destroying Edward's taste for war? Even if he didn't intend that association, could he prevent it?

He did give us one clear indication that he knew the tale could have political reverberations and that he wanted to control them: He left out the proverb in his French source on how troublesome it is to have a child as a king.[13] This deletion shows that Chaucer knew that the tale could be taken as a reference to Richard II's accession to the throne when he was still a

8. See L. Patterson, "'What Man Artow?'" 137; P. Olson, The "Canterbury Tales" and the Good Society, 119; G. Stillwell, "The Political Meaning of Chaucer's Tale of Melibee."

9. G. Stillwell, "The Political Meaning of Chaucer's Tale of Melibee"; W. Askins, "The Tale of Melibee and the Crisis at Westminster, November, 1387"; R. F. Yeager, "Pax Poetica."

10. J. L. Hotson, "The Tale of Melibeus and John of Gaunt."

11. V. J. Scattergood, "Chaucer and the French War."

12. J. Barnie, War in Medieval English Society; R. F. Green, Poets and Princepleasers; P. Olson, The "Canterbury Tales" and the Good Society; P. Strohm, Social Chaucer; L. S. Johnson, "Inverse Counsel."

13. "Et Salemon dit, 'Doulente la terre qui a enfant a seigneur. . . .'" Renaud de Louens in Sources and Analogues of Chaucer's Canterbury Tales, ed. W. F. Bryan and G. Dempster, 581, ll. 381–82.

young boy.[14] The deletion changes the French text to limit the interpretation of the tale.[15]

Despite taking out the reference to youthful kings, Chaucer left in his source's reference to youthful counsellors, which might have been almost as troublesome because Richard was accused of paying too much heed to his young counsellor, Robert de Vere.[16] In one case he removed the lines likely to cause offense; in the other he did not. Why the difference?

The formalist critics of the tale notice that it is occupied by the issues of war, peace, and advice that invite historicist readings. But by examining the way the issues are twisted and knotted, the formalists attack the notion that the tale straightforwardly comments on anything. They see the surface meaning of the tale as undermined by irony and paradox. Some of them use post-structuralist theory, but despite post-structuralism's interest in contradictions not intended by the author, they all attribute these hermeneutical games to Chaucer the poet.[17] They watch him pitting proverb against proverb and pulling morals out from under their exempla. As H. Marshall Leicester, Jr. says, Chaucer "decenters [the tale's] 'original' logocentric meaning as stable, timeless wisdom."[18] Or, as Daniel Kempton puts it in his equally deconstructive interpretation of the tale, in Chaucer's hands the "restless discourse of quotation undoes the idea of Holy Writ."[19] This approach would appear to see Chaucer as mounting an attack on the *Fürstenspiegel* as a genre and on its timeless wisdom, except that, as we have already seen, the *Secretum Secretorum* tradition is also riven with such fault lines. The *Melibee*'s self-contradictions put it firmly in the mainstream of the tradition.

The *Melibee* calls into question the possibility of its own project, edu-

---

14. For the date of the tale, see note 3. H. Cooper argues that the deletion itself does not date the tale because it could have offended before Richard took the throne and at any time during his reign (*Oxford Guides to Chaucer: The Canterbury Tales*, 311–12).

15. It is irrelevant to the *Melibee* but interesting to note that the proverb was cited as evidence of treason in a trial in 1444 (J. G. Bellamy, *The Law of Treason in England in the Later Middle Ages*, 118).

16. G. Stillwell, "The Political Meaning of Chaucer's *Tale of Melibee*," 442.

17. For a non-deconstructive version of this approach, see D. MacDonald, "Proverbs, *Sententiae*, and *Exempla* in Chaucer's Comic Tales," 456–57. MacDonald, who takes the *Melibee* as an exception to the rules of "comic misapplication," suggests that with very little alteration, Prudence could be made to sound like Pertolote, but implies that she doesn't.

18. H. Marshall Leicester, Jr., "Our Tonges Différance," 25. Also see R. Waterhouse and G. Griffiths, "'Sweete Wordes' of Non-Sense," Parts I and II.

19. D. Kempton, "Chaucer's Tale of Melibee," 274.

cating the ruler. Melibee's initial plan is to declare war on the enemies who wounded his wife and daughter (ll. 1009, 1050), but Prudence wants him to eschew vengeance and be reconciled with his foes: "'Certes,' quod she, 'I conseille yow that ye accorde with youre adversaries and that ye have pees with hem'" (l. 1675).[20] After hundreds of lines of instruction and advice on peacemaking, and even after Prudence has actually taken things out of Melibee's hands, making war unnecessary by winning the adversaries' acquiescence to her mediation of the conflict (ll. 1765–68), he resists her message. When she asks him what he intends to do, he replies that he will certainly exile and disinherit them all (ll. 1832–35).

As Lee Patterson says, since "Prudence's task is to teach Melibee how to interpret," this is "an aporetic moment that subverts the pedagogical program the *Melibee* simultaneously espouses and enacts." According to Patterson, this moment reveals "a systematic contradiction that inhabits the text as a whole."[21] Melibee's scant progress reveals the contradictions at the heart of the tale.

The "pedagogical program" of the tale is sabotaged by the failings of both the student and the teacher. Melibee is obtuse, of course. Even when he accepts Prudence's reasonable advice to call a council to discuss his response to the attack of his enemies, he gets it wrong. Prudence had told him to summon his "trewe freendes all" and his "lynage whiche that been wise," citing a maxim often included in the *Secretum Secretorum*, "Werk alle thy thynges by conseil, and thou shalt never repente" (ll. 1002–3). Yet he summons "a greet congregacion of folk" who were neither— including physicians and surgeons, flatterers and lawyers, old enemies to whom he was only superficially reconciled, and neighbors who fear him (ll. 1004–7). When he then ignores the advice of the few wise speakers and endorses the majority's call for war, Prudence has to start all over, critiquing his list of invited guests and reinterpreting their speeches, teaching him how to choose counsellors (ll. 1115–26), and finally doing the peacemaking herself.

Melibee is sometimes not merely obtuse, but illogical. For instance, after he has accepted the decision of his invited guests, he resists hearing Prudence's advice (ll. 1055–61). But his refusal to take her advice at this juncture is very peculiar because he has just done so: It was on her advice that he called the meeting that he now uses as a justification for not listening

20. *The Riverside Chaucer.*
21. L. Patterson, "'What Man Artow?'" 158, 157.

to any *more* advice (l. 1056). As if to highlight this inconsistency, Chaucer adds a phrase to his source, saying that Melibee convened his meeting "by the conseil of his wyf Prudence" (l. 1004). Melibee cannot refuse her advice now without impugning her earlier advice, and himself: "I seye that alle wommen been wikke, and noon good of hem alle. For 'of a thousand men,' seith Salomon, 'I foond o good man, but certes, of alle wommen, good womman foond I nevere.' / And also, certes, if I governed me by thy conseil, it sholde seme that I hadde yeve to thee over me the maistrie, and God forbede that it so weere!" (ll. 1057–58). These are debatable though plausible reasons not to have taken her advice the first time she offered it, but not the second. The quotation from Solomon notwithstanding, by bringing them up now he undermines his own authority.

Nor is Prudence's advice free of problems. Since we sometimes hear both her and Melibee's renditions of what others have said, we can compare their interpretations. At the initial council, for instance, the surgeons refuse to support the option of war against those who attacked Prudence and Sophie, paraphrasing the Hippocratic oath ("that we do no damage") and promising to try to heal Sophie's wounds (ll. 1011–15). Then the physicians speak: "Almoost right in the same wise the phisiciens answerden, save that they seyden a fewe woordes moore: / that right as maladies been cured by hir contraries, right so shul men warisshe werre by vengeaunce" (ll. 1016–17). Later, Prudence wants to know what Melibee thought of the surgeons' and physicians' advice, referring approvingly to the paraphrase of the Hippocratic oath and asking him particularly about his understanding of the physicans' extra words on the cure by contraries (ll. 1267–78). Melibee's version is "that right as [my enemies] han doon me a contrarie, right so sholde I doon hem another. / For right as they han venged hem on me and doon me wrong, right so shal I venge me upon hem and doon hem wrong; / and thanne have I cured oon contrarie by another" (ll. 1280–82). Prudence has a different interpretation:

Lo, lo . . . how lightly is every man enclined to his owene desir and to his owene plesaunce! / Certes . . . the wordes of the phisiciens ne sholde nat han been understonden in thys wise. / For certes, wikkednesse is nat contrarie to wikkednesse, ne vengeance to vengeaunce, ne wrong to wrong, but they been semblable. / And therfore o vengeaunce is nat warished by another vengeaunce, ne o wroong by another wroong, / but everich of hem encreesceth and aggreggeth oother, / But certes, the wordes of the phisiciens sholde been understonden in this wise: / for good and wikkednesse been two contraries, and pees and werre, vengeaunce and suffraunce, discord and accord, and manye othere thynges; / but certes, discord by accord, werre by pees, and so forth of othere thynges. (ll. 1283–90)

She goes on, adding an admonition from St. Paul.

The "fewe woordes moore" that the physicians add to the surgeons' sentiments transform them into their opposite, so that the narrator's judgment that the two groups are "almoost" the same seems comical or disingenuous. The issue—whether two things are opposite or alike—is exactly the issue raised by Prudence's interrogation of Melibee. After Melibee's fairly accurate reading of the physicians' advice, Prudence converts their meaning into its opposite by invoking a different sense of "contrarie." While the word can mean, as she suggests, "opposite," it can also mean "opposed," which fits a retaliatory attack. Prudence is using a semantic switch, as well as her frequent interjections of "Certes" and her hermeneutical lament—"Lo, lo . . . how lightly is every man enclined to his owene desir and to his owene plesaunce!"—to take a contrary view of contraries and distort the physicians' intentions. Despite Melibee's slowness to accept Prudence's point of view, these interpretive difficulties are Prudence's: She is interpreting according to "desir" and "pleasaunce."[22]

Thus, since both Melibee and Prudence have faults as interpreters, it is no wonder that the whole project of educating Melibee is called into question. It is also called into question by a conflict at its heart. As Daniel Kempton points out, there is a contradiction between her early principle, "Make no felawshipe with thyne olde enemys" (l. 1189), and her entire enterprise in the tale, producing a reconcilation between Melibee and his enemies.[23] Her ability to quote authorities on both sides of the question keeps her from justifying her choices between them at any given moment. The choices look pragmatic: When she wishes to displace Melibee's old enemies as advisers, she quotes one set of authorities. When she wishes to advocate peace, she quotes the other. Her wish to prevail overcomes her previous advice on the process of soliciting advice.

She makes obvious the lack of principle on which to base a choice when she tells Melibee's enemies,

Now sithen [Solomon] deffendeth that man sholde nat yeven to his broother ne to his freend the myght of his body, / by a strenger resoun he deffendeth and forbedeth

---

22. She also does this when she interprets Melibee's interpretation of the advice of the lawyers. They say, in essence, "Defend yourself" (ll. 1526–27); he adds "They said I should defend myself by building towers" (ll. 1333–34); and she interprets the towers allegorically as pride (l. 1335), but here there is no pretense of interpreting the lawyers' intentions.

23. D. Kempton, "Chaucer's Tale of Melibee," 268.

a man to yeven hymself to his enemy. / And nathelees I conseille you that ye mys-
truste nat my lord, / for I woot wel and knowe verraily that he is debonaire and
meeke, large, curteys, / and nothyng desirous ne coveitous of good ne richesse. . . .
Forthermoore I knowe wel and am right seur that he shal nothyng doon in this
nede withouten my conseil, / and I shal so werken in this cause that by the grace of
oure Lord God ye shul been reconsiled unto us. (ll. 1757–64)

She sounds logical as she explains Solomon's reasoning. But her "nathelees"
carries with it no evidence, just the personal testimony about Melibee's
good will (which, as we have seen, is hardly reliable), and her claims about
her influence over him. But nevertheless she glides past Solomon with a
smooth "And nathelees" — "nathelees" to acknowledge the conflict, but
"and" to gloss over it.

    Prudence's ability to jump from one maxim to its opposite stirs up
another threat to the project: her recognition of the dangers of advice itself.
While she is trying to correct the damage done by the incorrectly consti-
tuted council that Melibee summoned at her behest, she provides him
with advice about advice, material that sounds some traditional themes
from mirrors for princes like the *Secretum Secretorum*. In choosing counsellors, she counsels, start with God (ll. 1115–19): "Ye shul first in alle youre
werkes mekely biseken to the heighe God that he wol be youre conseillour"
(l. 1116). Of course this is impossible because he has started with Prudence,
both in calling the abortive council and now in letting her begin again by
telling her, "I wol governe me by thy conseil in alle thyng" (l. 1114). It is
too late for him to start with God.

    The next steps produce several additional problems: Melibee is to take
counsel in himself and keep the results secret because secrecy is the only
way to avoid being betrayed (ll. 1138–53). Neither friends nor foes are trustworthy (l. 1141). Then he is to choose a few tested friends who are faithful,
wise, and old to be counsellors (ll. 1154–65). He must not consult all his
friends, but just "a fewe" (l. 1166). Yet he must not have just one counsellor,
he should have "manye" (l. 1170). Not only is the recommended number of
counsellors unstable, it is not clear that it is a good idea to have counsellors
at all. This contradiction is fundamental. If one can safely tell secrets neither
"to thy foo ne to thy frend" (l. 1141), nor indeed to "any wight" (l. 1145),[24]
then the whole project is compromised. Like the liar's paradox, it is a self-
consuming artifact. If he takes her advice not to take the advice of other
people, he has already done so. Although I wrote about this contradiction

    24. Just in case we were tempted to think that wives might be a safe alternative to friends
and foes, this last category ensures that they are eliminated, too.

in the *Melibee* earlier,[25] I did not see then how consonant it was with other mirrors for princes. But we have already seen that advice, which a ruler must have, is a threat to him. Guicciardini's warning, which I use as the epigraph to this chapter, is a nice expression of the double bind. Prudence's warning that "whan thou biwreyest thy conseil to any wight, he holdeth thee in his snare" (l. 1145) echoes the *Secretum Secretorum*'s warnings that needing advice makes the ruler vulnerable (see Chapter 3). Prudence's willingness to tap into this tradition produces a conundrum that not only seems to make her inconsistent, but even jeopardizes her own goal of getting Melibee to do what she wants.

That the tale is riven with these contradictions threatens the historicists' claim that it seriously addresses topical matters. A serious comment on getting good advice — an idea supported by several critics — seems particularly unlikely. On the one hand, the amount of support both historicist and formalist approaches have garnered is testimony to their plausibility. But on the other, the fact that the two approaches seem incompatible attacks the plausibility of both.

There are possibilities outside the stark binary opposition between "it's topical about something" and "it shoots itself in the foot too often to be topical about anything." Critics have suggested other interpretations. For instance, the tale could be a religious allegory about forgiveness. The material that Chaucer adds at the end of the tale, including Melibee's characterization of his enemies as "sory and repentant of youre giltes" (l. 1879) and his hope that God will forgive all sinners at their deaths if they are "sory and repentant of the synnes and giltes" (l. 1885) they have committed, indicates his true intentions for the Melibee story.[26] Chaucer wishes to enhance the story's potential as an allegory of Christian penitence. But as Charles Owen has shown, the religious allegory is not altogether free of contradictions if it seems that Prudence, in asking Melibee to forgive his three enemies, is asking him to forgive their allegorical significations — the world, the flesh, and the devil.[27]

Another way to deal with the topical/nontopical opposition is to see it as the topic of the tale. Lee Patterson reads the *Melibee* as Chaucer's meditation on his own ambivalence about whether to use his poetry to

25. J. Ferster, *Chaucer on Interpretation*, 19–22.
26. J. Flynn noted these changes in "Reconstructing *Melibee*."
27. C. Owen notes such paradoxes and suggests ways around them in "The *Tale of Melibee*."

engage topical issues. Chaucer uses the recurring image of the child — Sophie, Melibee when domination by Prudence infantalizes him,[28] and Chaucer himself when Harry Bailly calls him "a poppet" in the *Prologue to Sir Thopas* (l. 701) — to dramatize his reluctant but necessary entrance into history.[29]

As appealing as these readings are — the religious one because it takes account of changes Chaucer made to the source that appear to indicate his intentions for the tale, Patterson's because it turns the problem into the solution — I am not yet ready to give up on the possibility of historicizing the tale in all its self-contradictory, self-consuming glory. But to make the connection between the tale and its time, we need more contextualizing information, particularly on relevant political events and on Chaucer's relationship to the court. These are the subjects of the next two sections.

England in the Late 1380s

The events between 1385 and 1389 that might have prompted Chaucer to write the *Melibee* bring together the issues of advice and military policy. Many of the historicists writing about the *Melibee* notice that the two issues are present, but they do not talk about their interrelations. These are crucial because, as we saw in Chapter 5, the great promoters of advice were also promoters of war. They were offended by the king's attempts to make peace with France, and offended that he tried to do it without consulting them. One chronicle reports that during the crisis of 1388, in which the Appellants tried a number of Richard's advisers for treason, they threatened to depose Richard "because it appeared that he preferred to govern through false traitors rather than through his most faithful friends the lords and nobles of the realm."[30] As magnates, the large land-holders of England, they felt that they had a right to advise the king that went back at least to Magna Carta (see Chapter 2).

The Appellants' complaints about the king's inner circle — that it was

28. L. Patterson, "'What Man Artow?'" 158.

29. L. Patterson, "'What Man Artow?'" In *Chaucer and His Readers*, S. Lerer interprets the version of the *Melibee* in the Helmingham manuscript of the *Canterbury Tales* as being adapted specifically for child readers (93–100).

30. *Polychronicon Ranulphi Higden Monachi Cestrensis*, IX, 103. Translated in A. R. Myers, ed., *English Historical Documents, 1327–1485*, 155. Also see *The Westminster Chronicle, 1381–1394*, ed. and trans. L. C. Hector and B. F. Harvey, 218–19. For accusations in the appeal that the advisers prevented others from having access to the king and monopolized his patronage, see, inter alia, 242–47.

too small and included the wrong people — were at least partly motivated by Richard's attempts to make peace with France. The Appellants had profited from the war and were sorry to see it pursued less vigorously.[31] The appeals of treason they initiated against the king's counsellors included the peace negotiations with France, especially those involving Calais.[32] Thus the people who supported peace were not the same as those who spoke movingly of their rights to advise the king. According to Anthony Tuck, "the appellants' purpose was to remove the favourites from their positions of influence over the king, ensure their own access to patronage, and initiate a more militant policy towards France."[33] They accomplished all this, having purged the king's household and installed themselves on the Council so that they controlled the government for the next year.

The commons in parliament did like peace, especially after the Rising of 1381, which ominously dramatized the domestic price of heavy taxes for war. They sometimes resisted appeals for money to prosecute the war, perhaps trying to avoid another outbreak of violence. In the years after the Merciless Parliament, Richard's policy of seeking peace with France may well have been motivated by his wish to be less dependent on the commons.[34] But the commons sometimes joined with the Appellants in their opposition to the king because of his lack of success in procuring peace and what looked to them like financial mismanagement.[35] When the Appellants, too, succumbed to financial corruption, the commons left the alliance.[36]

From 1386 to 1389, as the control of government shifted back and forth between the alliance of the Appellants and parliament and Richard and his advisers, foreign policy changed from peace to war and back again. Finally, because the Appellants were as unsuccessful in waging war when they controlled the government in 1388 as Richard had been in waging peace in 1387, they were themselves forced to resume negotiations with France for a truce. When Richard regained power, he continued the negotiations that led to the peace that had long been his goal.

---

31. One of the things Richard was blamed for was not sending aid to John of Gaunt in Ghent in 1385 during the supposed crusade.

32. L. C. Hector and B. F. Harvey, eds. and trans., *Westminster Chronicle*. On rumors of Richard's plans to relinquish all French territories except Aquitaine, see 204–5. For the complaint in the appeal that they were trying to surrender Calais, see 262–63.

33. A. Tuck, *Crown and Nobility, 1272–1461*, 196.

34. A. Tuck, *Crown and Nobility, 1272–1461*, 199.

35. J. J. N. Palmer, *England, France and Christendom, 1377–99*, 82–85.

36. J. J. N. Palmer, *England, France and Christendom, 1377–99*, 137.

Chaucer in the Late 1380s

Recent work on Chaucer's role in these turbulent years suggests that although Chaucer had some connection to the family of one of the Appellants (Chaucer's friend Sir William Beauchamp was the brother of the Appellant Thomas Beauchamp, earl of Warwick),[37] his connections were chiefly to royalists, including some of those killed by the Merciless Parliament (e.g., Tresilian, Thomas Usk, Brembre).[38] According to Paul Strohm, of the eleven men convicted of treason by the Appellants, Chaucer was associated in some way with eight.[39]

In 1386, when the Wonderful Parliament impeached the king's favorite, Michael de la Pole, John of Gaunt, often a moderating influence, was out of England pursuing his interests in Castile.[40] Chaucer may have felt vulnerable when the parliament presented a petition requesting that all controllers given lifetime appointments by the king be removed because of their corruption.[41] Chaucer's was not a lifetime appointment, but in December of 1386, less than a month after the anti-royalist council took over the government, he resigned his two controllerships (wool and petty customs). He also left his house and gave up his annuities. He seems to have been taking himself out of the line of fire as the Appellants began to move against the beneficiaries of Richard's patronage.[42] According to Derek Pearsall, "There was no 'king's party' in the strict sense of the word, since all who were in government were the recipients of royal patronage in some measure. But insofar as there was one, Chaucer was of it."[43] Distancing himself from the bureaucracy may have felt like a prudent way to ride out the period that turned out to be dangerous for a number of his friends and associates who had connections with Richard, some of whom were merely deprived of their jobs, others of whom were executed.

But Chaucer did not go very far. When he spent 1385–89 as a member

37. S. Sanderlin, "Chaucer and Richardian Politics," 173.

38. Thomas Beauchamp himself had royalist connections, having been Chamberlain of the Household from 1378 to 1380 (P. Strohm, *Social Chaucer*, 27).

39. P. Strohm, *Social Chaucer*, 27. "Politics and Poetics," 94–95.

40. On Chaucer's associations with John of Gaunt and his son Henry of Derby, see P. Strohm, *Social Chaucer*, 34–46. Henry's shifting relationships with the Appellants and the development of Gaunt's foreign polical ambitions are good indicators of the fluidity of political alliances during this period.

41. P. Strohm, *Social Chaucer*, 37.

42. D. Pearsall, *The Life of Geoffrey Chaucer*, 209. See also P. Strohm, *Social Chaucer*, 37; and "Politics and Poetics," 93. Lee Patterson doubts that Chaucer's departure was as voluntary as "taking himself . . ." implies. See his review of *Social Chaucer* in *Speculum* (April 1992): 487.

43. D. Pearsall, *The Life of Geoffrey Chaucer*, 209.

of the Peace Commission for Kent, and represented Kent in the Wonderful Parliament of 1386, he was probably still associated with Richard. As Lee Patterson points out, Chaucer's relationship with Kent may have been an example of "that meddling in local affairs of which men complained a decade later when they described Richard's tyranny."[44] Witnessing the Wonderful Parliament as a representative of Kent might have given Chaucer some vivid glimpses of the possible dangers to the king's friends in the erupting factional disputes.

The *Melibee* in the Late 1380s

The historical setting and Chaucer's place in it can help to reconcile the topicality of the tale with the contradictions that seem to destroy its ability to address contemporary issues. One possibility is that the elusiveness caused by its contradictions and paradoxes is a cover for its political intent (see Chapter 2 on constraints on political speech). The puzzles could be disguise. Lynn Staley Johnson notes both that Prudence urges Melibee to take responsibility for his own actions and that Chaucer himself takes evasive action in order not to be held responsible for political comment (for instance, by presenting himself as a "mere" translator). This contradiction may provide a link between the formalist and historicist readings. According to several commentators, the tale has to disguise its political commentary because it is so dangerous to take a side on the various conflicts.[45] The historicists use this notion of political disguise when talking about the tale's *generality*, which makes it hard to connect it to specific historical events.[46] But the notion of disguise could also be used to explain the fact that the tale is a self-consuming artifact. What better disguise is there than to pretend not to be saying anything at all?[47]

But what is the political comment that Chaucer is trying to soften by making the tale a conundrum? If one takes a bipolar view of late medieval English politics — the king versus everyone else — then advocating advice, as Prudence does most of the time, looks like advocacy on the side of the

44. L. Patterson, *Chaucer and the Subject of History*, 36.
45. L. S. Johnson, "Inverse Counsel," 154.
46. On generality as protection for the writer, see historicists such as G. Stillwell, "The Political Meaning of Chaucer's *Tale of Melibee*," R. F. Green, *Poets and Principleasers* (164); and J. Barnie, *War in Medieval English Society* (132).
47. See D. Lawton, "Dullness and the Fifteenth Century."

Appellants. But her calls for peace place her on Richard's side on the subject of the war with France. So the two issues had opposite valences. Those sympathetic to one were probably not sympathetic to the other.

Perhaps this split is the reason that Chaucer was willing to retain in the tale the criticism of young counsellors, just at the time Richard was criticized for having one among his favorites: Robert de Vere, although young, was not pro-war, as were the young counsellors in the *Melibee* (ll. 1035–36). As I said above ("England in the Late 1380s"), when the Merciless Parliament accused Richard's advisers, including de Vere, of treason, among the charges were treasonous dealings with France. That is, the Appellants were saying that attempts to create peace between the two countries were a betrayal of England.[48] Since de Vere was associated with Richard's peace policy, Richard would not have felt vulnerable to the charge that he was allowing inexperienced youths to drag him into war with France.[49]

Since Chaucer was likely to have been on the king's side in his struggle with the Appellants, maybe his treatment of both issues supports the king: Both Prudence's advocacy of peace and the deconstruction of Prudence's advice on advice could be ways of supporting or comforting the king. Perhaps Chaucer was trying to make advice look ridiculous by showing that its bromides self-destruct. If Chaucer wrote the *Melibee* for Richard when he was feuding with the parliament over who should choose his advisers, perhaps Richard was happy to be told that advice, praised though it was by his adversaries, produced its own problems. Maybe a deconstruction of the Appellants' ideology of advice was just what he wanted to hear.

In fact, the Appellants were rather like Prudence in that one of the reasons that they made such a fuss about advice was that they didn't like the ruler's policy. Prudence disliked war and they disliked peace, but all of them used talk about the process of advice, especially the choice of advisers, to oppose its outcome. Prudence went from advising Melibee about how to get good advice to actually implementing her own plan. The Appellants and their supporters implemented their own plan by replacing Richard's hated favorites on the council. In some sense, Chaucer is using the tale to expose the ways in which those who talk about process are sometimes really trying to manipulate it. Prudence's advisory coup echoes the Appellants' takeover of the government in 1388.

48. J. J. N. Palmer, *England, France and Christendom, 1377–99*, 115.
49. In addition, two of the Appellants, Thomas Mowbray and Henry Bolingbroke, were relatively young at this time.

The compartmentalization of the criticism of the *Melibee*, the separation of historicism from formalism, is unnecessary. The historicists can deal with the contradictions and paradoxes the formalists point out. And the formalists must understand that to point out contradictions and paradoxes is not to prevent the tale from having some political significance. The paradoxes and contradictions do not rule out politics; they merely make the tale's politics more complex.

As I noted in Chapter 1, following Pierre Macherey,[50] literature can test ideology by finding and exploring its gaps and contradictions. But the *Melibee* shows that such an activity does not necessarily free literature from the politics of its historical situation. In the late fourteenth century, to expose the contradictions in the ideology of advice was to take sides in the conflict between the king and the Appellants. When the tale appears to be referring to contemporary politics, it probably is. And when it appears *not* to be referring to contemporary politics, it may still be.

Chaucer in the 1990s

Because one of my general claims in this book is that even writers who are indebted to a powerful ruler (like James Yonge), or who wish to be so indebted (like Hoccleve), or who are just subject to him (like Gower) can criticize him, I must take account of how the *Melibee*, as I read it, fits in. To do that will also be to situate the tale with respect to the recent social and political interpretations of Chaucer.

Since Chaucer is so rarely overtly topical, a number of critics have focused on ways in which, as David Aers says, "linguistic, social, and subjective processes" are "bound together in the structure and history of particular communities."[51] Examining Chaucer's themes and style, they argue that he attacks the dominant ideology by showing that it is not only not unitary, but also not "natural" — that the categories it presents are socially constructed. Their argument is that Chaucer understood culture as disenchanted, to use H. Marshall Leicester's word — not God-given, but manmade.[52] For historicists like Aers, Paul Strohm, David Wallace, and Peggy Knapp, Chaucer knew that ideas that benefited a few were routinely pre-

---

50. P. Macherey, *A Theory of Literary Production*, 131–33.
51. D. Aers, *Community, Gender, and Individual Identity*, 3.
52. H. Marshall Leicester, Jr., *The Disenchanted Self*. Though not historicist in method, this book is very suggestive for historicism.

sented as divinely ordered for the good of all, and he challenged the hegemony of a "top down" social structure and the authority that justified it.[53] His response was to challenge ideology by deconstructing and multiplying it and thus toppling the hierarchy it supported.[54] When applied to the *Melibee*, this approach can emphasize the tale's anti-militarism, as Aers does.[55] Or, it can emphasize the importance of horizontal rather than vertical relationships. As Strohm reads it, the tale's promotion of counsel moderates "the ideology of the descending state ruled by a lord in the image of God."[56]

But the tale has also been read as more supportive of ruling class ideology. Stephen Knight emphasizes the utility to rulers of reforming their use of wealth and of winning peace to maintain order. The *Melibee* is a "serious and thoughtful address to the powerful on how to save their power." For Knight, it is the focus of Chaucer's conservatism in the *Canterbury Tales*.[57]

According to Larry Scanlon, the *Melibee*'s position on the power of rulers is paradoxical since Melibee must show he is worthy of sovereignty by giving it up (when he decides not to take vengeance on his enemies, who submit to him).[58] This paradox does not contradict Knight's view of the tale since the restraint is voluntary, but for Scanlon it has to do with the growing importance of statute law as adjudicatory process replaced the chivalric ideal of vengeance.[59]

As we have already seen, Lee Patterson provides another kind of historicist reading of the *Melibee*. Patterson argues that the tale's paradoxes and self-contradictions are Chaucer's way of rejecting the role of court poet. He

53. D. Aers, *Chaucer, Langland and the Creative Imagination*, "The *Parliament of Fowls*"; and *Chaucer*. In *Social Chaucer*, P. Strohm carefully places Chaucer in his social context and shows how Chaucer substitutes horizontal relations for the vertical ones of the dominant, hierarchical model. See also his "Politics and Poetics." Strohm has recently extended his investigation of literature's ability to perform "oppositional action" (9) in *Hochon's Arrow*. D. Wallace, "'Whan She Translated Was.'" P. Knapp, *Chaucer and the Social Contest*. Some of my readings of Chaucer's works in *Chaucer on Interpretation*—for instance, those of the *General Prologue*, the *Knight's Tale*, and the *Clerk's Tale*—fit into this "school" of criticism.

54. This approach is consonant with an earlier thread in Chaucer criticism in which Chaucer was seen as problematizing the verities of his culture. See, for example, Robert O. Payne's *The Key of Remembrance*; and Stewart Justman's "'Auctoritee' and the *Knight's Tale*," and "Medieval Monism and Abuse of Authority in Chaucer."

55. D. Aers, *Chaucer*, 28–29.

56. P. Strohm, *Social Chaucer*, 163. Strohm cites Paul Olson's view that the tale, like its source, supports "the consultative as opposed to the absolutist view of the prerogative of the King" (Olson, *The "Canterbury Tales" and the Good Society*, 120.)

57. S. Knight, *Geoffrey Chaucer*, 139.

58. L. Scanlon, *Narrative, Authority, and Power*, 213–15.

59. L. Scanlon, *Narrative, Authority, and Power*, 212–13.

refuses to give voice to "the traditional discourse of counsel" in favor of "a discourse that insists upon its autonomy from both ideological programs and social appropriations."[60] This view of the tale fits well with Patterson's approach to the rest of Chaucer's career in *Chaucer and the Subject of History*, where he argues that Chaucer is aware of the dynamic changes going on in his society, but tries to withdraw from them. For instance, he reads the *Miller's Tale* as a response to the economic and political dynamism of the rural peasant class that registers the counter-hegemonic energy to be found in the countryside.[61] For Patterson, the rest of the *Canterbury Tales* demonstrate "the extent to which the urgent social issues raised by the *Miller's Tale* have been disarmed."[62]

In my reading of the *Melibee*, I cross some of the categories I have set up here. I agree with the Chaucerians who affirm the ability of literature to perform a counter-hegemonic function. But in my reading of Chaucer's support for Richard II in the *Melibee*, I appear to be producing a conservative Chaucer like Stephen Knight's. However, I do not, as Knight seems to, accept that Prudence offers practical advice that could help a ruler rule better. I agree more with Patterson in his deconstructive reading of the tale, in which all advice collapses through its self-contradictions. But I do not find such deconstruction a block to topicality, for an attack on the efficacy of advice, along with the tale's ruminations on war and peace, would have had political resonance in the middle of the 1380s. Thus deconstruction and historicism can work together. As Patterson points out in a later article, "Making Identities in Fifteenth-Century England," deconstruction's aim to bring to light "the suppressions and elisions" of ideology is a fundamentally historical project.[63]

Thus, the anomaly in my treatment of Chaucer can be explained by the social placement of the tale. All of the other writers I consider in this book who were connected to rulers — as clients or would-be clients, or merely as subjects — took risks when they challenged or criticized those rulers. In the shifting political circumstances in which Chaucer probably wrote *The Tale*

60. L. Patterson, "'What Man Artow?' " 173.

61. This is one of Patterson's major differences with Strohm, who in *Social Chaucer* locates the chief engine for social change in the "middle strata" (142). See L. Patterson's review of *Social Chaucer* (486–87).

62. L. Patterson, *Chaucer and the Subject of History*, 277. Patterson does not argue against resistance for all medieval literature: see his *Negotiating the Past*, and "Making Identities in Fifteenth-Century England."

63. L. Patterson, "Making Identities in Fifteenth-Century England," 70, 71. For Patterson, when *The Siege of Thebes* deconstructs itself, it becomes a challenge to the ruler it addresses.

of Melibee, the Appellants' successful displacement of Richard II may have made support of the king as risky as criticism of him might have been in another time. In the context of the Appellants' struggles with Richard II, deconstruction of the ideology of advice has a strong political valence. The *Melibee* was a challenge not to the king, but to the ruling elite who had challenged him.

7

O Political Gower

[It is] a thing wanton, not sad but insolent.

—George Barclay, sixteenth-century translator,
explaining why he refused to translate Gower's
Confessio Amantis into modern English.[1]

WHILE IT IS GENERALLY AGREED that by the time Henry of Lancaster deposed Richard II in 1399, Gower was a Lancastrian,[2] attempts to define Gower's political ideas have produced a riot of opinion. According to Gervase Mathew, in 1385 he appeared to be "a moderate old-fashioned royalist with a strong distrust for the King's advisers."[3] Eric Stockton notes that Gower denounces the peasants in the Rising of 1381.[4] But according to George Boas, he "had great sympathy" for them.[5] Stockton sees him as "a rock ribbed conservative" in the *Vox Clamantis*.[6] George Coffman concurs, calling Gower "middle-class, conservative," and more inclined to look for improvements in government from kings than from parliament.[7] John H. Fisher says he started out "among the progressive thinkers of his day" for his emphasis on "legal justice and regal responsibility" for the common good, but finally became a Lancastrian "apologist" and "sycophant."[8]

1. Quoted by M. A. Manzalaoui, "'Noght in the Registre of Venus,'" 181.
2. Gower changed the dedication of the *Confessio Amantis* from Richard II to Henry in 1393. He also eliminated the poem's praise of the king. It is always significant when one removes such signs of respect for a monarch, especially given the story in the earlier versions that Richard had asked Gower to write the poem (Prologus 24ff. and *24ff.). But Gower's revisions were not predictions of the later usurpation. Henry and Richard were not enemies in 1393.
3. G. Mathew, *The Court of Richard II*, 81.
4. E. W. Stockton, trans., *The Major Latin Works of John Gower*, 19.
5. G. Boas, *Vox Populi*, 24. To support his description, Boas cites ll. 12721–32 of *Mirour de l'Omme*.
6. E. W. Stockton, trans., *The Major Latin Works of John Gower*, 23.
7. G. R. Coffman, "John Gower, Mentor for Royalty;" see 964.
8. J. H. Fisher, *John Gower*, 178, 133.

Derek Pearsall argues that there "is no sense that Gower is acting as a hired man, a Lancastrian propagandist."[9] According to Paul Strohm, during the reign of Richard II, because Gower was financially independent, he was also politically independent; unlike Chaucer, he was "effectively non-aligned."[10] But Russell Peck and Elizabeth Porter might call the attempt to pin down Gower's specific political views misguided because he treated political issues as moral ones. According to Peck, although Gower is an energetic social critic, for him "social issues resolve themselves in the personal lives of men." Gower aligns "social criticism with a benevolent psychology of personal ethics."[11] According to Porter, he took from other mirrors for princes the idea that "good governance of others depends on ethical self-rule."[12] Those who emphasize Gower as a moralist might think Chaucer's apostrophe to him — "O moral Gower"[13] — more appropriate than my title for this chapter.

One explanation for these contradictory assessments is the tumultuousness of the period in which Gower lived and wrote; any reasonable or reasonably prudent person might well have changed his mind several times during the late fourteenth and early fifteenth centuries. And Gower's assiduous revising is evidence that he did, on occasion, change his mind or his alliances. He was clearly engaged with major social and political issues. The part of the *Vox Clamantis* written after 1381 responds directly to the rising, and *Cronica Tripertita* tells the story of the deposition of Richard II by Henry Bolingbroke, formerly Henry of Derby. Even if the content of the *Confessio Amantis* were unquestionably apolitical, the change in its dedication from Richard II to Henry of Derby not long after the struggle between Richard and the Appellants, of whom Henry was one, would have catapulted the work into the political arena.[14] Like the *Melibee*, but drawing

9. D. Pearsall, *Old English and Middle English Poetry*, 209.

10. P. Strohm, *Social Chaucer*, 42, 31. Also see his "Form and Social Statement in *Confessio Amantis* and *The Canterbury Tales*," 37–38.

11. R. Peck, *Kingship & Common Profit in Gower's "Confessio Amantis*," xxi.

12. E. Porter, "Gower's Ethical Microcosm and Political Macrocosm," 135. L. Scanlon develops this idea — with greater emphasis on Gower as "a sophisticated political thinker" — in chapter 9 of *Narrative, Authority, and Power*; see 263. Gower makes the connection between politics and ethics explicit at the end of the *Cronica Tripertita*, taking Richard II as the example of a sinner who could not rule others successfully (E. W. Stockton, *The Major Latin Works*, 326).

13. G. Chaucer, *Troilus and Criseyde*, V. 1856.

14. See J. H. Fisher's account of the revisions in *John Gower*, 116–27. V. J. Scattergood, who sees Gower as politically "conventional" and generally supportive of the king, says that the changes in dedications of the *Confessio Amantis* indicate "some shifting of position." See his *Politics and Poetry in the Fifteenth Century*, 19. For an account of the change in the dedication as a response to events in 1390–91, see G. B. Stow, "Richard II in John Gower's *Confessio Amantis*."

more on the *Secretum Secretorum*, the *Confessio* responds to the turbulence of the late 1380s.

The turbulent times also meant that political discourse was probably dangerous. As we saw in Chapter 2, although it was not likely that a writer would be executed for a poem, it was also probably not wise to be openly critical of the faction in power, or the faction that might be in power to-morrow. Given that the king's struggle with the Appellants was couched in terms of advice, with their criticisms swirling around his counsellors, the years during which Gower wrote the first draft of the *Confessio Amantis* (1386–90) were highly charged ones in which to write a mirror for princes. The dangers plus the accompanying constraints on political speech help account for Gower's elusiveness, especially when he wrote in English. This chapter examines Gower's ideas about advice to the king and the role of "the people" in government by examining specific passages in the *Mirour de l'Omme*, the *Vox Clamantis*, the *Confessio Amantis*, and the *Cronica Tripertita*. It will explore Gower's politics to shed some light on the social function of the mirrors for princes.

The Languages of Advice

Since Gower wrote in all of the languages of the England of his day, it is very instructive to examine the different things he chooses to say to and about kings in Latin, French, and English. There is a range of directness. The earliest work, the *Mirour de l'Omme*, probably composed between 1376 and 1379,[15] may be the least direct. The section on kings (ll. 22225–23208) is full of examples of Biblical kings and general advice, little of it directed at a particular ruler. The pattern is, "kings who are good do this" or "if a king wants to be good, he should do that." But the *Mirour* has its moment of boldness, signaled by the word "meintenant" (l. 22808, "nowa-days,"[16]), which pointedly updates its traditional blandishments; when the narrator blames kings who are ruled by women (22803–12), he is gib-ing at Edward III, who was dominated by his mistress Alice Perrers. Since Edward was senile at this time but Perrers was not, perhaps Russell Peck's phrase for Gower, "a fearless critic of men in high places," should be taken

---

15. G. C. Macaulay, *The Complete Works of John Gower: The French Works*, xliii; J. H. Fisher, *John Gower*, 95.
16. *John Gower: "Mirour de l'Omme,"* trans. W. B. Wilson, 298.

to include women, too.[17] Of course, to judge just how fearless he was being, we should know the relationship of the composition of the poem, or at least this part of it, to the Good Parliament, so that we could tell whether Perrers was in a position to retaliate, or had been ousted from court, or had returned when the results of the Good Parliament were quickly undone. Unfortunately, scholars cannot pinpoint the date of the poem. But, however daring this passage was, it is the exception in the *Mirour*, which generally does not fashion barbs for contemporary figures out of its estates satire material.

One passage of the *Vox Clamantis* is bolder: It derides a competent king in his prime. Writing in Latin, Gower used plenty of general estates satire complaints, charging various groups in society with not fulfilling their proper functions. But he also levels a particular charge against the king, calling him an undisciplined boy who not only is *"indoctus"* — untaught, untrained, or ignorant — but also "neglects the moral behavior by which a man might grow up from a boy" (Book VI, Chapter 7, ll. 555–56).[18] Gower then excoriates Richard's equally irresponsible young advisers and selfishly greedy old advisers, and himself takes on the role of good adviser (VI.7.557–80) in order to bestow upon Richard the benefits of very traditional counsel from the *Fürstenspiegel* tradition (VI.8–18).[19] This might have been appropriate if Richard had actually been a young boy, but this passage is from the section of the *Vox* that Gower revised, probably in 1393.[20] Richard would have been of age with four years of full control of the government behind him. Gower's complaints about young advisers hark back to the late 1380s and Richard's conflicts with the appellant lords, whose criticisms of his rule included those about his young adviser, Robert de Vere (see Chapter 5, "Richard II"). Here, Gower's fearlessness is less equivocal than in the *Mirour*.

It is very illuminating to compare this passage from the *Vox* with related material from the *Confessio Amantis*. The English poem begins with either a dedication to Richard II in the Prologue (original version, *l. 24) or a revised dedication to England with a mere mention of Richard (ll. 24–

17. R. Peck, *Kingship and Common Profit in Gower's "Confessio Amantis,"* xx.

18. E. G. Macaulay, *The Complete Works of John Gower: The Latin Works*; E. W. Stockton, trans., *The Major Latin Works of John Gower*, 232.

19. Some of it, in another revised section, is made topical by *"nunc"* ("nowadays"), which makes its concerns current (VI.18.1179); E. W. Stockton, trans., *The Major Latin Works of John Gower*, 248.

20. E. W. Stockton, trans., *The Major Latin Works of John Gower*, 13. For the dates of the rest of the poem, see 11–12.

25), and then nestles the rest of the poem inside narration by a persona, the lover Amans, who in turn nestles some stories of kings from the *Secretum Secretorum* and other sources inside an inner frame in which Aristotle advises his pupil Alexander. The kings in the *Confessio* are from faraway places and long ago times, but as we shall see later in the chapter, the distance does not keep them from having some contemporary bite. What I am interested in here is Gower's different techniques for giving advice to a king in his different languages. In English, his criticism of the king is not quite so insolent, to use George Barclay's word from the epigraph to this chapter, as it is in Latin. It is more delicate, more hedged. Depending on the date of the *Mirour* and its relations to the phases of Alice Perrers's career, perhaps the French advice to the king is somewhere in between that in English and that in Latin on the "insolence" scale. But for Gower, English seems to require more tact and circumspection.

This contrast is complicated by the fact that in the *Confessio*, Gower does not leave the English to speak for itself, but surrounds it with Latin prose and poetry. According to Rita Copeland, even without the Latin commentaries and glosses, the English poem imitates various kinds of Latin academic discourse in order to transfer Latin authority into the vernacular.[21] According to Derek Pearsall, the Latin passages offer a particular academic interpretation of the English poem, which creates a kind of tension between the Latin and the English text.[22] Although I cannot define carefully all the relations between the English work and the Latin scaffolding that surrounds it, it is useful to note how, in the rhetorically elaborate Latin epigraph to the English prologue, the poet belittles his skills and condescends to his English poem and claims that it sings "of lesser things" (*minora*).[23] Derek Pearsall thinks that the implied comparison is to the *Vox Clamantis*.[24]

"*Minora*" might be one clue to reasons for the difference between the address to the king in the *Vox* and the address to the king in the *Confessio*. The subject matter is clearly not "lesser." It is the same, and it is great — the state of mankind, including all classes. But the rhetorical stance he can take toward it in English is less presumptuous. Gower is telling us, in an authoritative Latin modesty trope, that his English poem has less authority.

Some of this difference in authority must come from history and tradition — what has been said before in each language. Some perhaps comes

---

21. R. Copeland, *Rhetoric, Hermeneutics, and Translation in the Middle Ages*, 202–20.
22. D. Pearsall, "Gower's Latin in the *Confessio Amantis*," 20.
23. See Pearsall's excellent translation and discussion of this verse, "Gower's Latin in the *Confessio*," 16–17.
24. D. Pearsall, "Gower's Latin in the *Confessio Amantis*," 16.

from different historical circumstances and some from Gower's different circumstances. That the *Mirour* was his first major poem might explain some of its traditional character. But I wonder if some of the difference also comes from the different audiences the languages might have. I assume that the English audience is bigger than the Latin audience so that in some way what you say to your king in English is more public; perhaps in this less intimate, more open forum, it is wise to refrain from chastising him so directly. The rest of this chapter will examine Gower's techniques for chastising him discreetly.

The Hermeneutics of Counsel in the *Confessio Amantis*

That a king should have advisers, that they should tell him the truth rather than what he likes to hear, that the king should accept good advice and not bad, and that he should avoid flatterers are commonplaces of medieval advice literature, as we have already seen in the *Secretum Secretorum* and the *Melibee*. Gower invokes the importance of "good consail on alle sides" at the very beginning of the *Confessio*: It will keep the ruler "upriht" (Prologus.146–47).[25] But as we have also seen, such nostrums can get entangled and complicated until they are exposed as useless. Gower, too, affirms but then undermines the platitudes.

In Book VII of the *Confessio*, Gower praises truth-tellers partly by castigating flatterers, who give only good news and tell the king only what he wants to hear. They have no allegiance to truth and so distort the king's view of the world.[26] When speaking to the king,

> . . . thei by sleihte and be fallas
> Of feigned wordes make him wene
> That blak is whyt and blew is grene . . .
> . . . and sein
> That al is wel, what evere he doth;
> And thus of fals thei maken soth. . . .
>   (VII.2186–88, 2194–96)

---

25. K. Olsson notes the appropriateness of the poem's form as a compilation of examples to its exhortation to pay heed to diverse counsel (*John Gower and the Structures of Conversion*, 23–24).

All quotations from the poem are from *The English Works of John Gower*, ed. G. C. Macaulay. Reprinted as volumes 2 and 3 of *The Complete Works of John Gower*.

26. "So that here kinges yhe is blent / And wot not hou the world is went" (VII.2197–98).

This passage presents a number of binary oppositions — black/white, blue/
green, and most importantly, falsehood/truth — that show the narrowness
of the range of options for speech to the king. Advice is either on one side
or the other because reality is either on one side or the other. There is no
place in this formulation for gray or turquoise or ambiguity or the process
of interpretation. The world is as simple as the categories of the speech that
describe it.

The stories that follow challenge these simplistic formulations. For instance, almost immediately after the warnings about "flatours" (VII.2179),
Genius tells the story of Diogenes and Aristippus (VII.2217–2327), philosopher friends who part: Aristippus goes to court to flatter and become
rich, and Diogenes goes home to study and become wise. When Aristippus
finds Diogenes picking herbs in his garden, he chastises him for not seeking his fortune in court. Diogenes replies by chastising him for not seeking
reason, and advises him to consider picking herbs instead of seeking gain
in court. This story, told from an adviser's point of view, suggests that
since princes want only flattery, the wise should never even try to give
them good advice. If Diogenes had his way, princes would not get any
advice at all.

Other stories, rejecting this prohibition on advice, show rulers trying
to obtain advice. Tarquin and his son Arrons take over the town of the
Gabiens by a trick. Arrons wounds himself and throws himself upon their
mercy, claiming to be estranged from his father and prey to his father's
attacks. They trust him, and when the time seems right to Tarquin, Arrons
kills all the town's leaders. Tarquin marches in, slaughtering citizens, and
conquers the town.

The Gabiens' leaders do not welcome Arrons unthoughtfully. They do
several things right:

> Whan that the lordes hadde sein
> Hou wofully he was besein,
> Thei token Pite of his grief:
> Bot yit it was hem wonder lief
> That Rome him hadde exiled so.
> These Gabiens be conseil tho
> Upon the goddes made him swere,
> That he to hem schal trouthe bere
> And strengthen hem with al his myht;

And thei also him have behiht
To helpen him in his querele.
                      (VII.4641–51)

First, they take pity on him (VII.4643). Pity (VII.3103 ff.) is one of the five
points of policy that "yive entendement / Of good reule and good regiment" and "worthi governance" to the prince (VII.1701–2; 1708) and or-
ganize the major part of Book VII. Like the others, Truth (VII.1723ff.),
Liberality (1985ff.), Justice (2695ff.), and Chastity (VII.4215ff.), Pity is
meant to restrain the ruler. Thus, there is the same ambiguity about who is
being ruled in the *Confessio Amantis* as we saw in the *Secretum Secretorum*
and the *Melibee*. It is noteworthy here that not long after extensive praise of
pity as a policy for governing, Gower provides a story about how it visits
disaster upon leaders who try to exercise it.

The other thing the Gabiens do right is to seek counsel (VII.4646).
They ask for advice and they take it. They investigate Arrons's intentions
toward them as if they understand that the whole story could be fabricated.
Of course their mistake is to allow Arrons to be the sole witness about his
intentions, but the point is that in the face of deception, counsel and oaths
to tell the truth mean little. And because of the very nature of deception, it
is difficult to tell when it is intruding between words and intent.

What endangers the Gabiens besides deception is their predisposition
to be deceived. The Gabiens are partners in Arrons's treachery because of
how much they want him to be telling the truth. "But yit it was hem wonder lief / That Rome him hadde exiled so" (VII.4644–45). His story is
pleasant to them because it accords with their desire; their self-interest
governs their interpretations of his oaths and his pledges of aid. Counsel
and truth remain constantly in jeopardy not only from deceivers but also
from the desires of the deceived. None of these elements — pity, counsel, the oath, the Gabiens' pleasure — is present in Ovid's *Fasti*, Gower's
source.[27] Gower develops the story to demonstrate the tricky hermeneutics
of counsel.

The Biblical story of Ahab and Micheas sheds some interesting light
on the sad plight of the Gabiens, both reinforcing it and showing that the
opposite tactics — assuming someone is not telling the truth — do not work
very well either. King Ahab has to decide whether to try to recover some

---

27. Ovid, *The Fasti*, 77–78.

land from Syria. At the request of his son-in-law Josaphat, he assembles a group of prophets to advise him. Following the lead of the chief prophet Sedechias, the prophets all say that an expedition against the Syrians will be successful. Josaphat is suspicious, calling these predictions "fantosme" (VII.2589) and asking for some other prophet. Ahab produces Micheas, whom he had imprisoned because "yit he seide nevere wel" (VII.2603). Those who bring Micheas out of prison counsel him

> That he wol seie no contraire,
> Wherof the king mai be desplesed,
> For so schal every man ben esed,
> And he mai helpe himselve also.
>   (VII.2614–17)

Although Micheas has credibility precisely because he does not strive to please, his advisers tell him that everyone's welfare will improve if he tells the king what the king wants to hear.

At this point in the Bible, when Ahab asks his question about the advisability of fighting the Syrians, Micheas answers, "Go up, and prosper, and the Lord shall deliver it into the king's hands" (III Kings 22.15).[28] Since Ahab is conditioned to expect nothing but predictions of doom from Micheas, he refuses to accept that rosy answer and insists on the truth. Gower excises what the Biblical Ahab takes as Micheas's sarcastic joke at the king's expense and substitutes for it a straightforward reaffirmation of Micheas's commitment to truth (VII.2618–32).

In both the Bible and the *Confessio Amantis*, when Ahab presses Micheas, the prophet recounts his vision of God's wish to deceive Ahab:

And the Lord said: Who shall deceive Achab, king of Israel, that he may go up, and fall at Ramoth Galaad?
. . . And there came forth a spirit . . . and said: I will deceive him. . . . I will go forth, and be a lying spirit in the mouth of all his prophets. And the Lord said: Thou shalt deceive *him*, and shalt prevail: go forth, and do so. (III Kings 22.20–22)

> "In what thing mai I best beguile
> The king Achab?" . . .
> Tho seide a spirit ate laste,
> "I undertake this emprise. . . .

28. *The Holy Bible translated from the Latin Vulgate, Douay Rheims Version*, 383.

I schal," quod he, "deceive and lye
With flaterende prophecie
In suche mouthes as he lieveth."
                    (VII.2645–53)

Micheas goes on to predict defeat at the hands of the Syrians. Sedechias
strikes him, the king sends him back to prison, and his prediction comes
true: Ahab is killed, Josaphat is not. Both their sons rule after them, Ahab's
badly.

This is a shocking story. What hope does anyone have for discovering
the truth if the source of the difficulty is God himself? Since God is supposed to be the ground of truth, this is a radical idea. In Micheas's vision,
the center has no wish to hold. The changes that Gower makes soften this
story a little: God is not explicit about seeking Ahab's death. But the fourteen lines that Gower has added before the vision in his own and Micheas's
voice about Micheas's honesty support the truth of the vision. The insis-
tence that Micheas does not lie (along with the fact that he turns out to be
right) makes the story of God's deception even more discomfiting.

Another of the changes Gower makes in the story is to have the lying
spirit speak more precisely about his methods: He will put flattery in the
mouths of those Ahab believes (VII.2652–53). Thus Gower calls attention
to the problem—not only for this story, but for that of Arrons and the
Gabiens: People's interpretations are determined by their prejudgments.
The Gabiens believe what they think it is in their self-interest to believe.
Ahab believes what he wants to hear. In the Bible, he is not in the least
taken in by Micheas's sarcastic praise of the war since he is predisposed
to hear negative things from Micheas. And Josaphat also prejudges: Without any particular evidence, he refuses to believe the false prophecies.
None of them has any objective criteria for choosing between alternative
interpretations.

The final irony of the story is that Josaphat, despite his predisposition not to believe Sedechias and his troop of flatterers, follows Ahab into
battle. So even his accurate predispositions do not enable him to avoid defeat. Although his prejudices are closer to the truth than the Gabiens', they
do not help him very much. The advice the Gabiens get is proper, and
they follow it, but because they are interpreting Arrons through their own
desires, they choose wrongly and are destroyed. Josaphat is also interpreting through his prejudices, and though they are correct, he chooses
wrongly and is also destroyed. The story of the Gabiens is destabilizing

enough; with the addition of the story of Ahab and Micheas, the whole enterprise of getting advice from counsellors seems futile, or worse. And if Diogenes is right, the enterprise is futile from the point of view of the counsellors, too.

The King and His Counsellors

We can now see how the *Confessio Amantis* shares with the *Secretum Secretorum* and the *Melibee* the tendency to deconstruct the main paradigm of advice—a king requesting advice from men chosen as counsellors. This impulse to deconstruct the relationship between ruler and adviser may be related to the crack in the foundation of the *Confessio* that appears in the Prologue: that although the poem bewails and sets out to remedy the problem of division that plagues the world (e.g., VII.127, 348–51, 645–49, 706, 781–85, 889–90), division is inherent in the nature of man, who is made of four elements (VII.975–78). Love, the overall theme of the poem, is meant to align the parts of man properly, but it must work, in a sense, against the grain. Gower reminds us of this at the start of Book VII when Aristotle instructs Alexander in the divided nature of the world (VII.203–392) and of man (VII.393–489). Any attempts at spiritual order and unity have to contend with the fact that, like the earth, in his body man is "variatus" ("diversified," "varied"; see the Latin verse after VII.202). Given the disunity of man and the world he inhabits, perhaps it is no wonder that the systems he invents to promote knowledge and good governance do not work. The language in which Gower writes the poem is itself a sign of division, as he points out when he tells the story of Babel (Prologus.1017–31). Rita Copeland points out the paradox of Gower's announcing in Latin, in the first epigraph to the Prologue, his intention to write an English poem.[29] How could a vernacular poem ever heal division? The poem's major unity is in its theme of disunity.

But the poem's deconstruction of the paradigm of advice also has a social function in the *Confessio*. We can link Gower's skepticism about the wisdom produced by a king and his counsellors to Gervase Mathew's idea that Gower shows "a strong distrust for the King's advisers."[30] Gower's handling of some of the stories in Book VII both criticizes the king who

29. R. Copeland, *Rhetoric, Hermeneutics, and Translation in the Middle Ages*, 216–17.
30. G. Mathew, *The Court of Richard II*, 81.

listens only to a tight circle of advisers and suggests an alternative. In the late 1380s, the king's relationship to his advisers was scrutinized and publicly criticized when it became the subject of a destructive struggle between the king and the Appellants in which Richard was probably temporarily deposed and some of his advisers were executed (see Chapter 5). In this context, Gower threads his way very carefully among potentially controversial political issues as he tells the stories of Book VII. His politics are revealed when we note which stories he tells and how he changes his sources.

Gower takes from Livy the same story that appears in the *Canterbury Tales* as the *Physician's Tale*. It tells of how Apius, a corrupt *decemvir*, one of the ten rulers of Rome, tries to manipulate the laws in order to get possession of Virginia, a chaste young woman. Her father Virginius, in order to save her honor, kills her. In Livy's *Early History of Rome*, this story is overtly political. The *decemvirs* had come to power by overturning democratic laws. But the citizens of Rome are so stirred up by Apius's unjust claim on Virginia that they not only overthrow all the *decemvirs* but also overturn the whole system of government, replacing it with democratic elections. Virginia the oppressed maiden becomes a symbol of the oppressed city,[31] and Apius's designs on her symbolize the injustice of the *decemvirs*. Apius kills himself while awaiting trial, and the revolutionaries demonstrate their republican zeal by giving fervent speeches about the evils of tyranny and the rights of citizens.[32]

In the *Confessio Amantis*, the story is not about a revolution; an unjust ruler is removed, but the system of government is not transformed. The word "tyranny" is used, but applies narrowly to Apius's attempt to exploit Virginia (VII.5235–37, 5285–89). Apius is removed from office because he is an unjust man, not because he runs an unjust government. Only his personal morality is at stake. There is no mention of his death. The story is a moral exemplum:

> . . . rihtwisnesse and lecherie
> Acorden noght in compaingie
> With him that hath the law on honde.
>   (VII.5125–27)

---

31. Livy, *Early History of Rome*, 233.
32. Livy, *Early History of Rome*, 236.

Virginius laments his daughter's shame, not, as in Livy, her loss of freedom.[33] There is no republican oratory. What is in Livy a system of social injustice becomes in Gower's poem a "prive tricherie" revealed (VII.5287–89).

These changes may be the sort of thing that prompts some critics to call Gower "conservative,"[34] or makes him look like more of a moralist than a political commentator. But to say that he was not a republican is not to say very much. There were no viable alternatives to monarchy during the English Middle Ages, no serious debates about other governmental options. Even the rebels in the Rising of 1381 were monarchists who looked to the king for reform and redress of their grievances.[35] We should not treat Gower's revisions of the story of Virginia as a way of measuring his allegiance to monarchy, something that hardly needs to be measured in late fourteenth-century England.

Gower may be dodging issues by appealing to the medieval taste for moral generality and the common idea that the well-being of the state depends on the morality of the ruler. But he is not *just* playing it safe. For one thing, the morality of the ruler had political import, as it does today. The "character issue" plagued the reigns of Richard II's deposed great-grandfather, Edward II, who, some thought, had taken his favorite adviser as a lover, and his grandfather, Edward III, whose mistress was so powerful that finally *she* had to be "deposed" by the Good Parliament of 1376.[36] There were even rumors about "obscene familiarities" between Richard and his favorite, Robert de Vere.[37] Telling the story under the rubric of "chastity" does not depoliticize it.

Furthermore, Gower adds some unmistakable contemporary references. When he describes the citizens meting out punishment for the malfeasance, he says:

33. Compare Gower's VII.5247–52 with Livy, 238.

34. According to S. Delany, Chaucer went even further to mute the social criticism when he translated the story. "Politics and the Paralysis of Poetic Imagination in *The Physician's Tale*." But L. Lomperis provides an alternative reading of the political implications of the attempt, in the *Physician's Tale*, to control the body and sexuality of Virginia. See "Unruly Bodies and Ruling Practices."

35. R. Hilton, *Bond Men Made Free*, 229.

36. On claims that Gaveston and Edward II were lovers and a different way to interpret their relationship, see P. Chaplais, *Piers Gaveston*, esp. 109–14. On Alice Perrers's removal from court, see M. McKisack, *The Fourteenth Century 1307–1399*, 390.

37. ("familiaritatis obscoenae"), Thomas Walsingham, *Chronica Monasterii S. Albani, Thomae Walsingham, Quondam Monachi S. Albani, Historia Anglicana*, vol. II: *A.D. 1381–1422*, ed. H. T. Riley, 148.

Forthi, er that it worse falle,
Thurgh comun conseil of hem alle
Thei have here wrongfull king deposed,
And hem in whom it was supposed
The conseil stod of his ledinge
Be lawe unto the dom thei bringe,
Wher thei receiven the penance
That longeth to such governance.
And thus thunchaste was chastised,
Wherof thei myhte been avised
That scholden afterward governe,
And be this evidence lerne,
Hou it is good a king eschuie
The lust of vice and vertu suie.
(VII.5293–5306)

A number of important transformations are evident here. For one thing, Gower calls Apius not a *decemvir* but a king, and when he is removed from office, Gower says he is "deposed" (VII.5295).[38] In case that does not thrust the story into the fourteenth century, with the deposition of Edward II and the threats of deposition against Edward III and, most immediately, Richard II (see Chapters 2 and 5), in VII.5302–3 he pointedly applies it to his own time to warn modern kings "That scholden afterward governe."

To make things still less comfortable, Gower shows that both the misdeed and the deposition involve advice. Advice preceded the act; the consultation in VII.5297 may hark back to that in VII.5171. It also precedes the punishment. The phrase "comun conseil" (VII.5294), which describes the consultation of those who depose Apius, is an important idiom in late fourteenth-century England, used in chronicles and parliamentary records, in Magna Carta and the notices of Edward II's deposition.[39] It indicated that someone taking an action is not acting on his own will or whim. The use of the English idiom brings the story very close to the medieval context.

The phrase "of hem alle" that Gower adds to modify "comun conseil" in VII.5294 is also a significant claim in the Middle Ages because unanimity

38. L. Scanlon discusses these changes in *Narrative, Authority, and Power*, 294–95. In this story, Scanlon sees, not subjects' power to restrain the king, but kings' need to earn their power through self-restraint. I read the story as offering more threat to kings who do not restrain themselves; see below.

39. See the Appendix to this chapter.

was crucial—in parliament and in more local institutions and gatherings.[40] For instance, Froissart mentions a village speaking to Richard "all with one voice."[41] Unanimity was necessary for juries, which had to reach agreement on verdicts.[42] In contrast, it was technically not necessary for parliament. There, the concept of majority rule was introduced early. But in practice, the minority often gave way to the majority so that decisions could be reported as unanimous.[43] In affirming the impeachment of Latimer and Lyons in the Good Parliament of 1376, all the commons are said to have "cried in one voice."[44] Both houses speaking "with one voice" carried great weight. For instance, after the Rising of 1381, Richard offered them the opportunity to revoke the manumission and enfranchisement that he had— under duress—given all villeins during the rising. The parliamentary rolls show that both houses of parliament did so unanimously.[45]

In *Medieval Representation and Consent*, M. V. Clarke examines *Modus Tenendi Parliamentum*, a fourteenth-century treatise on the operations of parliament that gives the theoretical basis for the emphasis on unanimity in these documents. The treatise explains that "the proctors of the clergy of a single diocese have a greater voice in parliament, if they all agree, than the bishop himself."[46] They prevail, not if they outnumber him, but "si omnes sint concordes."[47] Decisions about the deposition of kings are often reported as having been made unanimously because unanimity carries authority.[48] (We will see testimony about unanimity in the *Vox Clamantis*.) Thus, in VII.5294 of the *Confessio Amantis*, Gower is telling us that the citizens of Rome are acting responsibly—as responsibly as citizens of England in similar circumstances.

That their responsible, citizenly wrath extends to the king's advisers (VII.5296–97) is striking in the context of the late 1380s, when the first version of the *Confessio* was written. Gower is coy about just what punish-

---

40. This idea is related to the unifying concept of the "community of the whole" that was so important in English political life. See Chapter 2, "England as a Political Nation."

41. R. B. Dobson, ed., *The Peasants' Revolt of 1381*, 316.

42. M. V. Clarke, *Medieval Representation and Consent*, 284.

43. J. Redlich, *The Procedure of the House of Commons*, vol. II, 264.

44. *Anonimalle Chronicle*, ed. V. H. Galbraith, 90.

45. R. B. Dobson, *The Peasants' Revolt*, 329. See also M. V. Clarke, *Medieval Representation and Consent*, 344ff.

46. M. V. Clarke, *Medieval Representation and Consent*, 336.

47. M. V. Clarke, *Medieval Representation and Consent*, 382.

48. For instance, M. V. Clarke cites the Lichfield Chronicle's report that Edward II was deposed "by the clamour of the whole people, unanimously. . . ." *Medieval Representation and Consent*, 185. When it came to accept the supposed "abdication" of Richard II in 1399, parliament spoke "unanimously and with one accord." Rolls of Parliament translated in B. Wilkinson, *Constitutional History of Medieval England 1216–1399*, vol. II, 310.

ment the advisers received—though he assures us that it was deserved. Criticism of a king's advisers puts Gower in the company of many who disapproved of Richard II's friends for their influence on governmental decisions and the king's personal behavior. Using the rather minimal dodge of seeming to speak through Livy, and suppressing the death of the king, Gower seems to be able to address not only the king but those surrounding him, warning the king that there are remedies for misgovernance, warning his advisers and would-be advisers that patience for all of them might grow thin. Citizens acting in concert could sweep them all away. Hedged or not, the story of Virginia constitutes a threat to the king.

Another of the threatening stories Gower recounts in Book VII is the Biblical story of Rehoboam, the king of Israel who caused the division of the kingdom into the two unequal parts of Judeah and Samaria (III Kings 12). He sparked the revolt that deprived him of most of his kingdom by refusing to moderate the heavy taxes imposed by his father. When his people asked for relief, he refused because he took the wrong advice: He listened to his young, foolish counsellors, not his old, wise ones.[49]

Although the story is presented under the moral rubric of Pity, and the presence in Book VII of the story of Solomon's sins shifts some of the blame away from Rehoboam,[50] its fourteenth-century political resonance is not far to seek. There were several taxes that could be candidates for the role of oppressive taxes that caused much grumbling: According to May McKisack, the people *were* overtaxed at the end of Edward III's reign.[51] According to Janet Coleman, taxes reached a new high in the first decade of Richard's reign, and taxes to support the war with France continued to be unpopular.[52] The poll tax of 1381 was the precipitating cause of the rising that Gower wrote about in the *Vox Clamantis*. Russell Peck says that Gower was using the story of Rehoboam to warn Richard that his taxes were making people restive, especially in London, and might cause another rising.[53]

---

49. John of Salisbury tells this story, with the same moral about the unwisdom of listening to unwise young counsellors, in *Policraticus* V.6. The trope of advisers who are inadequate because of their youth is still alive. In the spring of 1993, E. Yoder, Jr. was only one of many American political commentators to complain about the youth of President Clinton's advisers, who, he said, "however bright and dedicated, lack the sure touch that comes with experience and seasoning" ("Gergen May Change Clinton for the Better").

50. The story of Solomon's lust can be read as the preliminary cause of the division of the kingdom. Told some three hundred lines after the story of Rehoboam, it retroactively exonerates Rehoboam—because of his father's trespass, no matter what he did himself, the kingdom would have been divided (VII.4469–4545).

51. M. McKisack, *The Fourteenth Century: 1307–1399*, 385.

52. J. Coleman, *Medieval Readers and Writers*, 85.

53. R. A. Peck, *Kingship & Common Profit in Gower's "Confessio Amantis,"* 150.

The word "taillage" (l. 4045) gives the story another topical twist, since tallages were well-known and well-hated in the fourteenth century, and they were mentioned in the parliament of December 1381 as one of the causes of the rising.[54] In addition, Rehoboam's people justify their proposal for a reduction of taxes by pointing out that his father's great building projects are finished (ll. 4039–49), and Richard's predecessor, his grandfather Edward III, had also carried out a "massive building programme."[55] Another likely contemporary reference is in the aspersions cast on young counsellors. Robert de Vere, one of the royal favorites attacked by the Appellants, was only five years Richard's senior and was widely considered too young to have so much influence. He was accused of treason in 1387 and 1388, and was a much-vilified symbol of Richard's supposed susceptibility to bad advice.

The very choice of a story with these elements argues for Gower's intent to comment on issues of his own time. He also tells it in a way that enhances its contemporary bearing. In the Bible, the group that comes to the king to request tax relief is a "*multitudo*" — a "crowd," or a "mob" (*Biblia Sacra*, III Kings 12.3). In the *Confessio Amantis*, it is a parliament:

> The poeple upon a Parlement
> Avised were of on assent,
> And alle unto the king thei preiden,
> With comun vois. . . .
>   (VII.4031–34)

In fourteenth-century England it was widely recognized that the function of the commons in parliament was to respond to the king's requests for taxes.[56] The commons had won the right to approve.[57] They rarely refused,[58] but they occasionally resisted and put conditions on their approval, so that there was some negotiating between crown and commons.[59] Gower

54. *Rot. Parl.*, III.98–103; see R. B. Dobson, *The Peasants' Revolt of 1381*, 330.

55. C. Given-Wilson, *The Royal Household and the King's Affinity*, 259.

56. The phrase "comun vois," especially in conjunction with the verb "preiden," could well evoke the commons in parliament. See the Appendix under "preiden."

57. M. McKisack, *The Fourteenth Century*, 191–93. It was a right that was not definitively won once and for all, but had to be periodically reasserted.

58. J. Coleman, *Medieval Readers and Writers*, 85.

59. One of the most famous examples was in the Good Parliament of 1376, when the commons' unwillingness to discuss the granting of new taxes led to the dismissal of some of the king's counsellors and the appointment of new ones. See M. McKisack, *The Fourteenth Century*, 387–93.

depicts this process when the parliament offers Rehoboam an incentive to accede to their request:

> And *if* thee like to don so,
> We ben thi men for everemo,
> To gon and comen at thin heste.
>   (VII.4059–61; emphasis mine)

What is at stake in this process of advice and consent is the very basis of the king's ability to rule: the support of the people.

As in the story of Virginia, Gower describes the people's actions as being unanimous. They speak with "on assent" and "comun vois," an important claim, as we saw in the story of Virginia. They also couch their plea in language very like that used by the parliament:

> Oure liege lord, we thee beseche
> That thou receive oure humble speche
> And grante ous that which reson wile,
> Or of thi grace or of thi skile.
>   (VII.4035–38)

Addressing the king as their liege lord, praying, beseeching him, asking him to grant something, describing themselves as humble, and appealing to his reason are all rhetorical moves in the repertory of the commons in parliament.[60]

By using this contemporary vocabulary for the relationship between a king and his people, Gower makes the story topical for his fourteenth-century audience, bridging the distance between fourteenth-century England and Biblical Israel.[61] But this distance was not as great as it might seem because the story of Rehoboam was already functioning as a political code. It was a recognized way to criticize a king for listening to the "wrong" advisers, no matter what their age.[62] A famous example, already

---

60. See Appendix for examples.

61. This topicality provides one of Macaulay's arguments in his introduction to his edition that Book VII is a digression from the main purpose of the *Confessio* (*The English Works of John Gower* vol. I, xix). R. F. Yeager defends Book VII as an integral part of the work's structure in *John Gower's Poetic*, 196–216.

62. According to Bishop Stubbs, Rehoboam had already been used against a king (Edwy) in Anglo-Saxon times. *The Constitutional History of England in Its Origin and Development*, II, 382.

discussed Chapter 5 ("Edward III"), is Archbishop of Canterbury John Stratford, who, during his 1340–41 struggle with Edward III, wrote Edward a letter that was widely circulated (Stratford was trying to marshall support for himself) and subsequently incorporated into several chronicles.[63] When Stratford admonishes Edward about his choice of advisers, he lists several bad kings, among them Rehoboam, who "left the good counsel . . .of . . . aged and wise men who had been with his father, and did according to the counsel of young men who would fain please him and who knew little; whereby he lost all the land of Israel, save only the twelfth part. In like manner have many kings of Israel and of other lands been brought to trouble by evil counsel."[64] Stratford cites the counsellors' faults — their inexperience, their wish to please — and makes the link to other times and other places (for instance, fourteenth-century England) — "In like manner. . . ."

We can also see an explicit application of this story to Richard in the chronicle that Adam of Usk wrote after Richard's death. After discussing Robert de Vere, Adam says that "this Richard, with his youthful councillors, may well be likened to Rehoboam, son of Solomon, who lost the kingdom of Israel because he followed the advice of young men."[65]

Thus the Rehoboam story was used in a political fight with one king and to justify the deposition of another. I believe that it was part of a code for criticizing the king, and that when Gower told it in the *Confessio Amantis*, it had enough currency to have political resonance. As with the story of Virginia, despite a few moves to blunt the story's political effect, it is unmistakably critical of Richard II. And, as with the martyrdom of Virginia, Rehoboam's loss of his kingdom includes, as an integral element in the story, criticism of Richard's advisers.

The King and His People

As I have said, criticizing the king's advisers was one of the most common forms of political discourse in the Middle Ages. The king was often under-

---

63. For an account of the conflict, see R. M. Haines, *Archbishop John Stratford*, 278–327.

64. *Adae Murimuth: Continuatio Chronicarum. Robertus de Avesbury: De Gestis Mirabilibus Regis Edwardi Tertii*, ed. E. M. Thompson, 327. The original French is on 325. Thompson's translation of Stratford's letter is also printed, along with several other documents and accounts of the crisis, in B. Wilkinson's *Constitutional History of Medieval England, 1216–1399*, vol. II: *Politics and the Constitution, 1307–1399*, 188–203. A Latin version of the letter appears in Walsingham's *Chronica Monasterii S. Albani*, vol. I, *A.D. 1272–1381*, 231–47.

65. *Chronicon Adae de Usk: A.D. 1377–1404*, ed. and trans. E. M. Thompson, 35 (Latin); 149–50 (English).

stood to determine the character of the government,[66] which made him the person whom it was most appropriate and yet most dangerous to criticize. Censuring his advisers was safer; it was a way to complain about the government without attacking him.

But king and counsellors can also appear to form an inseparable unit, each determining the essence of the other. Gower portrays this symbiosis in a pair of contradictory stories. After the story of Rehoboam comes the question of which is more important:

> Wher it be betre for the lond
> A king himselve to be wys,
> And so to bere his oghne pris,
> And that his consail be noght good,
> Or other wise if it so stod,
> A king if he be vicious
> And his conseil be vertuous.
>   (VII.4150–56)

Although it is hard to imagine a historical situation in which this binary opposition could occur, the question is answered: It is better to have good advisers because they outnumber the king. It is therefore more likely that they could convert him than that he could convert them (VII.4157ff.).

This is a rational choice, as long as one accepts its dubious premise that persuasion is a matter of majority rule,[67] but it contradicts a story that comes just before that of Rehoboam. When King Lucius asks two counsellors about his reputation among the people, each flatters him in a different way. One says he is well thought of; the other, deploying the common tactic even against himself, says that the people excuse the king but blame his counsellors. The fool, contradicting what Genius says in VII.4147–66, then breaks in, scorning them both and telling the king that if he were good, his counsellors would be good, too (VII.3989–97). Lucius, inspired by this revelation, converts to the ways of virtue, reforms his counsel, and rights every wrong in his kingdom: "The poeple was nomore oppressed, / And thus stod every thing redressed" (VII.4009–10).

These stories cancel each other out, producing a chicken-and-egg conundrum. But as he is making a transition between the story of King Lucius

---

66. A. B. Ferguson, *The Articulate Citizen and the English Renaissance*, e.g., 9.
67. As we saw in Chapter 6, when Melibee uses this principle to sort through different advice he receives at a conference of advisers, Prudence rejects the results.

and the negative example of Rehoboam, Gower escapes the conundrum. If both king and counsellors are good, he says, vices disappear, virtue triumphs, and God is pleased (4011–18). He then slips in another comment:

> For if the comun poeple crie,
> And thanne a king list noght to plie
> To hiere what the clamour wolde,
> And otherwise thanne he scholde
> Desdeigneth forto don hem grace,
> It hath be sen in many place,
> Ther hath befalle gret contraire;
> And that I finde of ensamplaire.
>   (VII.4019–26)

With the surprising conjunction "For," which implies a hitherto unacknowledged causation, the unanswerable questions about the king and his counsellors are jettisoned in favor of the relationship between the king and his people. Since the king's true counsellors are the people, he should listen to their complaints. The key to his success is not his choice among aristocratic advisers, but his willingness to bend to hear the complaints of the commoners. The ultimate criticism of the king's advisers is to dismiss them. This comment introduces the story of Rehoboam, which, with its realistic portrayal of parliament, is the story with perhaps the clearest contemporary reference in Book VII. Thus, it becomes not only a story about a king choosing inexperienced advisers, but a story about a king who let the wrong advisers separate him from his people. Whereas Richard II's struggle with the Appellants made the important conflict appear to be between the king and the magnates, Gower seems to be saying that the more important dyad consists of the king and his people. Advisers matter less than the people as a whole.

Gower's emphasis on the king's direct relationship to his people is particularly striking in contrast to the advice of the *Secretum Secretorum*, which tells kings to make themselves scarce rather than mixing too freely with the people. Aristotle sounds like Shakespeare's Henry IV, who chastises his son for being too exposed publicly and explains his own popularity by his aloofness.[68] Rather, says Aristotle, kings should have advisers who keep open

---

68. *1 Henry IV*, III.2.39–91. M. Manzalaoui notes the relevance of Shakespeare's play to Gower's departure from the *Secretum Secretorum* ("'Noght in the Registre of Venus,'" 177). The relevant passage in the modern English translation of the Arabic *Secretum Secretorum* is on

court and speak with subjects in the king's stead.[69] Gower sweeps away the advisers' mediation and the king's reserve because destabilizing overtaxation occurs when he does not bend to hear.[70]

It is important to test this reading of the story of Rehoboam against what Gower says about the actions of the people in two important contemporary events: the Rising of 1381 and the deposition of Richard II. Gower's writing about contemporary events in Latin rather than English would seem to be evidence of his elitism,[71] especially in light of his famous vilification of the peasants in the Rising of 1381. But in fact, the *Vox Clamantis* is surprising because of the way it manipulates its eponymous motif of the voice. If we map the relationship between the narrator's voice and the people's voice, we can see several aspects of Gower's politics.

In several places Gower uses the aphorism "Vox populi, vox dei" ("The voice of the people is the voice of God"). When Gower quotes it, he does so approvingly, unlike Alcuin, who counsels Charlemagne not to believe it because actually, "the clamor of the crowd [vulgi] is very close to madness."[72] Such accusations of madness are a favorite medieval method of discrediting peasants.[73] The oppositions between voice and clamor and between godliness and insanity define two important poles for Gower. Book I of the last version of the *Vox*, Gower's horrified denunciation of the Rising of 1381, envisions groups of peasants turning into animals, that is, losing their human intellect: "They who had been men of reason before had the look of unreasoning brutes" (54),[74] and became "stupid and wild," "senseless" (55), "mad" and "filled with a devilish spirit" (57). Any bystander could

---

185; the Latin translation is on 49 (R. Steele and A. S. Fulton, eds.). According to H. R. Haldeman, when Richard Nixon was president he occasionally articulated a wish to be less available to the public. He wanted be "aloof, inaccessible, mysterious," and cited de Gaulle, who believed that "over-exposure detracts from impact. Shouldn't be too chummy, etc." (*The Haldeman Diaries: Inside the Nixon White House*, 59; also see 125).

69. Arabic, 238–39; Latin, 143 (R. Steele and A. S. Fulton, eds.).

70. P. R. Coss confirms that it was necessary for a late medieval king "to make a reality of that direct relationship with his subjects" ("Bastard Feudalism Revised," 62).

71. Not that the choice of English for the *Confessio*, with its formal structure, Latin glosses, and address to the learned (VIII.3112–14), was populist, either. For the significance of these features of the *Confessio*, see R. Copeland, *Rhetoric, Hermeneutics, and Translation in the Middle Ages*, 202–20. See also D. Pearsall, "Gower's Latin in the *Confessio Amantis*."

72. G. Boas, *Vox Populi*, 9.

73. See Lee Patterson's "'No Man His Reson Herde,'" 113–55 in *Literary Practice and Social Change in Britain, 1380–1530*, ed. L. Patterson, 135, 145–46. Another version of this essay is chapter 5 in Patterson's *Chaucer and the Subject of History*.

74. *The Major Latin Works of John Gower*, trans. E. W. Stockton. I refer to this translation in parentheses in the text. The Latin is in Macaulay's *Complete Works of John Gower: The Latin Works*.

tell that they were insane and possessed because they refused to work (54–57), instead behaving like their betters—that is, they usurped upper-class prerogatives (58, 61, 63). Very tellingly, they cried out "with the deep voices of monsters" (67), and the sound they produced was "noise" (66–68) of a particular quality: It was not unison, but rather, "they kept making various noises in various ways" (67).

Nevertheless, at other places in the work the voice of the people sounds healthier and is, in fact, merged with the narrator's. For instance, he ends the *Vox* by saying, "What I have set down is the voice of the people [plebis], but you will also see that where the people [populus] call out, God is often there" (Bk. VII, ch. 25. l. 1470; E. W. Stockton, 288). The "but" ("set") is striking here. It implies that the idea that the people have anything worth-while to say will be strange to the audience, as if to say, "I speak the words of the people, but listen anyway." This passage was probably written before Book I, with its disgust for the people and their inhuman voices. However, if we read the work in the current order, with Book I coming first, the "but" has a great deal of work to do to persuade us to accept this claim of author-ity based on God's alignment with their distress.[75]

In the *Cronica Tripertita*, which follows the *Vox*, the voice of the people plays a very active role. In the movement to overthrow Richard in favor of Henry, there are a number of voices: the "voice of the Commons" in par-liament (295), the voice of the people, and the voice of the narrator. The parliament brings charges against those who counsel the king badly and commit offenses in his name. The voice of the people is instrumental in the substitution of Henry for Richard, but it is unlike the voice of the people in Book I of the *Vox*. Here the people are very expressive and articu-late: They grumble at Richard, shout their praise of Henry (320), sing "in their hearts" and burst into "ringing speech" when Henry is chosen king (321), shout their agreement when Henry nullifies Richard's most recent decrees (322), and cry out for the vindication of the murdered duke of Gloucester (322).

Was Gower merely an opportunist, excoriating the people when they threatened his interests as a landowner and extolling their wisdom when they happened to agree with him? Or did he change his mind gradually over

---

75. In *Writing and Rebellion*, Steven Justice discusses the relationship between Book I and the rest of the *Vox* and its bearing on Gower's claim to speak for all, noting some of the passages I examine here. He says that Gower wants to distinguish his own voice crying from the peasants' clamor: "book I of the *Vox* turns a profound threat to his public self-commission into a strategy for extending it" (209).

the years in which he wrote the *Vox*, the *Confessio*, and the *Cronica Tripertita*? It is difficult to tell, of course, but there are some clues, even in the *Vox*, that he did not reject all peasants or blame only them for the rising. For one thing, he says that the ruling class shares the blame for the rising.[76] For another, he isolates the peasants who committed the worst crime of the revolt, the killing of Simon of Sudbury, Archbishop of Canterbury, and thus distinguishes between "the crazy peasantry" and "the people as a whole" (74). Furthermore, the way the work stands in its revised form, the horrors of peasant depredations in Book I are followed closely by assurances in Book II that all creatures, including — significantly — wild animals, obey a just man and rebel against a sinful one (103–6). The examples include Biblical kings like David, Saul, Nebuchadnezzar, and the Egyptian Pharaoh. Even though Book II was written earlier, this passage implies that Richard was to blame for the Rising of 1381. It is not far to the story of Rehoboam.

According to John H. Fisher, Gower's claim to speak for all the people is related to the tradition of Old Testament prophecy, but also "the notion of the universal voice had political overtones in the fourteenth-century struggle toward parliamentary sovereignty."[77] We can hear those overtones more clearly if we return to a concept I have already mentioned: unanimity. When in Book I of the *Vox* Gower disdains the people during the Rising of 1381, their voices are various, plural, not unanimous, and therefore, "noise." When in the *Cronica* he concurs with the people's voice, it is singular: The people speak "as though one man" to approve Henry's coronation (322). When Gower says that Henry was elected king "with *all the people*," and in fact "all the earth," praising him (320, emphasis mine; 321), he is being consistent with the medieval emphasis on unanimity, especially for depositions, and with his own description in the *Confessio Amantis* of the unanimous deposition of Apius, the corrupt Roman *decemvir*.

There is one other way in which Gower is echoing and reinforcing contemporary language about government. He says he does not speak for himself. "I am not speaking of these things on my own part," he says in the Prologue to Book III of the *Vox*; "rather, the voice of the people has reported them to me, and it complains of their adverse fate at every hand. I speak as the masses [vulgus] speak . . ." (III Prologus.11–13; E. W. Stock-

---

76. "Just as the lioness rages when robbed of her nursing cub and attacks the cattle near her, so the angry peasantry, bereft of the safeguard of justice, attacked the nobles with greater ferocity" (71).

77. J. H. Fisher, *John Gower*, 105. See also A. Middleton's "The Idea of Public Poetry in the Reign of Richard II."

ton, 113). As we saw in Chapter 2 ("England as a Political Nation"), this was the foundation of the idea of representation: that a person not speak for himself, but for those for whom he holds *plena potestas*. Gower is being self-aggrandizing in claiming to speak for all, because it was not literally true since he was not an MP. But he is careful to use the right formula for his claim: He does not speak *per se*.

Examination of these passages and ideas from three of Gower's major works alongside contemporary events reveals several things: first, that when he seems to dismiss aristocratic advisers in the *Confessio*, Gower is being consistent with his view that the people are the king's best advisers because they are the source of his power[78] and second, that Gower was in tune with some important principles of government in his time. When he spoke of the king, his advisers, and his people, and when he claimed to be speaking in the people's voice, he was often articulating some of the common understandings of fourteenth-century government, especially ones espoused by those who worked against the accumulation and arbitrary use of royal power. In some ways, then, Gower *was* speaking for—on behalf of and in defense of—the people.

Sad (Hi)Stories of the Deposition of Kings

In Gower's treatment of members of the government, there is some subservience, but also some subversiveness. When he writes in English, the language accessible to greater numbers of readers, he praises Richard (in the first version of the *Confessio Amantis*, which was copied even after he had revised the poem)[79] and does not speak directly of contemporary events. It might be seen as concessionary to use classical and Biblical tales instead of commenting on politics explicitly, but then it is hardly concessionary to make the story of Virginia into the story of the deposition of a king. And the vilification of the peasants in Book I of the *Vox Clamantis* is tempered by oblique blame of the elite—including the king—for the rising. In the passages I have examined, Gower shows just the mix of deference and veiled challenge to authority that both James C. Scott and Annabel Patterson describe in people whose speech is constrained.[80] The story of Rehoboam is

78. See E. W. Stockton, *The Major Latin Works*, 321.
79. J. H. Fisher, *John Gower*, 116–17.
80. J. C. Scott, *Domination and the Arts of Resistance*; A. Patterson, *Censorship and Interpretation*. For comments on both, see Chapter 1.

the perfect equivocal example. It is a Biblical tale far from the contemporary scene but brought closer by the inclusion of contemporary governmental language, and it was probably already readable, through a not-very-secret code, as a critique of the government. Having made the gesture of writing about long ago and far away kings, Gower seems to have felt free to criticize his own. The language of advice allows him to do it safely.

The language of advice had its value for the politicians, too. We have already seen in Chapter 5 that what lay behind the magnates' anger at Richard II for taking advice from the wrong people were actually other issues. Robert de Vere's real sins were that he channeled royal gifts and favors away from the magnates and helped Richard stifle the war with France that had been enriching them.[81] But, since to talk about their real complaints — loss of patronage and war profits — could have appeared too greedy and selfish, they needed covers, codes to avoid naming their interests (see Chapter 5). So the idioms of advice served the peers as well as the poets, providing for each acceptable language for opposition. When opposition to Richard erupted again in 1399 and Henry permanently usurped the throne, the poet's use of the language of advice in a fairly popular English poem may have mattered. According to Chris Given-Wilson, when he was finally deposed in earnest, Richard had plenty of noble supporters. The group of lords working against him was rather small. The crucial lack in his support was the gentry — minor land-owners like John Gower. After Richard had declared the end of his minority in 1389, he had cultivated them, perhaps attempting to create the more direct relationship with his people that Gower advocates in Book VII of the *Confessio*.[82] But their support for him ebbed away after 1397 when his policy changed to concentrate his attention on Cheshire; by 1399 his affinity had very narrow representation, which made him much more vulnerable to a revolt by a small elite.[83] This reversal of their loyalty may have coincided with and been reinforced by the *Confessio Amantis*, which some members of that class were reading between 1390 and 1399.[84] Perhaps as they allowed Rich-

---

81. A. Tuck, *Richard II and the English Nobility*, 86, 102, 127; *Crown and Nobility, 1272–1461*, 196.

82. P. R. Coss, "Bastard Feudalism Revised," 62.

83. C. Given-Wilson, *The Royal Household and the King's Affinity*, 255, 267; "The King and the Gentry," 96, 101–2; P. Morgan, *War and Society in Medieval Cheshire, 1277–1403*, 203–6.

84. See J. H. Fisher's analysis of the dating of manuscripts of the *Confessio Amantis, John Gower*, 117. In "English Books in and out of Court from Edward III to Henry VII," A. I. Doyle agrees with Fisher that some extant copies of the poem may have originally been made for "country gentry and London citizens"; even if not the original owners, they certainly owned them in the fifteenth century (171). Also see Doyle and Parkes, "The Production of Copies of

ard to be deposed and killed, they were remembering Gower's Apius and Rehoboam.[85]

And perhaps Henry of Lancaster, dedicatee of the revised *Confessio* (Prologus.87), was, too.[86] As we saw in Chapter 5, when Henry needed the support of the gentry, he used the language of advice again. At his accession, the Archbishop of Canterbury is reported to have said that Henry wished to be advised not only by the nobles but "by common counsel."[87] Thus, the language of advice used to oppose Richard was also used to legitimize as king the man who usurped his throne. Gower's work contributed to the erosion of support for Richard by helping to make the language of advice part of political discourse, honing it as an instrument for criticizing the king.

Appendix on Idioms

Here are examples of some uses, mostly in governmental documents, of idioms that Gower picks up in the *Confessio Amantis*. Each phrase from the *Confessio* is followed by references to historical uses of it.

ABBREVIATIONS

CA   *Confessio Amantis*

SM   *Sources of English Constitutional History: A Selection of Documents from A.D. 600 to the Interregnum*, vol. I, rev. ed., ed. and trans. by Carl Stephenson and Frederick George Marcham. The documents are translated and numbered continuously.

---

the *Canterbury Tales* and the *Confessio Amantis* in the Early Fifteenth Century" (with M. B. Parkes), 208–9.

85. Another overthrow of a government by popular uprising in the *Confessio Amantis* occurs after the rape of Lucrece, VII.5115–30. J. Coleman points to the socially engaged literature (e.g., *Mum and the Sothsegger, Wynnere and Wastoure*, the complaint poems of the MS Digby 102) that was helping the middle classes develop their "own political, critical voice." See "English Culture in the Fourteenth Century," 60.

86. It is likely that Henry was given a copy of the poem. According to C. Meale, it might have been Huntington MS EL.26.A.17, which would then have been inherited by Henry V at his father's death. "Patrons, Buyers and Owners," 203.

87. *Rotuli Parliamentorum*, III, 415. A. R. Myers, *English Historical Documents: 1327–1485*, no. 221, P. 415. S. B. Chrimes and A. L. Brown, eds. *Select Documents of English Constitutional History: 1307–1485*, 194. See also B. Wilkinson, *Constitutional History of England in the Fifteenth Century (1399–1485)*, 43.

LT   *English Constitutional Documents: 1307–1485*, ed. Eleanor C. Lodge and Gladys A. Thornton. The documents, in the original languages, are not numbered continuously.

M   *English Historical Documents: 1327–1485*, ed. A. R. Myers. The documents are translated and numbered continuously.

BW   Bertie Wilkinson (see footnotes for specific source).

RP   *Rotuli Parliamentorum*

THE IDIOMS

1. *CA* VII.4033 **"thei preiden"**
    LT #18, p. 141 *RP* II, 165, 8 (1348)
    LT #19, p. 141 *RP* II, 203, 30 (1348)
    LT #22, p. 143 *RP* II, 257, 13
    LT #29 pp. 147, 150, 149 ("les dites Communes prierent humblement a nostre Seignur le Roy en dit Parlement"), *RP* II, 321–60 (1376)
    LT #30, p. 151 *RP* II, 364, 10, 20 (1377)
    SM #63B, p. 235 (1378)
    SM #63F, p. 238 (1386), "the commons very humbly pray . . ."
    SM #63I, p. 241 (1397), "the commons prayed the king . . ."

2. *CA* VII. 4035 **"liege lord"** [an address to the king]
    SM #63A, p. 234 (1377)
    LT #33, p. 153 (1377), "Seignur lige" (see SM #63A)
    LT #30, p. 151 (1377)

3. *CA* VII.4036 **"humble speche"**
(The following are claims by petitioners to be humble or speak, beseech, pray, etc. humbly to the king):
    LT #29, pp. 149, 150 (1376)
    SM #63A, p. 234 (1377)
    LT #33, p. 153 (1377, see SM #63A)
    SM #63E, p. 237 (1381)
    SM #63F, p. 238 (1386)
    SM #63H, p. 241 (1397)
    LT #53, p. 165 (1414)

4. *CA* VII.4037 "**grante ous**"

(The following are requests to the king or descriptions of his or the parliament's actions in terms of granting or grants):

SM #62H, p. 229 (1353)

LT #30, p. 151 (1377)

SM #63A, pp. 233, 234 (1377)

LT #33, pp. 152, 153 (1377; see SM #63A)

SM #63C, p. 236 (1379)

SM #63G, p. 240 (1388)

SM #64E, p. 245 (*Statutes of the Realm*, 1391)

SM #63I, p. 241 (1398)

5. *CA* VII. 4037 "**reson**"

SM #63A, p. 234 (1377), "it seems reasonable . . ."

6. *CA* VII.5294 "**comun conseil**"

SM #44, pp. 117, 118 (Magna Carta, 1215)

SM #59, p. 205 (notice of Edward II's abdication, 1327)

LT #9, p. 21 (notice of Edward II's abdication in French: "commun conseil et assent")

SM #62H, p. 229 (1353), "by the counsel and common assent"

Anonimalle Chronicle: 1333 to 1381, p. 81

BW (*RP*, III, 415; "Henry IV's promise to rule with counsel and consent") [88]

BW (Summons of representatives of the counties and boroughs, *plena potestas* [1295]) [89]

---

88. Translated and excerpted in B. Wilkinson, *Constitutional History of England in the Fifteenth Century (1399–1485)*, p. 43. Also in M no. 221, p. 415. Also in S. B. Chrimes and A. L. Brown, *Select Documents of English Constitutional History: 1307–1485*, p. 194.

89. B. Wilkinson, *Constitutional History of Medieval England, 1216–1399*, vol. III, 308.

8

A Mirror for the Prince of Wales: Hoccleve's *Regement of Princes*

It is necessary for thee, O Alexander, to select writers of thine orders [rolls]. . . . [I]t is necessary to employ such writers as would make use of perfect meanings and put them in beautiful words well written. . . . And as the scribe is thy confidant in secret matters he ought to be trustworthy, honest, acquainted with thy intentions and with the consequences of thy affairs. . . . Thou shouldst favour him according to his faithfulness and painstakings in thy interests, and give him the rank of one free-born, whose fortune or misfortune is bound up with thine.[1]

CRITICS AND HISTORIANS WHO VALUE Thomas Hoccleve's major work, the *Regement of Princes*, are divided about its chief virtues. Some focus on the work's apparently autobiographical elements, and there is an engaging argument about whether the autobiography is individually distinct or merely borrowed.[2] Others emphasize its direct comments on the contemporary scene.[3] In this chapter, I hope to show that in Hoccleve's case the

1. A. S. Fulton, "The Secret of Secrets," in *Opera hactenus inedita* . . . , ed. R. Steele and A. S. Fulton, 242.

2. P. Doob has seen the autobiographical details in all of Hoccleve's poetry as conventional descriptions of mental disorder and therefore literary, not personal (*Nebuchadnezzar's Children*, chapter 5). Others claiming that Hoccleve's self-revelations are genuine include J. Burrow, who reminds us that the way people experience themselves and the world is, after all, "shaped by conventions" ("Autobiographical Poetry in the Middle Ages," 394). Also see S. Medcalf, "Inner and Outer," S. Kohl, "More than Virtues and Vices," and J. Mitchell, *Thomas Hoccleve*, chapter 1. This discussion contributes to the debate about the emergence of individualism in the Middle Ages.

3. While A. C. Reeves is unimpressed by the specificity of Hoccleve's contemporary references ("Thomas Hoccleve, Bureaucrat," 202, 211–12), A. B. Ferguson sees Hoccleve as a "hack-writer and time-server" whose "lapses into originality" produce a few useful observations about government (*The Articulate Citizen and the English Renaissance*, 89). V. J. Scattergood appreciates the poem's comments on issues like the election of bishops, abuses by liveried retainers, and the possibility of settling the conflict with France through a royal marriage (*Politics and Poetry in the Fifteenth Century*, 274–79, 222–25).

division between autobiography and topicality is a false one. Although the poet seems remarkably self-centered, from his complaint about the physical effects of writing all day as a clerk in the office of the privy seal (ll. 993ff.) [4] to his self-castigating accounts of past misbehavior (ll. 4362ff.) and plaintive requests for help in getting his tardy annuity paid (ll. 825ff.), his political comments are not flukes, momentary distractions from his personal obsessions. On the contrary, he is responding in very precise ways to real issues of the reign. His insistent humility but surprising boldness track major political battles and some of the uncertainties about monarchical power that haunted the first reign after the deposition and murder of Richard II. Not only do the personal and political themes echo each other throughout the poem,[5] but they are interwoven so tightly as to be inseparable.

Since, like Gower in the *Confessio Amantis*, Hoccleve claims to be able to speak for "the people," his repeated declarations of poverty seem not only to reveal personal information but also to position him politically. His claim to worthiness as an adviser for Henry, Prince of Wales, to whom he addresses the poem, rests on his representing others. It also echoes the *Secretum Secretorum*, which, in the passage that serves as the epigraph for this chapter, asserts the importance of clerks, not just as scribes but as advisers, and also concerns itself with their remuneration.[6] Therefore, Hoccleve's identity in the poem depends radically on his position in the society. The dialectic between the personal and the political also calls forth images of both the upward and downward political pressures that we have seen operating in other mirrors for princes. The links between Hoccleve's personal and political concerns appear when we locate the poem as specifically as possible in its historical situation at the end of Henry IV's reign and in the *Fürstenspiegel* tradition.

The date of the poem, crucial for any exploration of how it addresses its context, has been the subject of several contemporary discussions. In *Selections from Hoccleve*, M. C. Seymour dates the poem between the burning of John Badby on March 1, 1410 (ll. 281–329) and the death of Henry IV, when the Prince of Wales became king in March of 1413. He then

---

4. The text referred to in parentheses is F. J. Furnivall's edition, *Hoccleve's Works III. The Regement of Princes*. When quoting the poem, I do not follow Furnivall's indentations of the left margins or his diacritical marks.

5. D. C. Greetham, "Self-Referential Artifacts."

6. One Middle English version uses the word "remvneracion" where the English translation of the Arabic reads "favor" (M. A. Manzalaoui, ed., *Secretum Secretorum*, 83, MS Ashmole 396).

moves the second date back to 1411 by saying that the advice not to hold councils on holidays (ll. 4964–65) would not be relevant after the prince left the council in November of 1411, and by reference to the events of Hoccleve's life mentioned in the poem.[7] Derek Pearsall agrees with the narrower range of dates, but for him the reasons are not only that it would not be tactful to address the prince as someone in charge of councils after November of 1411 but also that Hoccleve's 1411 annuity was paid up in February of 1412 so that his complaints about delinquent payments would be unnecessary.[8]

I am not convinced that advice about when to hold councils would ever become irrelevant to the heir to the throne, or that it would have been a breach of decorum to note the fact that he would later regain control of council meetings. And since, as we will see, Hoccleve had a tendency to shape his life for the purpose of his arguments (and the annuity, though paid, was paid late), I am leery of taking his autobiographical claims literally. Since Seymour says that two of the manuscripts could have been produced "shortly after 1411" (114), I see no reason to discard 1412 as a possible date for completion of the poem, as F. J. Furnivall suggests on his title page. But the outer limits for the date are obviously correct.

Begging and Advising

As Larry Scanlon has shown, when Hoccleve asks Prince Henry to help him collect his tardy annuity, he produces a great deal of tension in the *Regement* by turning a mirror for princes into a begging poem. These two genres have conflicting assumptions: The poem-as-petition "postulates a royal *voluntas* that acts entirely at its own pleasure," whereas the *Fürstenspiegel* "posits a king who relies on counsel."[9] Scanlon sees that this tension inhabits many mirrors for princes because the writers and translators depend on the rulers they address. The rulers are often patrons, or the writers wish them to be,[10] so that the poet's attempt to control or "govern" them,

7. M. C. Seymour, *Selections from Hoccleve*, 114–15.
8. D. Pearsall, "Hoccleve's *Regement of Princes*: The Poetics of Royal Self-Representation," 387–88.
9. L. Scanlon, "The King's Two Voices," 230. Material from this essay is reworked in Scanlon's *Narrative, Authority, and Power*; see 301.
10. In "The King's Two Voices," Scanlon cites John of Salisbury's relation to Becket, Aegidius Romanus's to Philip the Fair, and even Aristotle's to Alexander (230–31). We can add Chaucer's to Richard II, Gower's to Richard and then Henry IV, and James Yonge's to the earl of Ormonde.

to submit them to "regement," seems presumptuous and counterproductive. Scanlon suggests several ways that Hoccleve resolves this conflict of genres, including the introduction of the wise old man, who serves as a buffer between Hoccleve and the prince, and a series of exempla that demonstrate that a king who is perfectly free can, of his own will, accept restraint.[11] Since the restraint keeps him from looking like a tyrant, what he gets in return for it is "a significant gain in political power."[12]

Scanlon emphasizes the interdependence of vernacular poet and ruler: The "God-givenness of kingship" helps to authorize vernacular authors. At the same time, the shaky Lancastrian dynasty needs the authority of vernacular literature to make it legitimate.[13] Hoccleve helps to make Prince Henry the legitimate heir to the throne by treating him as if that is what he is.[14]

Derek Pearsall takes this idea of poetry's ability to legitimate the regime one step further and speculates that Prince Henry, a master of public relations, actually commissioned the poem from Hoccleve.[15] Hoccleve's various expressions of fear of offending could have been a cover for Henry's request for the poem.[16] It was not that Henry really wanted advice from a clerk in the office of the privy seal, but that he needed to appear receptive to it.[17] Jeremy Catto supports the idea both that Henry used propaganda and that, especially while he headed the council, he might have had direct contact with clerks of the office of the privy seal.[18]

Scanlon's description of the tension in the poem and Hoccleve's attempts to resolve it are very useful. Pearsall, while offering no direct evidence of a commissioning, offers a contextualization of the poem that makes it at least possible. But both characterizations make the poem too quietistic, too tied into the ideology of monarchical power. Hoccleve, for all his humility, does not merely embrace the power of the king. He also counsels, pressures, and criticizes. The advice not to hold councils on Holy

---

11. See L. Scanlon, "The King's Two Voices," 236 for the old man as mediator, 243–44 for the exempla on voluntary restraint. The poem also emphasizes the king's restraint by promoting a number of virtues that require it, such as "mercy," "pity," and "patience." Scanlon, *Narrative, Authority, and Power*, 315–18.

12. L. Scanlon, "The King's Two Voices," 244; *Narrative, Authority, and Power*, 316.

13. L. Scanlon, "The King's Two Voices," 226.

14. L. Scanlon, "The King's Two Voices," 232–33; *Narrative, Authority, and Power*, 301–2.

15. D. Pearsall, "Hoccleve's *Regement of Princes*," 393; see also G. L. Harriss, "Introduction," in *Henry V*, 8.

16. On the characteristic deference of the writers of mirrors for princes, see R. F. Green, *Poets and Princepleasers*, 165.

17. D. Pearsall, "Hoccleve's *Regement of Princes*," 386.

18. J. Catto, "The King's Servants," in G. L. Harriss, *Henry V*, 80–81.

Days, when the prince had done or was still doing exactly that, is only a small example.[19]

To be sure, both critics see that the narrator need not be entirely submissive. For example, according to Scanlon, when Hoccleve attributes Richard's fall to anything other than his own failures as king (Hoccleve calls it a fall through Fortune; ll. 22–25), he "stops just short of indecorous confrontation."[20] The Lancastrian party line was that Richard deserved to be deposed, and Hoccleve was not toeing it.[21] But the weight of both arguments falls on the side of the ruler's power and the subject's lack of it. My argument seeks to redress the balance and to show that the alignment between Hoccleve's politics and Lancastrian politics is not simple. The answer to the question, "Whose side was Hoccleve on?" is far from straightforward.

Perhaps the acuteness of the conflict between genres in the *Regement of Princes* comes from the fact that Hoccleve's request of Prince Henry is so specific, and his social status as a poor privy seal clerk is so low. How can such a petitioner be a counsellor? At times the conflict appears to disrupt the poem. For instance, because Hoccleve emphasizes both the ruler's financial behavior and the danger of flatterers, when he adds the story of his financial woes and his expectation that the prince will solve them (ll. 1779–85, 4385–89), the tension between petition and advice becomes excruciating. Praise of the prince for generosity ("O liberal prince," l. 4387) looks calculating and manipulative; the extensive discussions of the relative moral weight of avarice, liberality, and prodigality sound compromised because they aim to enlist the prince in the effort to get Hoccleve's annuity paid, and the repeated warnings about flattery make Hoccleve look stupid or insensitive. How could he overlook the conflict beween the warnings and the praise of the prince, which must look embarrassingly obsequious, blindly self-serving, and insultingly insincere? It appears that he thinks his readers, including the prince, cannot understand the import of the poem. Or else *he* can't. Either he thinks we are very stupid, or he is.

But there is evidence that these unattractive alternatives are not the

19. G. L. Harriss, "Introduction," *Henry V*, 9.

20. L. Scanlon, "The King's Two Voices," 233–34. Cf. Scanlon, *Narrative, Authority, and Power*, 303.

21. Some others think that attributing Richard's fall to Fortune was Hoccleve's way of siding with the Prince of Wales rather than his father, since the prince had been fond of Richard, and, in one of his first acts as king, reburied him with more honor in Westminster Abbey. For an account of the reburial of Richard, see M. W. Labarge, *Henry V: The Cautious Conqueror*, 43. In *Henry V*, C. Allmand attributes the reburial of Richard to political not personal motives (436).

product of Hoccleve's incompetence or underestimation of his audience, but intentional. First, there are his selections from among his sources, which offered many topics that Hoccleve could have used to avoid the subject of the ruler's finances. Even within that topic there are choices of attitude. For instance, both the *Secretum Secretorum* and *De Regimine Principum* discuss the ruler's spending habits, and the *Secretum* has passages that are somewhat harsh, warning the king that his prodigality could stir God to anger and the people to rebellion. The example is the Chaldean rulers, who were so wasteful in their expenditures that they grabbed the goods of their people, who called to God for help. God sent a terrible, destructive wind; then "insurrexit populus contra eos, et nomina eorum de terra penitus deleverunt" ("the people rose up against them, and completely erased their names from the earth").[22]

From the available options Hoccleve chooses a much more lenient view of prodigality, which, according to *De Regimine Principum* is much preferable to avarice, and happens to further his own aims.[23] Certainly, the warnings against prodigality are present: Spending the kingdom down to nothing is bad, and liberality is the ideal mean between avarice and prodigality (ll. 4740–46).[24] The old man also gives one Boethian exhortation (ll. 1072–1127) to forgo wealth because it merely promotes insecurity. Though it sorts oddly with a poem that asks for money,[25] this exhortation does temper the poem's pro-liberality stance. But if a ruler has to indulge in one financial vice, he should opt for prodigality over avarice, and the form his free spending should take is, not surprisingly, giving too much to his people. This sin is preferable because it can help the needy (ll. 4641, 4642–55, 4684–94; see also 2474–76). Thus, Hoccleve's recommendations for liberal financial policy fit his own personal hopes.

But we cannot properly understand Hoccleve's petition to Prince Henry without putting it into the larger context of the politics of finance in the early fifteenth century, and the reward for doing so will be an appreciation of Hoccleve's willingness to confront the prince on national policy issues. The need to find the right balance among avarice, prodigality, and liberality was the major preoccupation of Henry IV's reign. It was the sub-

22. R. Steele and A. S. Fulton, eds., *Opera hactenus inedita Rogeri Baconi*, 44.

23. L. Scanlon, *Narrative, Authority, and Power*, 319.

24. R. Steele and A. S. Fulton, eds., *Opera hactenus inedita Rogeri Baconi*, 43. Aegidius Romanus, *De regimine principum libri III*, 60 (column a).

25. This may be the old man's response to Hoccleve's earlier bitterness when he remarked that having nothing left to lose is the only truly secure estate (ll. 29–35).

ject of the struggles between Henry and the parliament, and also between King Henry and his son, the Prince of Wales. The struggles come directly out of those in the reign of Richard II. In 1390, after Richard had just declared himself of age and regained control of the government from the Appellants, parliament passed "an ordinance for the government of the king's Council." It said that the council should meet daily and should be consulted on financial matters. The approval of two out of four chief councillors was needed for every gift or grant that the king wanted to make that would decrease revenue. This protocol was in place until 1397, when Richard took over the council and made many grants without them.[26] At the shaky beginning of Henry IV's reign, because he wanted to reward those who had supported his usurpation and woo those who hadn't, he continued Richard's policy of making grants on his own.[27] Since he also had to fight a number of rebellions, including a long series of Welsh uprisings, the early years of his reign were plagued by financial trouble that set the stage for political conflict.

At the beginning of his reign, Henry IV gave far more grants and annuities than Richard II had.[28] Average yearly expenses rose steadily above those for Richard's reign.[29] Predictably, he had to borrow money to pay them and support the wars, especially in 1400, 1402, and 1407–8.[30] Even so, the exchequer, unable to pay out all the money it owed, resorted to issuing promises of future revenues instead of cash ("assignments"). When creditors objected to what were essentially bad checks, the exchequer sometimes took them back and counted them in a way that historians have called "fictitious loans." According to G. L. Harriss, the obligations paid by cash sank by over 10 percent in Henry's reign, as compared to Richard's, and the obligations paid by assignment and by fictitious loans rose more than 10 percent.[31] Since these figures include the whole reign, those for the early years alone were probably higher, because the nervousness about whether the realm was credit-worthy stirred parliament to discipline the king.

26. K. B. McFarlane, *Lancastrian Kings and Lollard Knights*, 86–87.
27. K. B. McFarlane, *Lancastrian Kings and Lollard Knights*, 87.
28. G. L. Harriss, "Financial Policy," in his *Henry V*, 160.
29. They were one hundred and twenty thousand pounds for Richard's reign, one hundred and thirty thousand in 1401, and by 1404–6, one hundred and forty thousand pounds per year. E. F. Jacob, *The Fifteenth Century*, 87–88.
30. E. F. Jacob, *The Fifteenth Century*, 76.
31. "Financial Policy," 161. Harriss used the figures compiled by A. B. Steel in *The Receipt of the Exchequer, 1377–1485*. For Steel's conclusions about the worsening state of national finances under Henry IV, see Steel, 117–18, 133, 134, 140, 143, 145.

The commons first asked Henry to seek the advice of the council before making grants in 1399.[32] This effort was paralleled by their wish to have
the members of council at least announced in parliament, if not approved
by parliament.[33] They did not fully succeed until the long parliament of
1406, and even then, not permanently. The story of the process contains
human drama of much variety, including political maneuvering, courage on
the part of the speakers, parliament's willingness to withhold taxes, the
king's periodic illness, his attempts to manipulate parliamentary elections,
royal temporizing, and the king's indignant speeches on his prerogatives
and liberties.[34] The resolution of what G. L. Harriss calls the "crisis of confidence in royal credit" was that the council was given control of the realm's
finances and then instituted fiscal planning, estimating expenses, and allo-
cating revenue.[35] England was put on a budget. This regimen lasted until
November of 1411, when King Henry dismissed the council and replaced it
with one made up of his own supporters.

Two important things for us to note in this long evolution of financial
policy are the parts played by the idioms of advice and the Prince of Wales.
Because the struggle was over the relative power of the king and the council,
much of it, as well as the 1406 parliamentary victory, was cast in terms of
advice. Although, as K. B. McFarlane says, the ordinances of that parliament "had the effect of transferring all power to the hands of the councillors," one of them read, "In all matters the king should govern by the advice
of his councillors and trust them."[36] That is, the documents used advice as
a screen to obscure the fact that the king was no longer in charge of the
government.

The person who *was* in charge of the government was the Prince of
Wales. He began attending meetings of the council in December of 1406,
when the Welsh revolt, of which he had been given charge almost from the
start of the reign (when he was just thirteen years old), had died down. He
headed the council, which was made up of his supporters, beginning in the
fall of 1407. When parliament took power from the king, they handed it to

32. In a sense they were taking him up on Archbishop Arundel's rhetoric of advice just
after the usurpation: "[The king] does not wish to be governed by his own will, nor by his
willful purpose or singular opinion, but by common advice, counsel, and assent . . ." (See
Chapter 5, note 70).

33. K. B. McFarlane, *Lancastrian Kings and Lollard Knights*, 87–89.

34. For excellent accounts of the stages of the process, see K. B. McFarlane, *Lancastrian
Kings and Lollard Knights*, 86–101; and E. F. Jacob, *The Fifteenth Century*, 73–90.

35. G. L. Harriss, "Financial Policy," 162.

36. *Rotuli Parliamentorum* III.572–73, quoted and commented on by K. B. McFarlane,
Lancastrian Kings and Lollard Knights, 91.

his son. The king did not take it back until a bout of illness abated and he reasserted himself in November of 1411.

In other words, when Hoccleve addressed the *Regement of Princes* to Prince Henry, recommending that rulers choose liberality over avarice in order to benefit their people, especially the poor, Henry was in the midst of (or had just finished) his attempt to cut the king's spending in order to restore the credit of the government. The prince was probably not very receptive to Hoccleve's praise of liberality, or his comparison of the king to a well that serves a large population and so needs a wide mouth (ll. 4649–55).[37] Hoccleve's project might have been something like trying to convince the speaker of the U.S. House of Representatives, Newt Gingrich, in 1995—as the Republicans were trying to fulfill their "Contract with America"—that the proper role of the federal government is financial assistance of the poor.

But there were other parts of Hoccleve's message, and the prince could take his pick. For instance, the dangers of foolish largesse might have struck a sympathetic chord (e.g., l. 4745). And surprisingly, the part of Hoccleve's message that appears to us to be most self-interested, the request to Henry to expedite the payment of Hoccleve's annuity, might have been the most welcome to Prince Henry's ears, since enabling the government to honor its debts was exactly his project. The fact that Hoccleve's annuity was "al behynde" (l. 4385) was the government's biggest problem writ small.

The long exemplum about John of Canace (ll. 4180–4354) dramatizes the need for good credit. Hoccleve tells it in order to discourage foolish largesse, and uses it as an occasion to confess his own prodigality and ask for the prince's aid (ll. 4355–75).[38] That puts him in a position very like that of the government itself. Hoccleve, having spent too much, must ask for help: "So haue I plukked at my purse strynges, / And made hem often for to gape & gane" (ll. 4369–70) that relief must come from the prince (ll. 4373–75). But since John of Canace's story involves borrowing to produce an illusion of prosperity, it is also an image of the government's predicament: Having given away too many resources, both John and the government must borrow money to keep up the appearance of wealth, which is crucial to their welfare.

Hoccleve's recommendation to the prince about how to prevent finan-

---

37. D. Pearsall also notes that the prince might have objected to the old man's specific suggestion in l. 1879 about how to get the annuity paid by transferring it from one office to another. (See "Hoccleve's *Regement of Princes*," 387n. 5.)

38. C. Blyth calls Hoccleve's juxtaposition of a story against foolish spending with his confession of his own, "elaborately nervy wit" ("Thomas Hoccleve's Other Master," 354).

cial problems like his own and that of John of Canace was very close to the
prince's own recommendations about how to solve the government's:

> Now, if þat ye graunten by your patente
> To your serauntes a yeerly guerdoun,
> Crist scheelde þat your wil or your entente
> Be sette to maken a restriccioun
> Of paiement; for þat condicioun
> Exileþ þe peples beneuolence,
> And kyndeleþ hate vndir priue scilence.

> Beeth wel avised, or your graunt out go,
> How ye þat charge may performe and bere;
> Whan it is past, obserue it wel also,
> ffor elles wole it yow annoye and dere;
> ffor your honur it muchel bettre were,
> No graunt to graunt at al, þan þat your graunt
> Yow preeue a brekere of a couenaunt.
>
> (ll. 4789–4802)

With its use of official terminology, the first of these stanzas is very specific
in its approach to royal finance. "Serauntes" (l. 4790) is official vocabulary.
In the first grant Hoccleve received from Henry IV, Hoccleve is described
as "seruiens noster." [39] Also, "patente" was a word used in official records
like the parliamentary rolls and the proceedings of the privy council, where
Hoccleve spent his working life. Hoccleve used it when writing to the chancellor about his own annuity. [40] His 1400 grant was established "per literas
suas patentes." [41] Since the granting of annuities with the explicit intention
of not paying immediately (ll. 4791–92) was precisely the issue between the
king and the parliament, language that would sound familiar in parliament
or council amplifies this bit of advice.

The second stanza deftly uses "grant" as two different parts of speech
in line 4801 and is then capped by the climactic rhyme, "graunt / coue-
naunt," which makes the contract seem formal or even sacred and justifies
the claim that what is at stake in the performance of it is "your honur." Like

---

39. F. J. Furnivall and I. Gollancz, eds., *Hoccleve's Works: The Minor Poems in the Asburn-
ham Ms. Addit. 133*, li.
40. *Middle English Dictionary*, "Patent(e."
41. F. J. Furnivall and I. Gollancz, eds., *Hoccleve's Works: The Minor Poems*, lii.

Hoccleve's concern that the kingdom pay back its debts to merchants, thus keeping its "couenantis" (ll. 2374–80),[42] the rhyme expresses well the fit between Hoccleve's message and Prince Henry's mission during his years at the head of the council.

In fact, although many annuities were paid late, it is not clear that Hoccleve's was late. Because the medieval records are not perfectly reliable, it is hard to determine just when he was paid. Modern examiners of the records reach different conclusions about the payments, and thus also about whether or not Hoccleve was telling the truth in his begging poems.[43] For my purposes, the truth of Hoccleve's autobiographical claims does not matter. Either he used his own financial worries to address the kingdom's financial crisis, or he invented some plausible ones in order to address one of the most important issues of the reign. If he invented them, that underlines the paradox that Hoccleve's seemingly selfish concerns have broad applicability and fit closely with the prince's program in his father's government. Hoccleve was perhaps inventing a self to make his political case all the more trenchant.

Begging as Advising

The intimate connection between Hoccleve's real or fictitious personal troubles and England's financial and political troubles should help us to understand the tension between the petitionary poem and the hortatory poem in a new way. As we have already seen in Gower's *Confessio Amantis*, the two genres' contradictory assumptions about the ruler's power and his freedom to use it get linked when the speaker claims to represent the people who are not otherwise represented in government. Therefore, it is in Hoccleve's interest to appear to be of convincingly low estate. He must emphasize the chasm that separates him from the prince. The prince is "hye & glorious" (l. 2020), while Hoccleve is "humble" and impotent (ll. 2019, 2035). Although he is rich in "beneuolence" (that quality "exiled" by restricted annuity payments in l. 4794), his goods are "skant" (l. 2032). While the prince is so wise and learned that he needs no counsel (ll. 2136–37), Hoccleve's very unlikeliness is what makes him a likely counsellor.

42. Many versons of the *Secretum Secretorum* recommend concern for the welfare of merchants, though the concern takes different forms. E.g., R. Steele and A. S. Fulton, eds., *Opera hactenus inedita* . . . , 50 (Latin), 186 (English translation of Arabic); R. Steele, *Three Prose Versions of the Secreta Secretorum*, 13.

43. M. Richardson, "Hoccleve in His Social Context," 319.

Þe moste lak þat han þe lordes grete,
Is of hem that hir soothes shuld hem telle;
Al in þe glose folk labour and swete;
Thei stryuen who best rynge shal þe belle
Of fals plesance, in þat hir hertes swelle
If þat oon can bet than other deceyue;
And swich deceyt, lordes blyndly receyue.
                              (ll. 1926–32)

The greater the ruler the more he needs advice from those who are not great, and the more those who are marginalized have to offer him. The less pleasant the truth, the more he needs to hear it. Hoccleve uses the familiar trope to express this theme: "Thus, my gode lorde, wynneth your peples voice; / ffor peples vois is goddes voys, men seyne" (ll. 2885–86).

There is another aspect of Hoccleve's unlikeliness that may seem surprising, appearing as it does relatively soon after Richard II's deposition: Hoccleve says he is young. Although he has the backing of the wise old man, he presents himself as young and foolish (ll. 146–47), even childish (l. 2058).[44] Hoccleve later tells the story of Rehoboam and his young counsellors that was mobilized in opposition to Edward III and Richard II ("Ware of yong conseyl, it is perilouse; / Roboas fonde it so, whan he forsoke / Olde conseil, and to þe yong hym toke," ll. 4947–49), but he also returns to the earlier attitude of the *Secretum Secretorum* that not only the lowly but the young might be sources of wisdom:[45]

And if þat a man of symple degree,
Or pore of birth, or ȝonge, be wel conseile,
Admytte his resoun and take it in gre. . . .
                              (ll. 4880–82)

The characteristics of the counsellor cannot reliably distinguish good counsel from bad. The prince must judge on his own. Hoccleve, the young counsellor, shores up his authority with his revered old sources. Since Hoccleve claims to have worked in the privy seal office for twenty-four years (ll. 803–5), he cannot actually be young.[46] He is shaping his auto-

44. His relationships to both the old man and Chaucer are filial (ll. 1953, 1961).
45. R. Steele, *Three Prose Versions of the Secreta Secretorum*, 34. For a discussion of this issue, see Chapters 3 and 7 above.
46. I am grateful to Charles Blyth for pointing this discrepancy out to me. As he noted, in this case the youth/age trope takes precedence over autobiography.

biography in order to make a point, harking back to the *Secretum Secretorum*'s approval of young counsellors to promote himself as an unlikely adviser from whom the prince needs to hear.[47]

Not only was Hoccleve not as young as he claims, but his actual social status was not as precarious as he implies. According to Frederick Furnivall and Israel Gollancz, he had very respectable associates and friends.[48] But he needed to exaggerate his destitution in order to qualify as the spokesman of the poor because the *Fürstenspiegel* tradition teaches kings to listen to the complaints of the poor. A king must know "What fame þat his poore peple him bere" (l. 2545) so that he can learn their grievances and redress them (l. 2547–50). The story of Edward III venturing "In-to contre, in symple array allone" to find out his people's opinion of him, is held up as an example to be imitated (ll. 2556–62).

This sentiment, although traditional, was probably not inert in the context of the financial reform over which the prince had recently presided. The council he had directed (beginning in December 1409) was unusually small and elite since it excluded knights and esquires, who had served on previous councils.[49] Whether the dominance of the aristocracy was Prince Henry's choice or not is uncertain. Since his leadership was so strong at this time, it may have been, and although knights and esquires were probably not seen, by others or themselves, as representatives of the lowest ranks, it is tempting to interpret Hoccleve's promotion of advice from the lower ranks of society as a criticism of that policy. The crown's ability to pay off its debts to large creditors may not have been important to the truly common people, some of whom undoubtedly got squeezed as the council tried to rein in grants to improve the government's credit. Their more pressing concern may have been the benefits they lost as the government tried to refurbish its credit.[50] Perhaps it is these people Hoccleve is claiming to represent through his own "poverty."

Another group whose cause he takes up is a different kind of servant

---

47. At the same time, he may be complimenting the prince, who joined the council at age nineteen and who had just turned twenty when he began to run it (and thus the government) in 1407.

48. F. J. Furnivall and I. Gollancz, eds., *Hoccleve's Works: The Minor Poems*, xxxiv–xxxv.

49. E. F. Jacob, *The Fifteenth Century*, 105. A. L. Brown, "The Commons and the Council in the Reign of Henry IV," 24, 26. A. L. Brown, "The King's Councillors in Fifteenth-Century England," 103–5. C. Allmand, *Henry V*, 39.

50. A modern parallel is the left's criticism of President Bill Clinton's economic proposals early in 1993 to decrease the budget deficit. Those who think that the deficit is a problem mainly for the very wealthy criticized Clinton for trying to fix the deficit at the cost of neglecting the poor. See D. Henwood, "Putting Bondholders First," 1.

of the government, the soldier. Just before he documents his dependence on the annuity (his other income never exceeds six marks per year, he says; ll. 932–35), he claims that his future might be mirrored in the plight of soldiers who "Ben in-to pouert falle" (l. 921). The date of completion of the poem is crucial for the historicizing of this passage. Almost from the beginning of his father's reign, Prince Henry had been in charge of soldiers, and had great difficulty keeping them supplied and paid. He complained, for instance, that he was not given enough money to pay his soldiers in Wales.[51] After he left the council in 1411, he was accused of misappropriating funds meant for soldiers while he was in charge of the garrison at Calais. He was eventually cleared, in either the summer or the fall of 1412.[52] If the poem was completed after the prince had left the council (which, as I said earlier, is possible), but before the exoneration (which is very likely), Hoccleve might have been able to expect that the prince would be sensitive on the subject of the financial state of soldiers. Like the poet's identification with the poor, his identification with soldiers, both part of his creation of himself as unlikely adviser, might have been at least a little irritating to the prince.

The Discipline of Advice

The truths that princes do not necessarily want to hear can be dangerous. They can certainly be dangerous to the truth-tellers. Some of those who could speak, refrain out of fear; they "fro drede of any lord or syre, / Hydeth þe trouthe" (ll. 4453–54). Like the warnings of Mum in *Mum and the Soth-segger* about the persecution of truth-tellers, the reasons for silence are compelling. The *Regement* provides a number of stories, which I will discuss shortly, about counsellors who are punished.[53] But danger also lurks for the rulers. We have already gotten a hint of this in stanzas I quoted (see "Begging and Advising") about the restriction of grants. If grants are not paid, the people's benevolence disappears, and the hatred that takes its place will burn under the cover of a dissembled peace (ll. 4796–4802). Hoccleve uses

51. E. F. Jacob, *The Fifteenth Century*, 77; C. Allmand, *Henry V*, 28–29.
52. C. L. Kingsford, ed., *The First English Life of Henry the Fifth* . . . , xxiv; C. Allmand, *Henry V*, 58.
53. The writer's fear of his audience is also figured in his fear of "the audience / Of women" after he delivers a misogynistic interpretation of the relationship between Adam and Eve. To compensate for the slight, he then produces a lengthy defense of women (ll. 5097–5194). This passage might have been inspired by Chaucer's *Legend of Good Women*.

what James C. Scott might call the trope of the hidden transcript as a threat against the ruler (see Chapter 2, "The Poets Speak of Silence"). The broken promise will not only annoy him, but also "dere" — "injure" or "wound" — him (l. 4799). The menace that haunts the *Regement* for both counsellor and ruler charts both the downward and upward political pressures that I have discussed in earlier chapters.

In a rich, suggestive article, Anthony J. Hasler reads the *Regement of Princes* in terms of Foucault's idea that power works "through its hold on the body."[54] In his watershed book on this process, *Discipline and Punish: The Birth of the Prison*, Michel Foucault emphasizes the way the ruler's power is registered on the subject's body.[55] Hasler sees that in Hoccleve's poem, both the body of the subject and the body of the ruler are at stake. The lines of force travel not only downward, from ruler to subject, but upward, as well.

Hoccleve provides many reasons for would-be advisers to fear the ruler. For example, a clever craftsman tries to please his tyrannical lord by building a brass bull in which to burn objects of the tyrant's wrath. It converts the victims' cries of pain into the bellowing of a bull, so that they are deprived not only of life but of their humanity: "Hir woys was lyke a boles euer-mo, / And nothyng lyke a mannys voise in soun" (ll. 3022–23). The tyrant used it first on its creator, so that the flattering adviser is destroyed for his sycophancy. As Larry Scanlon says, the story reveals and punishes the competitiveness of the adviser and also exposes both how cruel the ruler must be to be first in cruelty and how vulnerable advisers are to the displeasure of rulers.[56] In another story, when Theodorus, adviser of the "kyng of Lysemak," confronts him with his faults, the king crucifies him (ll. 2570–83). Telling truth to power is dangerous. But Theodorus compounds the danger by cursing false counsellors from the cross, predicting that they, too, will suffer "This peyne, or othir like þer-to" (l. 2575). All counsellors, regardless of their veracity, will be punished.

Although these stories seem to represent an extreme of barbarism, the man Hoccleve seeks as a patron is not exempt from implications of cruelty. After the old man advises Hoccleve to tell his troubles to Prince Henry, he offers his own body and voice as a warranty:

54. A. J. Hasler, "Hoccleve's Unregimented Body," 164. Hasler was influenced in this work by two important articles by Louise Fradenburg, "The Manciple's Servant Tongue: Politics and Poetry in the *Canterbury Tales*," and "Spectacular Fictions: The Body Politic in Chaucer and Dunbar."
55. M. Foucault, *Discipline and Punish*, esp. 3–31.
56. L. Scanlon, "The King's Two Voices," 245–46.

Compleyne vnto his excellent noblesse,
As I haue herd þe vn-to me compleyne;
And but he qwenche þi grete heuynesse,
My tonge take, and slitte in peeces tweyne.
                                        (ll. 1849–52)

Since in some ways the old man stands for Hoccleve and since, as I have
noted, Hoccleve also complains about the terrible effects of writing on his
body (ll. 981-1029), the old man's promise implicates Hoccleve, as well. It
expresses the jeopardy he feels the poem puts him into.

One of the first stories the old man tells Hoccleve in the attempt to
draw him out and cure his despair[57] is that of the burning of John Badby.
The old man tells it to warn Hoccleve, who had complained of being
"thoghty" (l. 80), of the dangers of too much thinking, which is "perillous"
(l. 267) because it can lead to heresy. But the story of Badby has other
messages, as well. It introduces the Prince of Wales as one who has the
power to put aside the fire to offer the heretic another chance to recant, as
well as the power to start the fire. The subject's body and thus his very
existence depend on the ruler's power. It is probably not accidental that
what Hoccleve notices about this incident is the prince's offer of financial
support if Badby recants:

If he renounce wolde his errour clene,
And come vn-to oure good byleue ageyne,
He schulde of his lif seure ben & certeyne,
And sufficiant lyflode eek scholde he haue
Vn-to þe day he clad were in his graue.
                                        (ll. 304–8)

The ruler can offer both life and livelihood, but the subject must accept
them on the ruler's terms. This is a stern lesson for a petitioner looking for
timely payment of his pension, since dependence on the ruler for patronage
means acceptance of the ruler's doctrine. Dependence means ideological
submission.

But the story of Badby is not just testimony to the extent of the ruler's
power to impose his will. It also testifies to the subject's power of resistance.
As Anthony Hasler says, Badby's refusal to recant "means that to the last he

57. The process is similar in many ways to the "talking cure" the narrator of Chaucer's
Book of the Duchess tries to work upon the Black Knight.

remains out of order, retains the potential for rivalrous signification."[58] Although the cost is high, his silence speaks.

A story in which the subjects are not silent but still bear the cost is that of the unnamed knight who imposes just but "sharp" and "streyte" laws on his people (ll. 2950–89). According to Charles Blyth, there are two traditions for this story, one in which the ruler (the Athenian Lycurgus), delighted with the harmony resulting from the laws, wants to make them permanent. He convinces his subjects to swear not to change them until he returns from a trip and then departs, never to return. This is how John of Salisbury tells the story in the *Policraticus* (34) and how Gower tells it in the *Confessio Amantis* (VII.2917–3028). In the other tradition, the ruler prompts the oath-taking and leaves the city because his people complain about the strictness of the laws. This is the version Hoccleve chooses.[59] The people, who were "froward" to begin with (l. 2953), continue in their obstreperousness:

> And when þei [laws] weren byfore hem [people] I-radde,
> Þei made hem wondir wroth, & seyden al
> Þei were not so nyce ne so madde
> To hem assent, for ought that may befalle;
> They wolden nat hem to þo lawes thralle,
> And wold han artyd þis knight hem repele,
> Makyng ageyn him an haynous querele.
>
> (ll. 2955–61)

The narrator's sympathies do not seem to be with the quarreling people, and their defiance wins them nothing except a long-term extension of the troublesome laws. But, as Blyth says, it is significant that Hoccleve chooses this version of the tale at all, when the more placid alternative was so easily available in the *Confessio Amantis*.[60]

But both Gower and Hoccleve allow this story to expose the manmade quality of the laws and the ruler's pretense that they are god-given. For Gower, the revelation comes when Lycurgus tells his people how he must leave to confer with the god who originally handed down the laws. Lycurgus has decided "to feigne" (VII.2947), inventing an excuse to leave

---

58. A. J. Hasler, "Hoccleve's Unregimented Body," 172.
59. On these two traditions, see C. Blyth, "Thomas Hoccleve's Other Master," 355–57.
60. For Blyth, Hoccleve's choice shows that he is more attuned to complaints from the people than Gower is. "Thomas Hoccleve's Other Master," 357–58. For other episodes in which Gower was sensitive to such complaints, see Chapter 7 above.

the city so that his subjects will swear to uphold the laws in his absence. But not only is the godly summons feigned, but the entire story of the origin of the laws is a lie as well (VII.2953–91). Larry Scanlon notes that "As Lycurgus emphasizes the divine source of his authority, Gower emphasizes his fabrication of it."[61] Hoccleve makes the same point when he clearly attributes the origin of the laws to the ruler ("lawes ful iust he made, and in streyte kinde," l. 2954) but allows him to claim "I mad hem naght, it was god appollo" (l. 2963). Both of these poets are "disenchanted," to use H. Marshall Leicester, Jr.'s term,[62] unmasking as partial and self-interested an ideology that claims to be universal. And both show that the burden of the ruler's imposition of the law is borne by his people. In the *Confessio Amantis*, although the laws guarantee that every man can keep "his encress" (VII.2927) and common profit also increases (VII.2930–32), one of the chief benefits of the law is that "the pouer / Of hem that weren in astat / Was sauf" (VII.2932–34). The laws work to benefit the ruling class. In the *Regement*, despite the narrator's seeming approval of the just ruler's just laws (ll. 2951, 2954), the ruler himself acknowledges as he leaves that the laws are "to streyte" (l. 2974). The people pay the price in perpetuity.

The reciprocal dynamic shows that the price is sometimes high for the ruler, too. After all, the poem is called the *Regement of Princes*, and partakes of the paradox of the *Fürstenspiegel* that the powerful are supposed to submit to the discipline of those who have only enough power to counsel them. And, as in many mirrors for princes, the regimen starts with the body; Hoccleve advises Prince Henry on drinking and eating (ll. 3844–71). The poem includes harsher disciplines, as in the story of Marcus Regulus, who advises his people not to ransom him and insists on returning to prison and certain death to save his honor and his people's (ll. 2248–82). There is also the Roman consul who sacrifices an eye to uphold the law (ll. 2738–72).[63] These stories, though striking, are, as Larry Scanlon points out, examples of voluntary restraint on the part of the ruler,[64] examples of rulers' self-mutilation, not the result of their subjects' resistance.

The fact that these stories are from classical Rome makes them seem

61. L. Scanlon, *Narrative, Authority, and Power*, 288; also see C. Blyth, "Thomas Hoccleve's Other Master," 356–57.

62. H. Marshall Leicester, Jr., *The Disenchanted Self: Representing the Subject in the "Canterbury Tales."* See Chapter 6 ("Chaucer in the 1990s") for the significance of this kind of analysis for Chaucer studies.

63. James Yonge tells this story in his translation of the *Secretum Secretorum* for James Butler, earl of Ormonde (R. Steele, ed., 128).

64. L. Scanlon, "The King's Two Voices," 243; L. Scanlon, *Narrative, Authority, and Power*, 315.

distant from the contemporary scene. Like Gower in the *Confessio Amantis*, Hoccleve may be using the old stories as a disguise for his political intent, a shield for his most aggressive impulses toward the prince. If so, Hoccleve avails himself of this protection only a little. He pointedly updates the stories of Marcus Regulus and the Roman consul (ll. 2288–89, 2769–72), looking for the heirs of such virtue in England, pointing out the current rulers' failure to live up to these high moral standards. Furthermore, he mentions many other issues that cannot be calculated to soothe sensitive monarchs. I have already discussed the ways in which his recommendations on finance might not find favor with Prince Henry. In addition, he draws on *Fürstenspiegel* tradition to remind Henry that even kings die: Ancient emperors were measured for their tombs as soon as they were crowned, to remind them of the transitory world and the need to govern well while they lived (ll. 2857–2884). Not content with the truism and its moral, Hoccleve addresses Henry directly: "In your prosperite and in your welthe, / Remembreth euer a-monge, þat ye shul dye . . ." (ll. 2892–93). He does the same thing with the story of Alexander's death, which is followed by an apostrophe: "O worthi princes two,[65] now takiþ hede! / As hardy, deth is yow for to assaille / As sche dide Alisaundre . . ." (ll. 5363–65). With this rhetorical flourish, Hoccleve reminds kings of their mortality. He animates cliché with direct address.

Several leveling moves might also seem aggressive, as when Hoccleve promotes mutual advice-giving among a universal brotherhood:

Of counceill & of helpe we be dettoures
Eche to other, by right of bretherhede. . . .

Euery man owiþ studien and muse
To tech his brothir what þing is to do. . . .

And þus he mote conseille his brothir, lo!
"Do þat right is, and good, to goddes pay. . . ."
(ll. 2486–98)

For a prince it might be bad enough to be told by a preachy and poor young petitioner—one of the prince's servants—to do the right thing, without having him claim equal status with royalty. Hoccleve seems to be presum-

---

65. He is addressing the kings of England and France.

ing upon, even exaggerating, the intimacy described by the *Secretum Secretorum* in the epigraph to this chapter.

The aggressiveness is also apparent in Hoccleve's emphasis on the importance of a king's keeping his coronation oath; kings who fail to do so, like the Scythians and Arabians, are destroyed along with their people (ll. 2227–2240). This story is suitably removed by temporal and geographical distance from the contemporary scene, but since Edward II's failure to keep his coronation oath was used to justify his deposition,[66] the contemporary threat could not have been buried very deep. The people of a faithful king are obedient (l. 2212), the people of an unfaithful one hide their anger: "Thogh men dare not opynly him diffame, / Thei þinke, al be it þat þei no thing speke" (ll. 2406–7). The trope of the hidden transcript returns here to threaten the ruler because his lack of faith leads directly to the rebellion of the poor against the wealthy:

> And doutelesse, if þat fordone be lawe,
> A princes power may goo pley him þenne;
> ffor þei þat nought ne haue, with knyfe I-drawe,
> Wol on hem þat of good be myghty, renne,
> And hurt hem, and hir houses fire & brenne,
> And robbe and slee, and do al swich folye,
> Whan þer no lawe is, hem to iustifie.
>
> (ll. 2780–86)

Labeling such a rebellion illegal insanity (ll. 2785–86)[67] may be a way for Hoccleve to protect himself from charges of favoring or even supporting such a rebellion. In 1412 the Rising of 1381 was surely still vivid in collective memory; tales of the chaos and destruction would not have been forgotten. But the self-protection does not hide the threat in this passage. It would be palpable, especially since Hoccleve has so often characterized himself as one of those "þat nought ne haue," and since the deposition of Edward II was also well-remembered. Just in case the prince misses the point, Hoccleve lets Aristotle make it explicit: "Ther is no hye estate so sadde and stable, / Remembre wele, lat it nat be for-ʒete, / But he to falle in perile is ful able" (ll. 4068–70).

Considering that he is willing to threaten the future king with rebel-

66. B. Wilkinson, *Constitutional History of Medieval England*, vol. II: *Politics and the Constitution*, 170–71.
67. See the discussion of Gower's use of this trope in Chapter 7.

lion and deposition, it is no wonder that he is also willing to cross him on financial policy, as we have seen, and stir up other trouble. For instance, he advises Prince Henry to live on his own money ("Of your good propre," l. 4833) rather than public funds, even though the funding of the king's household had been an issue during several reigns. The extravagance of Richard's household had drawn fire from the Appellants in the late 1380s, and we have already seen how sensitive Richard was to Thomas Haxey's complaints about it in 1397 (See Chapter 2, "Limitations on Speech in Parliament"). Failure to support his household was one of the charges made against him at his deposition, and Henry IV had promised to reverse that failure.[68] In short, the financing of the household was one of the very sensitive issues during these two reigns, and the storms around it involved monarch, magnates, and parliament.[69] Although the prince might have been sympathetic with the goal, the phrase is a contentious way to raise the issue in the context of contemporary conflicts and with deposition lurking ominously in the background.

In addition, Hoccleve promotes reconciliation with France: "forthi may / By matrimoigne pees and vnite / Ben had" (l. 5393–95). According to Derek Pearsall, Hoccleve's program "is not a rebuke to the Prince's martial ardor but exactly the policy that Henry V claimed to be following throughout his French campaigns and put into practice after the conquest of Normandy."[70] The French proposed a number of marriage partners for the Prince of Wales, and a marriage did take place after Agincourt, but while he headed the council, his main concern was protecting and increasing English land in France. As part of his struggle with his father, he had for a number of years supported more military action on the French front, not less.[71] In September of 1411, Thomas, earl of Arundel, one of the prince's supporters who was on the council, led a military expedition to France without the authorization of the king.[72] According to G. L. Harriss, this operation was one of the reasons King Henry exerted himself in the parliament of November 1411 to take back control of the government by replacing the prince's men on the council with his own.[73] It could not have helped

---

68. On Richard: C. Stephenson and F. G. Marcham, eds. and trans., *Sources of English Constitutional History*, no. 66, 252; on Henry: C. Given-Wilson, *The Royal Household and the King's Affinity*, 140; P. Morgan, *War and Society in Medieval Cheshire, 1277–1403*, 208.

69. C. Given-Wilson, *The Royal Household and the King's Affinity*, 138–41.

70. D. Pearsall, "Hoccleve's *Regement of Princes*," 389.

71. E. F. Jacob, *The Fifteenth Century*, 110–11; M. W. Labarge, *Henry V*, 35–36.

72. C. Allmand, *Henry V*, 49.

73. G. L. Harriss, "The Management of Parliament," in *Henry V*, 142.

familial relations that King Henry's decision not to go himself to lead a French expedition in 1411 was probably the occasion of the suggestion by Bishop Beaufort, half-brother of the king and wholehearted supporter of the prince, that the king abdicate in favor of his son.[74] Although the prince and the king agreed on English goals in France such as the securing of rights to Aquitaine, at the end of the reign, they differed more and more on means, and even differed on which side to support in the French civil war, the prince supporting the Burgundians, the king the Armagnacs.[75] Military policy on France was one of the irritants in the at-times difficult relationship between father and son. While the poem was being composed, the peace with France cannot have been a soothing subject for the Prince of Wales. Hoccleve's pacifism could not have pleased him.

Larry Scanlon reads Hoccleve as essentially signing on to the project of legitimizing the Lancastrian reign by treating the prince as his father's heir. Once the prince is accepted as heir to Henry Bolingbroke, the orderly succession lends sanction to a dynasty that had a dubious start. Hoccleve rhetorically creates a prince whose legitimacy is signaled by his receipt of a mirror for princes.[76] David Lawton suggests that Hoccleve is not supporting the Lancastrians in general but, rather, choosing the prince over the king.[77] It is hard to separate these two projects. The usurpation begins the Lancastrian dynasty on which the Prince's right to rule depends; the poem supports — helps to create — his legitimacy by treating the prince as a prince.

But Hoccleve is legitimating not only Prince Henry, and through him the Lancastrian kings, but himself as adviser to kings. Hoccleve is submissive and takes certain precautions to reassure the prince that although he foresees possible sources of danger to his rule, he is not currently one of them himself. But as adviser, he is willing to criticize the prince and risk riling him. In, around, and through his submissiveness, he is very assertive about his status as a representative citizen whose experience with and in the government authorizes him (quite literally) as an adviser. He does not conform to the picture of the ideal scribe/adviser in the *Secretum Secretorum* in a simple way. His "trustworthiness" does not preclude his raising the most troubling and divisive issues of the reign or crossing the man whose patron-

74. E. F. Jacob, *The Fifteenth Century*, 112.
75. C. Allmand, *Henry V*, 53–54.
76. L. Scanlon, "The King's Two Voices," 232; *Narrative, Authority, and Power*, 301–2.
77. D. Lawton, "Dullness and the Fifteenth Century," 776–77.

age he hopes for. In the relationship between prince and poet, there are risks for both. In the terms of the poem, the key to legitimacy for both is their willingness to submit to the discipline of advice.

Since our records of Hoccleve's life are incomplete, it is probably hasty to draw conclusions from the fragments, but it might be significant that in September and December of 1413 — that is, less than a year after the death of Henry IV and the ascension of Henry V to the throne — Thomas Hoccleve received payments of his pension "with areers." [78]

78. F. J. Furnivall and I. Gollancz, eds., *Hoccleve's Works: The Minor Poems*, lix–lx.

9

Machiavelli's *Prince*

Þe dome of hym þat sekyth counsel is robbyd or drawn owte of
wylle.

— *Secretum Secretorum* [1]

OF ALL THOSE written in the Middle Ages and the Renaissance, there is
only one currently famous *Fürstenspiegel* — Machiavelli's *Prince*. Because it
is often seen as at once the culmination and the strongest critique of the
tradition, this book would be incomplete without a discussion of it. I
am interested here in two matters: the relationship between Machiavelli's *Prince* and the medieval mirrors for princes I have been examining,
and that between Machiavelli and his prince.[2] These topics are linked by the
question of whether or in what way Machiavelli's mirror for princes is subversive. Although it was written to curry favor with the Medici, some say
it subverts the genre, and some say it subverts the ruler's authority. The
Prince will provide a new lens with which to see the medieval mirrors for
princes. If I am right that both deference and criticism, both flattery of the
prince and subversion of his government, are present in the medieval
works, then this same combination in the *Prince* cannot be seen as subversion of the genre. The genre was already "subverted."

---

1. M. A. Manzalaoui, ed., *Secretum Secretorum*, 185.
2. Machiavelli originally wrote the book for Giuliano de' Medici. After Giuliano died
in 1516, he dedicated it to Lorenzo. For the sake of simplicity, wherever possible I refer to
Machiavelli's princely audience as "the Medici."

The *Prince* and the Medieval *Fürstenspiegel*: What's New?

Although some modern historians of political theory see the *Prince* as different from all political writing that came before it,[3] others see it as "new wine in old bottles." The recognition of the "old bottles" in this formulation comes from the acceptance of Allan Gilbert's 1938 work in *Machiavelli's Prince and Its Forerunners: The Prince as a Typical Book de Regimine Principum*, a meticulous, chapter by chapter commentary on the *Prince* and its analogues.[4] That acceptance is usually reluctant and qualified, however. For instance, although Mark Hulliung says that "Gilbert's scholarship is impeccable" and his contribution "undeniable," he complains that Gilbert "nearly loses [Machiavelli] in a glut of continuity with the Christian Middle Ages."[5] Quentin Skinner, while basically accepting Gilbert's work, says his claim is "overstated."[6] Maybe Gilbert's title is part of the reason for these reactions. In a sense, the title is the overstatement, since the book acknowledges that Machiavelli contributes new elements to the genre. Gilbert does not claim that Machiavelli is *merely* typical. But for those who want to see the Renaissance in general and Machiavelli in particular as breaking radically with the Middle Ages, "a glut of continuity" is unsettling.[7]

Despite the fact that the *Prince* shares most of its major categories of thought with the medieval *Fürstenspiegel* and that its language is, as J. G. A. Pocock says, "irritatingly orthodox,"[8] it is not merely modernists' longing for the Renaissance to be more modern than the nonmodern Middle Ages that makes the *Prince* look different from its predecessors. The *Prince* is certainly more openly hostile to Christianity or at least to the papacy and its malign political influence on Italy. It also more consistently promotes

3. Felix Gilbert says that Machiavelli marks the beginning of modern political thought (*Machiavelli and Guicciardini*, 153). For other references, see Q. Skinner, *The Foundations of Modern Political Thought*, I.129, esp. n. 1.

4. Since Machiavelli refers to no predecessors by name, Gilbert does not claim that the parallels he finds are indications that Machiavelli used any of the works as sources. Among the works in Gilbert's pool of analogues are the *Secretum Secretorum*, Gower's *Confessio Amantis*, and Hoccleve's *Regement of Princes*.

5. M. Hulliung, *Citizen Machiavelli*, 24.

6. Q. Skinner, *The Foundations of Modern Political Thought*, I.129.

7. As Brian Stock says in *Listening for the Text*, "The Renaissance invented the Middle Ages in order to define itself" (69). Many modern scholars follow the Renaissance definition by seeing the Middle Ages as naive and static, or having whatever quality will contrast with the sophisticated and dynamic Renaissance.

8. J. G. A. Pocock, *The Machiavellian Moment*, 170.

imperialism,[9] is more interested in rulers who have not inherited their kingdoms,[10] and is more accepting of the leader's occasional need to behave immorally.[11] There are several other themes that don't appear in medieval mirrors for princes. But when Felix Gilbert says that the difference is in "its corroding analysis of the common assumption that a prince ought to be liberal, magnanimous, loyal and beloved,"[12] we should be careful about where such an assumption lies. Surely Arthur Ferguson is right when he says that the medieval *Fürstenspiegel* makes the well-being of the commonwealth dependent on the moral character of the ruler and holds up ideals for him to imitate (the source of Ferguson's impatience with the genre).[13] But Allan Gilbert has shown how predecessors of the *Prince* had already corroded the moral ideals of the tradition.[14] We must therefore explain why those ideals seem perennially shiny and smooth, regenerately virginal, and always newly vulnerable to corrosion.

If I am right that the medieval authors of mirrors for princes routinely had to disguise their criticisms of rulers and regimes, the habitual ambiguity that they used as a disguise may explain why Allan Gilbert finds individual passages in Machiavelli's predecessors that undermine the ideals while Felix Gilbert continues to believe that the ideals are still intact. Since the critiques in the medieval works are sometimes visible only through careful juxtaposition of passages, broad overviews of whole works and very close readings of individual passages can yield very different results. For many reasons, some of which I will discuss later, in the *Prince* Machiavelli rarely uses ambiguity in the same way. This is one of the differences that we feel when reading him. His attacks on traditional morality are short, sharp, and clear, not buried under mounds of contradictory precepts and narratives. One need not be an archeologist to be offended, because Machiavelli

9. Although the *Secretum Secretorum* starts out as advice to a conqueror, not all its translations and heirs continue its interest in war and conquering other peoples. Some of the versions, like Hoccleve's, even promote peace. See *Regement of Princes*, ll. 5202–15. For Machiavelli's enthusiastic promotion of imperialism, see Mark Hulliung's *Citizen Machiavelli*, e.g., 220.

10. Chapters 2 and 3 establish this theme, continued throughout. See Allan Gilbert, *Machiavelli's Prince and Its Forerunners*, 21–23.

11. The Arabic version of the *Secretum Secretorum*, *Kitab sirr al-asrar*, countenances the "breaking of agreements in state policy . . . in certain situations" (A. S. Fulton, ed., "The Secret of Secrets," 190). According to W. Berges, there are Arabic tales with the same theme (*Die Fürstenspiegel des hohen und späten Mittelalters*, 111).

12. F. Gilbert, *Machiavelli and Guicciardini*, 165.

13. A. Ferguson, *The Articulate Citizen and the English Renaissance*, e.g., 73, 80.

14. For Machiavellianism before Machiavelli, see also B. Guenée, *States and Rulers in Later Medieval Europe*, 72–74.

has already done the excavating. But Machiavelli is not the first to have introduced this material into a mirror for princes. He has merely exposed it more clearly to view. Even in the light of Michael McCanles's deconstructive reading, the *Prince* seems not different in kind from the *Fürstenspiegel* tradition. McCanles sees the work as a self-consuming artifact that lays down rules only to demonstrate that not following them and following them will equally lead to failure.[15] As we have seen in a number of the previous chapters, the English mirrors for princes are full of contradictory advice that cannot be reconciled and contradictory stories with incompatible morals. They both say and "unsay" their best counsel, and slyly note their own unreadability. If this is also true of the *Prince*[16] — and I think it is — then it is not uniquely so, and this is not a way to distinguish the *Prince* from its medieval analogues.[17] The tradition is already deconstructed.

The issue of public finance will serve as an example of the way that Machiavelli echoes and changes the tradition's polishing and corroding of the ideals. Included in Felix Gilbert's common wisdom is the idea that the ruler should be liberal and magnanimous, which Machiavelli contradicts when he says in chapter 16 that liberality is dangerous because it can force a ruler to refill his coffers by raising the taxes on his people, which will win him no friends (56).[18] It is certainly true that many of the medieval mirrors for princes (starting with the Arabic source[19]) recommend liberality.[20] One of them is, of course, Hoccleve, who does so because he is trying to extract money from the prince he addresses. But a number of them also warn that

15. M. McCanles, *The Discourse of Il Principe*. This thesis runs throughout the book. There are helpfully clear formulations of it on 44, 45, 47, and 50.

16. I called McCanles's reading of the *Prince* "deconstructive," but he attributes the text's dialectical turning upon itself not to the nature of language, but to the nature of power (power based on dependence is not power, and all power is dependent; 44) and on Machiavelli's intention. That is, Machiavelli sees the paradoxical nature of power and tries to reveal it in his work. Therefore, some would not call McCanles's reading properly deconstructive. But the issue is complicated because Machiavelli nowhere announces the paradox, and it is up to the reader to ferret out the thesis that "is present everywhere in Machiavelli's text and visible nowhere" (45). In some sense, we have the same interpretive problems with the paradoxes of the *Prince* that we have with the English mirrors for princes.

17. McCanles cites the whole of Allan Gilbert's book to support his claim that the "radical difference" between Machiavelli and his forerunners is that "for him the Christian lexicon of moral judgments ceases to provide the privileged and circumscribing vocabulary to which are subordinated all other terms for describing human behavior" (61). I hope to show in this chapter that Gilbert's evidence does not provide straightforward witness on this "radical difference."

18. Page numbers refer to Quentin Skinner's edition of the *Prince*, R. Price, trans.

19. *Secretum Secretorum*, ed. R. Steele and A. S. Fulton, 181.

20. According to Allan Gilbert, "the weight of exhortation was on the side of free-handedness" (*Machiavelli's Prince and Its Forerunners*, 89).

overgenerosity is unwise because rulers who ruin their people and their kingdoms do not deserve to rule.[21] As we saw in Chapter 8, Hoccleve joins this latter group, as well. In a stanza that Allan Gilbert does not cite, Hoccleve follows the *Secretum Secretorum* in warning against giving to the unworthy and giving so much that poverty weakens the ruler and "Victorie ʒeueth to his enemys" (l. 4143; see also ll. 4152–56). So the comparison beween the *Prince* and its analogues is muddied by Machiavelli's single-mindedness on this issue and the analogues' wish to have it both ways. Some of the earlier works do polish the ideal of liberality and magnanimity in a king. But, in itself, steering rulers away from generosity is not new.

There is a similar compilation of citations for mercy in Machiavelli's chapter 17. Again, the weight of advice in the medieval mirrors for princes favors it, thus preserving the ideal, but because they recognize the inadvisability of taking even virtues to extremes, they also mark its limits. Hoccleve is one of the writers who reins in pity (ll. 3144–92),[22] but also polishes the ideal by recommending it elsewhere (ll. 2997–3003). So Machiavelli's acceptance of certain kinds of cruelty to avoid social disorder is startling not because it is new, but because it is stated more baldly. It is also less surrounded by advice that flatly contradicts it.[23] In many cases, Machiavelli seems to feel no need to hedge or to soften his message.

In fact, he announces its novelty.[24] As he introduces the final series of chapters, in which he takes on a number of issues that are standard topics for mirrors for princes (starting with liberality in chapter 16), he apologizes with what may really be a boast:

21. Allan Gilbert refers to one of the Middle English translations of the *Secretum Secretorum* edited by R. Steele (Gilbert, *Machiavelli's Prince and Its Forerunners*, 88; R. Steele, *Three Prose Versions of the Secreta Secretorum*, 7, 8). This mirror for princes defines foolish largesse as giving money to undeserving people and warns that spending oneself into poverty puts one at the mercy of his enemies (7; see 52 for another example), but also warns that poverty leads rulers to take "the goodis and possessiones from her sugetis" and thus causes rebellions. Heavy taxes and the disturbances that follow are exactly Machiavelli's concerns. As we saw in Chapter 5, this is one of the tropes of advice the Appellants appropriated in their conflict with Richard II in the late 1380s.

22. On 101, Allan Gilbert cites stanza 453 (ll. 3165–71).

23. At the beginning of chapter 17, Machiavelli does recommend acquiring a *reputation* for mercy. His polishing of the ideal often comes in this form. Another matter on which he wants it two ways is whether a ruler should try to be loved or feared. In one place, he says that fear is easier to guarantee than love, and less fickle (chapter 17), but in another reflects that "the best fortress a ruler can have is not to be hated by his people" (chapter 20, 75). On this matter, his behavior is quite medieval.

24. This is consonant with what J. G. A. Pocock sees as the work's theme of innovation (*The Machiavellian Moment*, chapter 6) and its consistent focus on nonhereditary—that is, new—princes.

It now remains to consider in what ways a ruler should act with regard to his subjects and allies. And since I am well aware that many people have written about this subject I fear that I may be thought presumptuous, for what I have to say differs from the precepts offered by others, especially on this matter. But because I want to write what will be useful to anyone who understands, it seems to me better to concentrate on what really happens rather than on theories or speculations. For many have imagined republics and principalities that have never been seen or known to exist. (Chapter 15, 54)

The new "reality principle" that needs this apology is the idea that a prince must "learn how not to be good." Although we are unable to determine just what his sources said because he does not name them, as we have seen, the idea that virtues can cause trouble for a ruler would not have shocked many medieval writers in this tradition. What would have struck them as new is the announcement of newness. The whole genre is structured around the prestige of Aristotle as an authority. The English writers I have examined who do not assume Aristotle's mantle — Gower, Chaucer, and Hoccleve — invent authoritative personae (Genius, Prudence, and the old man, respectively) as purveyors of wisdom.[25] None of them claims novelty. None promises wisdom culled from experience (as Machiavelli does in his dedication of the work — quoted below in "The *Prince* and the Prince"). They do not value what Chaucer calls "newfangleness." The premium on novelty is what is not medieval here, and it is interesting that the idea of newness is what has shaped a great deal of the discourse about the *Prince*. Modern commentators, including me, are still trying to define what is new about Machiavelli's mirror.

The *Prince* and the Prince

The reason Machiavelli puts a premium on the newness of his work may have to do with his relationship to the patron he was angling for. During the Florentine republic of 1498–1512, while Machiavelli was a secretary to the Second Chancery (one of the divisions of the government), he became an important assistant to Pietro Soderini, who from 1502 to 1512 was

---

25. As Annabel Patterson notes, the appeal to authority is often an attempt to avoid cenure and dodge the censors, and it was used regularly by Renaissance writers (*Censorship and Interpretation*, 57). But while appeals to authority are often present in both medieval and Renaissance works, claims of novelty are not.

Gonfaloniere (head of the government) of Florence.[26] When Pope Julius II drove Florence's French allies from Italy, the republic fell and the pope installed the Medici to rule the city. Machiavelli was the only official of his rank fired from his job, probably because of his close association with Soderini; he was banished from Florence for a year and fined the large sum of 1000 gold florins.[27] The Florentine aristocrats who supported the Medici opposed Soderini and his close associate.[28] When Machiavelli's name was found on a list of people from whom two republican conspirators thought they could get help, he was arrested and tortured.[29] Upon his release, he retreated to a farm near the city where, craving political involvement, he wrote works in many genres that he hoped would get him employment in the Medici government. One of those works was the *Prince*. Like James Yonge's translation of the *Secretum Secretorum* for the earl of Ormonde, Machiavelli's mirror for princes was part of a job application, though for himself, not a patron.

A mirror for princes was a strange choice of genre for an ardent republican. That the republican should use it to seek employment from the prince whose rule he had opposed is even stranger. Certainly the theme of newness with which I began this section might have been part of Machiavelli's attempt to attract the attention of such an unlikely patron, along with the emphasis throughout on advice for nonhereditary rulers and, in chapter 5, on rulers who wish to tame a city that once ruled itself. Machiavelli was perhaps trying to tempt the Medici with the opportunity of learning the secrets of the enemy. The complex and ambivalent display that Machiavelli uses to attract his unlikely audience is worth discussing in more detail because it is another key to the relationship between the *Prince* and its forerunners.

The dedicatory letter at the start of the *Prince* makes rhetorical moves that will be familiar to readers of mirrors for medieval princes — the authorial self-deprecation and both manipulative praise and sly critique of the recipient. Machiavelli notes that those who wish "to gain the favor of a prince" seek out riches of various kinds to give them:

Wishing myself to offer Your Magnificence some token of my devotion to you, I have not found among my belongings anything that I hold more dear or valuable

---

26. Machiavelli also became secretary to the "Ten of War," and was thus involved, through the Second Chancery, in domestic issues, and, through the Ten of War, in foreign affairs. See Q. Skinner, *Machiavelli*, 6.

27. R. Ridolfi, *The Life of Niccolò Machiavelli*, 131, 133.

28. F. Gilbert, *Machiavelli and Guicciardini*, 173.

29. R. Ridolfi, *The Life of Niccolò Machiavelli*, 136.

than my knowledge of the conduct of great men, learned through long experience of modern affairs and continual study of ancient history. . . .

And although I consider this work unworthy to be presented to Your Magnificence, I trust very much that your humanity will lead you to accept it. . . .

And if Your Magnificence, from the heights of your exalted position, should sometimes deign to glance down towards these lowly places, you will see how much I am unjustly oppressed by great and cruel misfortune. (3, 4)

Machiavelli is humble and frankly eager to please, and despite the fact that his book will warn against flatterers (chapter 23), he flatters. Hoping to call forth Medici kindness, he claims to be sure of his reader's "humanity." But he is also not shy about trying to call the high lord's attention down to his own plight. What is especially piquant about this bid for attention is that all his pain — mental, physical, and financial — though he delicately attributes it to "misfortune," was caused by the Medici. And he points out that he was "unjustly oppressed." The only people with the resources to solve his problem are the ones who caused it in the first place. Praise of the lord and blame are inseparable.

Since Machiavelli's "experience of modern affairs" includes watching the Medici and their allies, some of the advice for the lofty lord actually constitutes criticism of his party. As Quentin Skinner notes, to tell the prince to live in the principality he has conquered (chapter 5) is implicitly to criticize Louis XII of France and Guiliano de' Medici, the first dedicatee of the *Prince*.[30] And to advise against the use of mercenaries (chapters 12 and 13) is implicitly to criticize the practice of all rulers except Cesare Borgia.[31] The gift that Machiavelli offers the "lofty lord" thus contains some barbs.

If the lord noticed these implied criticisms, he might then be sensitive to the parts of the work that would seem to lead to the conclusion that Machiavelli is one of the last people that he should consider employing. For instance, at the climax of an important chapter mostly taken up with an account of Cesare Borgia's correct but finally unsuccessful strategies, we learn that Borgia's ultimate, ruinous error was appointing Julius II, a former enemy, as pope.[32] As Machiavelli explains, "Anyone who thinks that new benefits make important men forget old injuries is mistaken" (chapter 7, 29).[33] If this principle applies also to less high personages, then the

---

30. See Q. Skinner's edition of the *Prince*, xi and xiii.
31. Q. Skinner, *Machiavelli*, 18.
32. Of course, Julius is also an enemy of Machiavelli.
33. Although Allan Gilbert does not find appropriate analogues for this passage (48), we have already seen (Chapter 6 above) that Chaucer provides one in the *Melibee* when Prudence

relative positions of Julius before elevation to the papacy and Cesare Borgia
are analogous to those of Machiavelli and the Medici. Deftly making himself parallel to the man who defeated him, Machiavelli also seems to be
saying that the Medici should not become his patron on the expectation
that new favors will cancel out old injuries. Is Machiavelli working against
his own purpose?

The question seems even more urgent because Machiavelli gives other
seemingly self-defeating advice in the *Prince*. For instance, in chapter 23 he
tells the Medici not to take unasked-for advice. This is a rather clever plan
for getting advice but limiting the amount of it by having the ruler take
advice only from chosen sources.[34] But it produces a paradox, since the
Prince is itself unasked-for advice. If the ruler takes Machiavelli's advice, he
will already have violated it. But if he takes the advice in the book, he will
reject the book. Shades of Prudence in the *Melibee*.

If the Medici were attentive enough to be amused at this conundrum,
these passages are not necessarily self-defeating because, if nothing else,
they prove that Machiavelli is not self-serving in the advice he gives; in the
Prince, as in all the other mirrors for princes that I have examined in this
book, the good adviser does not favor his self-interest. Machiavelli does not
recommend the familiar false financial crisis and picking the man to be adviser who offers his own money, as the *Secretum Secretorum* does, but he
counsels the prince to reject any man if it appears that "he is thinking more
about his own affairs than about yours, and that all his actions are designed
to further his own interests" (chapter 22, 80). In giving advice that would
hurt his chances, Machiavelli certainly passes that test.

But there is one more change to ring on this theme of the autobiographical significance of the advice in the *Prince*. The book does offer some
advice that can appear self-serving. For instance, Machiavelli several times
repeats warnings to a nonhereditary ruler against trusting those who helped
to put him in power: "[Y]ou cannot retain the friendship of those who have
helped you to become ruler, because you cannot satisfy them in the ways
that they expect. Nor can you use strong medicine against them, since you
have obligations to them . . ." (chapter 3, 7). This and the similar warning
against king-makers in chapter 20 (80),[35] amply fulfilled in Shakespeare's
1 Henry IV, sweep away many of the Medici's likely choices for advisers by

tells her husband that he has made a mistake in consulting his old enemies. She offers the
opposite advice to his new ones as she tries to make peace, quoting Solomon at both junctures.

34. Allan Gilbert mentions no analogues for this idea.

35. Allan Gilbert offers no analogues for these warnings.

casting doubt upon Machiavelli's opponents in the Florentine struggles before 1512. Conveniently enough, the remaining choices for rulers include "those men, whom at the beginning of their power they regarded with suspicion" (chapter 20, 79). In a word, Machiavelli.[36]

I have already indicated some skepticism about whether the Medici were able or willing to do this kind of reading. Maybe they weren't, or maybe they were and just didn't buy the argument. All we know is that Machiavelli's bid for employment was rebuffed.[37] As a job application, it did not work. But it is important to note that despite his startling clarity and claims of novelty on some issues, on this one Machiavelli gives contrasting ideas in different places, piles up opposing opinions, and allows ambiguities to resonate. He offers two clear admonitions: "don't hire me" and "hire me." In other words, when he writes in ways that implicate him, he looks quite medieval.

His circumspection might have to do with the fact that there are other ways of interpreting the *Prince*, other functions it could have performed in its social context besides being part of a job application. According to some modern commentators, it was not a sincere attempt by Machiavelli to ingratiate himself with the Medici by helping them rule more effectively. Rather, it was an attempt to expose the methods by which princes rule their subjects in order to make tyranny more difficult. One of the chief modern proponents of this view is Antonio Gramsci, in his *Prison Notebooks*:

> Machiavelli himself remarks that what he is writing about is in fact practised, and has always been practised, by the greatest men throughout history. So it does not seem that he was writing for those who are already in the know. . . . One may therefore suppose that Machiavelli had in mind "those who are not in the know," and that it was they whom he intended to educate politically. . . . Who therefore is "not in the know?" The revolutionary class of the time, the Italian "people" or "nation," the citizen democracy which gave birth to men like Savonarola and Pier Soderini.[38]

Gramsci is following the line earlier laid down by Jean Jacques Rousseau, who also saw the *Prince* as exposé of princely tactics meant to aid those who

---

36. Q. Skinner agrees that this passage is meant to have autobiographical significance, but because it is contradicted in the *Discourses*, he calls it "special pleading," a violation of Machiavelli's "normally objective standards of argument" (*Machiavelli*, 22). I am arguing that the contradiction resides within the *Prince* itself and do not want to privilege one side of the contradiction as "objective" or "normal" and the other as "not."

37. According to one account, Lorenzo thought that the work was not full enough of "grandiloquent phrases." (Alvisi, quoted in Federico Chabod's *Machiavelli and the Renaissance*, 17).

38. A. Gramsci, *Selections from the Prison Notebooks of Antonio Gramsci*, 135.

oppose them.[39] The virtue of this kind of interpretation is that it saves Machiavelli from being a traitor to the republican cause, a thought so troubling that modern commentators have worked hard to reconcile the *Prince* with Machiavelli's more republican writings like the *Discourses on the First Ten Books of Titus Livius*.[40] Mary Dietz objects to this line of argument because there is no evidence that Machiavelli intended his book to reach an audience of republicans. She says that as far as we know, he attempted to have it reach only the Medici.[41]

The *Prince* did, however, have audiences other than the Medici. Not published until 1532,[42] it was "circulated in manuscript during Machiavelli's lifetime, surreptitiously copied and corrupted, and [it] achieved an underground fame."[43] Just what was it about the book that meant its life as a manuscript had to be surreptitious?

Even Machiavelli seems to have imagined that the *Prince* could be used as a revolutionary handbook. The story is told about his response to seeing how Lorenzo de' Medici received his gift: Lorenzo was more grateful for a pair of hounds. "Wherefore Machiavelli went away in great indignation, telling his friends that he was not the man to conspire against princes, but that if they persisted in their ways conspiracies would surely occur — as if he meant that his book would provide him with his revenge."[44] Since the *Prince* seemed to have such revolutionary potential, it is quite appropriate that as a young man Frederick the Great of Prussia wrote a refutation of it. This is an indication that a very specific audience read it as a pro-republican document. But another audience is also relevant. In 1527 the pope was defeated and the Medici overthrown in Florence. When the republic was

39. J. J. Rousseau, *On the Social Contract*, 88.
40. Mark Hulliung has a particularly trenchant summary of modern thought on this issue (229–37). Hulliung's own view is that there should be no difficulty in reconciling the two works because republicanism is not Machiavelli's ultimate concern. Machiavelli is primarily interested in imperialism, which motivates both works. Republics are desirable because they can accomplish "the greatest triumphs of power politics" (5); Machiavelli valued Rome because it created a great empire (197).
41. M. G. Dietz, "Trapping the Prince: Machiavelli and the Politics of Deception," 779. Dietz's own theory also assumes that Machiavelli was an ardent republican, but proposes that he supported republicanism in a different way: by purposely giving the prince bad advice to make him more vulnerable to republican opposition. Her theory does not depend on Machiavelli's wanting to reach republican readers. She and John Langton debated her theory a year later in "Machiavelli's Paradox," with Langton claiming that in the *Prince* Machiavelli's nationalism overcame his republicanism so that his offer to help the Medici was genuine.
42. Q. Skinner, *The Foundations of Modern Political Thought*, I.250.
43. Machiavelli, *The Prince and The Discourses*, M. Lerner, "Introduction," xxx.
44. Alvisi, *Introduction* to the *Lettere Familiari*, xiv, quoted in Chabod's *Machiavelli and the Renaissance*, 106.

restored, Machiavelli rushed back to the city, hoping to be restored to his old job. The Council rejected him resoundingly. Perhaps they read the *Prince* as anti-republican. Perhaps they were encouraged to do so by the fact that his *History of Florence* had been commissioned by a Medici, and Machiavelli had been drawing a salary from the Medici for the previous six years.[45] In the context of his later actions, it might have been easy to see the *Prince* as traitorous. According to Machiavelli's contemporary, G. B. Busoni, at this time, "everyone hated him because of the *Prince*."[46]

So it seems that the *Prince* made Machiavelli no friends whatsoever. Its lack of success in providing Machiavelli what he wanted from so many different audiences is testimony to its ultimate ambiguity, especially when drawn into a hermeneutical circle with its author's life and career. It provoked at least suspicion in people of all political persuasions. It is interesting to reflect that Voltaire, who had encouraged Frederick the Great's treatise answering Machiavelli, nevertheless made this ironizing comment in his *Memoirs*: "If Machiavelli had had a prince for disciple, the first thing he would have recommended him to do would have been to write a book against Machiavellism."[47] The game of exposing the tyrant and exposing the exposers can go on endlessly.[48]

Thus, all the while that he is being deferential, even flattering to the prince he addresses, and self-abnegating even to the point of defeating his own purposes in writing the book, there are a number of ways he can be interpreted as being hostile to the prince and also self-promoting, whether by just reminding the prince of the pain he had caused Machiavelli, criticizing the prince's allies, by addressing the prince as one who might have attained his position "through wicked means,"[49] or by exposing the tyrannical methods of all princes. While all texts are susceptible to multiple interpretations, this particular text's ambiguities may be a sign of the large stakes involved. Not only had Machiavelli been fired, banished, fined, and tortured by the Medici, his relative Girolano had been tortured and killed (by Cosimo de' Medici) "for having expressed himself openly

45. Q. Skinner, *Machiavelli*, 87.

46. Quoted in R. Ridolfi, *The Life of Niccolò Machiavelli*, 248.

47. Quoted by M. Lerner, "Introduction," *The Prince and The Discourses*, xli.

48. A recent round of the game concerns a book called *The Machiavellian Manager's Handbook for Success*. In an irreverent column called "FYI," the *News and Observer* of Raleigh, North Carolina ("We're Not Naming Names," April 21, 1993, D1) noted that the book is advertised as a guide for amoral office manipulation, but that the author, "L. F. Gunlicks, who works in the Department of Justice, says that his intentions are honorable: By exposing the Machiavellian manager and all his tricks, it's possible to neutralize him."

49. From the title of chapter 8, 30.

against government by oligarchy."[50] Ambiguity, though it had its costs, may have been wiser than openness.

Novelty Again

As Allan Gilbert has shown, from the vantage point of the medieval mirrors for princes, Machiavelli's contribution to the genre was not to sully for the first time the ideal of the benevolent, loving, kind, generous ruler. The ideal had already been tarnished. If the modernists have not been able to absorb the full implications of Gilbert's study, the reason may be partly Machiavelli's own self-presentation as an original. But it may also be partly the brevity of Gilbert's interpretations of the texts he quoted to show their parallels with the *Prince*. His range of reference is so broad that he could not possibly have done full readings of all the texts he quoted from, which was not, after all, the purpose of his study. As I said earlier, in the context of the English works that I have studied in this book, it is not the fact of the tarnishing of the ideal that makes Machiavelli stand out, but the way he trumpets it and announces its novelty. It is also that he does not hedge it around with contradictions. Far from burying it under restatements of the ideal, he highlights it. This sometimes makes the *Prince* seem shocking. But Machiavelli is not doing it for the first time; rather, he is merely claiming to, and he is doing it in a dramatic way. Many of his thoughts on the moral standards for rulers' behavior are not new. His rhetoric of novelty is.

As I have already suggested, he may have felt a certain freedom to claim amoral tactics for himself because the Medici had already done their worst by him. He does not seem to have been limited by the inhibitions of the medieval writers, who were not free to abandon the ideals entirely. And perhaps the waning of the medieval obsession with authority also emboldened him. But where he deals with material that is relevant to him and his relationship to the Medici, he is much more medieval: His self-promotion and hostility to the prince are blurred by overlays of self-abnegation and deference.

And, of course, despite the bold assertions of amorality and the claims to novelty, the book is ambiguous in its social setting. To a prince, it may read like a handbook for reigning; to a member of the opposition, like a handbook for destablizing a reign. Thus it could be presented to a prince,

---

50. R. Ridolfi, *The Life of Niccolò Machiavelli*, 2.

but had to circulate in manuscript secretly, just as for the medieval mirrors for princes, deference was a necessary cover, but criticism was possible. For both, ambiguity was always useful. But to say that the *Prince* fits into the *Fürstenspiegel* tradition is not to say that it is a straightforward defense of conventional pieties. The *Prince* fits in because the tradition itself is full of works that are also not straightforward defenses of convention. It does not promote simple, stable meanings. It is not monolithic or monovocal but rather contains enough complexities, enough ambiguities, and enough contraditions that we can say the *Prince* belongs there without demeaning either. Perhaps Allan Gilbert's title — *Machiavelli's Prince and Its Forerunners: The Prince as a Typical Book de Regimine Principum* — is not an overstatement, after all.

10

Conclusion

[L]iterature challenges ideology by using it.[1]

SINCE THE ISSUES OF ADVICE PERSIST, the fictions of advice continue to circulate and to fascinate us today. Some of the important tasks that the *Secretum Secretorum* outlines for the head of government and that medieval political actors fought over — distinguishing, for instance, between good counsellors and bad, and then surveying the counsel they offer and distinguishing the good from the bad — remain crucial. During the time I have been working on this book, they have surfaced repeatedly. Just as I was writing for the first time about the *Secretum Secretorum*, the Iran-Contra hearings were, I thought, distracting me from my project. Then I heard congressional committee members pressing Secretary of State George Shultz about why he had not prevailed when he told President Ronald Reagan that it was impolitic and illegal to exchange weapons for hostages with Iran and divert the resulting funds to the Nicaraguan Contras. They wondered why, since he was right, he had not succeeded. Shultz responded with his theory of advice: that the adviser can only recommend; the president has to be the one to decide. Here were the two sides of the paradox of advice that we have seen throughout this book — that the ruler is the head and yet must be willing to be governed — being used for the interlocutors' respective purposes: In order to hold the adviser accountable, the elected representatives claimed that the ruler could be ruled, whereas the cabinet member emphasized the ruler's responsiblity in order to deemphasize his own.

Since that summer of 1987, presidential candidates have selected running mates to be their chief advisers and had their judgments second-guessed, and the successful candidates have tried to get their nominees for

---

1. P. Macherey, *A Theory of Literary Production*, 133.

high office confirmed by the Senate, with some public hearings broadcast to spellbound audiences. Some presidents' staff members have been accused of blocking access to the president or being too young and inexperienced to offer good advice. When America went to war against Iraq, pundits worried that Saddam Hussein was not getting good advice because those around him would be too afraid of him to tell him "no" (as Prudence warned her husband in the *Melibee*). The country also watched to see whether Congress would approve the war or say "no" to President Bush. In the meantime, a series of books by advisers to former presidents has appeared, including George Shultz's *Turmoil and Triumph: My Years as Secretary of State*, Clark Clifford's *Counsel to the President*, H. R. Haldeman's diaries of his years with Richard Nixon, and, most notably, Robert McNamara's *In Retrospect: The Tragedy and Lessons of Vietnam*. Some of these books have been best-sellers; all have attracted serious reviews and comment.

The question that repeatedly engaged the public was one that has concerned me in the course of this book: whether or not heads of government could be opposed, by whom, how, and to what effect. In one sense, my readings of some of the medieval works (especially the *Secretum Secretorum* in Chapter 3) might lead to the conclusion that they cannot be opposed, at least not through advice, because advice can never be correctly heard or successfully implemented. It is not necessarily that the regime is so powerful that it contains any moves against it, but, rather, that the conditions of discourse prevent rulers from hearing anything that contradicts their policies. Even if they want advice, the viciousness of the hermeneutical circle destroys their chances of hearing it (Melibee is too caught up in vengeance and war fever to give real credence to the peace party), or the inability of language — especially in narrative — to present plain meaning plainly (what *is* the moral of the story of the Magus and the Jew?) prevents advice from having any bite. The temptation to this deconstructive reading is strongest when we look at the *Fürstenspiegel* tradition unhistorically, as I do in Chapter 3. In contrast, looking at history or literary works in the context of history highlights elements of advice literature that are not likely to be part of the containment of opposition, but which rather support my claim that opposition is not consistently contained. In the period I study here, there were a number of episodes in which power was taken from kings by peers or parliament: the depositions of Edward II and Richard II; the Good Parliament of 1376, which removed from court close advisers and the mistress of Edward III; the Appellants' takeover of the government in the Wonderful Parliament of 1386 and the Merciless Parliament of 1388; the parliamentary limitations placed on Henry IV starting in 1406; and the installation of the Prince of Wales as head of the government in all but name until 1411. Neither literary writers nor their works wielded explicit political power in these actions. But many of these actions deployed the language of advice as it was sustained and revivified by the writers and translators of the *Fürstenspiegel* tradition. And the deconstruction of the advice tradition may even have been turned to political account in the *Tale of Melibee*. Perhaps the most persistently self-contradictory of the works I discuss here, the *Melibee* may use the deconstruction of advice to oppose the Appellants when they were in power, thus participating in a disempowered monarch's resistance to the forces arrayed against him.

The language of advice served the writers and the politicians alike. For the writers, it provided a rich repository of principles and stories that could be shaped into an instrument for pursuing their own interests, sometimes promoting themselves, sometimes criticizing their rulers. It provided some protection for political speech, for under the mantle of the *Fürstenspiegel* tradition they could speak more freely than if they addressed contemporary issues in their own voices and in the present tense. The mix of oppositional and conciliatory gestures available through the advice tradition is encapsulated in Donald Reilly's cartoon of the minstrel being introduced to the gatekeeper of a castle: "He says his ballads sing of the brotherhood of man, with due regard for the stabilizing influence of the nobility" (Figure 2). In Reilly's drawing, it is meant to help the minstrel get past the gatekeeper, in effect a censor who might exclude any disquieting ideas. For the poets and translators of the late fourteenth and early fifteenth centuries, it furnished a similar sort of protection, as it did also for the political actors who deployed it to oppose their kings and who needed to appear less self-interested than they usually were. The Appellants used the tropes of advice to oppose Richard partly because they were available to them through the manuals and treatises of the *Fürstenspiegel* tradition. That tradition was an integral part of political thought, supplying ways of perceiving sociopolitical processes and a repertoire of roles actors could appropriate.

By historicizing what we usually call "literature," we can watch this process at work. For instance, we can see tropes of advice familiar from the mirrors for princes used against Richard II by the Appellants, and picked up by Gower in the *Confessio Amantis* in all likelihood because they had been made current by the Appellants' battles with the king. The Appellants adapted the story of the king swayed by bad advice from young counsellors

*"He says his ballads sing of the brotherhood of man, with due
regard for the stabilizing influence of the nobility."*

Figure 2. Drawing by D. Reilly; ©1988 The New Yorker Magazine, Inc.

to fit Richard II. Then, when Richard was deposed, his story was easily
incorporated into new works, joining Rehoboam as an exemplary figure of
an ill-advised king. Late medieval political discourse enriched and was in
turn enriched by the flowering of the literary genre of the mirrors for prin-

ces. Literature was not quarantined from political affairs but, rather, helped to constitute them.

Out of their very different perspectives, all the participants in this dialectic helped to form the language of advice. Literary writers and historical actors dug up old stories, invented new ones, and traded them back and forth. They groomed the fictions of advice, highlighting their contemporary relevance as it suited them, supplementing and refining them, keeping them polished, keeping them current. Even as they used them in their different conflicts, they were all cooperating to forge a language for political action.

In addition, while forging a tool for politicians to use, the writers wielded it, too. James Yonge both advised his patron and supported him as a candidate for lieutenant of Ireland in his competition for the job with his rival Talbot (see Chapter 4); Chaucer supported his king in his conflict with the Appellants (see Chapter 6); Gower turned away from noble advisers and advised his king to pay attention to the people (see Chapter 7); and Hoccleve contributed to Lancastrian legitimacy, supported the Prince of Wales in his conflict with his father, and, along the way, offered some stern advice of his own to the prince (see Chapter 8). These writers did not just preserve the language of advice and hand it over to politicians, they also shaped it to their own purposes in order to participate in public discourse in their own right.

Who was listening? Who was the potential audience for vernacular works on public themes in the late fourteenth and early fifteenth centuries? Mirrors for princes were numerous, with old ones being translated and new ones being written by important writers like Chaucer, Gower, and Hoccleve.[2] If we want to understand why this literature bloomed during this period, these questions about audience are crucial. It would be helpful to know not only who read or heard these works and what class they belonged to but also how they interpreted them and whether the works influenced their thoughts and actions.

Unfortunately, because of the paucity of information on readers' reactions to literature and even ownership of books,[3] these questions are difficult to answer. Of the many critics who have addressed this question, some emphasize the courtly nature of this literature, while others look to the growing middle class. On the one hand, Richard Firth Green notes the

2. For a fuller survey, see R. F. Green, *Poets and Princepleasers*, chapter 5.
3. R. F. Green, *Poets and Princepleasers*, 7, 99.

association of many late medieval writers, including Chaucer and Hoccleve, with the royal court, and the flourishing of reading and writing in and around the court. And he is surely correct to see the traditional *Fürstenspiegel* as courtly since aristocrats owned Latin and French mirrors for princes, perhaps in imitation of rulers who showed interest in them by commissioning translations.[4] No one with aspirations to lead others could be without a mirror. But it is unclear whether kings or lords had a taste for this sort of literature in English, because many of their books were in French and Latin.[5] But the *Secretum Secretorum* began appearing in English "[s]oon after 1400" with "The Governance of Lordschipes,"[6] and perhaps this date, however fuzzy, is something of a watershed after which the aristocracy paid more heed to books in English. Other translations of the *Secretum Secretorum* followed, at least one, as we have seen, commissioned by an earl. One manuscript of the *Regement of Princes* bears the arms of John Mowbray, second duke of Norfolk, and John Tiptoft, earl of Worcester, had a copy of Lydgate's *Fall of Princes*.[7] Two other manuscripts of the *Regement* were fine enough to be given to members of the aristocracy, and one may have been presented to the Prince of Wales.[8] If the story is true that Richard requested that Gower write an English poem, he may have read the *Confessio Amantis*, and Henry IV owned a copy of it that his son inherited.[9] Henry V promoted English in a number of ways,[10] and it seems likely that the aristocratic readership of serious literature in English grew over time.

In addition to this evidence for increasing aristocratic interest, there is also evidence for interest in vernacular works among members of the middle class. Janet Coleman's list of middle-class readers includes "urban merchants and gild members ranging from the rich to the relatively poor, country gentry ranging from those bearing arms to lesser squires and humble free tenant farmers." That class was "fluctuating . . . wide-ranging," and "newly literate and newly vocal." She tends to group together many kinds of "Middle English poems dealing with contemporary conditions,"[11] including anonymous lyrics, Lollard and anti-Lollard literature, antiwar

4. R. F. Green, *Poets and Princepleasers*, chapters 1–3, 140–42.
5. V. J. Scattergood, "Literary Culture at the Court of Richard II," 36.
6. MS Lambeth 501, R. Steele, ed., *Three Prose Versions of the Secretum Secretorum*, 41.
7. K. Harris, "Patron, Buyers and Owners," 168–69.
8. D. Pearsall, "Hoccleve's *Regement of Princes*," 395–96.
9. See Chapter 7, note 86.
10. J. H. Fisher, *The Importance of Chaucer*, x, 8–9, 144–45; M. Richardson, "Henry V, the English Chancery, and Chancery English."
11. J. Coleman, *Medieval Readers and Writers*, 61–64.

poetry, alliterative debate poems, *Mum and the Sothsegger*, and the works of Langland, Gower, Lydgate, and Hoccleve as addressed to this inclusive class.[12] She singles out some complaint, especially that expressing sympathy for peasants, as meant not for peasants themselves, but for "the lower echelons of the middle class."[13] She also speculates that Gower's "most obvious readership" may have been "trilingual chancery clerks who copied in Latin and French, as well as creating a correspondingly official language in English."[14] We know of at least one clerk—from the office of the privy seal, not the chancery—who was indeed involved in the creation of official language through work on a formulary (it "contained nine hundred forms for letters") and who knew the *Confessio*: Hoccleve copied Trinity College MS RIII 2 (581).[15] In "English Culture in the Fourteenth Century," Coleman separates out the *Vox Clamantis* and other English mirrors for princes as "testimonies to the voice of a gentry and urban 'middle class' developing its own political, critical voice" (60), emphasizing the gentry represented in parliament (33–39).[16] Since not all courtly readers and hearers were noble, and since Richard Firth Green agrees that some courtly literature acquired middle-class readers in the fifteenth century (as "an extension of the aristocratic reading public rather than a replacement for it"[17]), the idea of a middle-class audience seems inescapable, but not exclusive.

We can define more precisely the relationship between courtly and middle-class audiences. Several critics have focused on a limited group of literary works to make the useful distinction between the different places of literary production and literary consumption, for much of the poetry produced in the court for a courtly audience—including most of the literature discussed in this book—was written with a wider public in mind. It is one of Anne Middleton's seminal insights in "The Idea of Public Poetry in the Reign of Richard II" that although the first version of the *Confessio Amantis* was addressed to the king, the poem was always intended for a wider public: "The king is not the main imagined audience, but an occasion for gathering and formulating what is on the common mind."[18] Indeed, according

12. J. Coleman, *Medieval Readers and Writers*, 58–156.
13. J. Coleman, *Medieval Readers and Writers*, 63.
14. J. Coleman, *Medieval Readers and Writers*, 127.
15. On the formulary, see J. Catto, "The King's Servants," 80. On Hoccleve as copyist, see A. I. Doyle and M. B. Parkes, "The Production of Copies of the *Canterbury Tales* and *Confessio Amantis* in the Early Fifteenth Century," 182–85.
16. J. Coleman, "English Culture in the Fourteenth Century," 60, 33–39.
17. R. F. Green, *Poets and Princepleasers*, 10.
18. A. Middleton, "The Idea of Public Poetry," 107.

to Paul Strohm, much courtly literature was "disseminated among an enlarged public."[19]

Ultimately, if we focus on the gentry,[20] professionals, and the upper ranks of the urban ruling class who were taking greater and greater roles in government, the division between courtly and noncourtly audiences seems less strict. Since some of these men were moving in and out of court to hold offices in royal government, some of the members of the court were middle-class. Others were moving in and out of government as holders of offices in the shires that were connected to the royal government (e.g., as members of parliament, sheriffs, and justices of the peace).[21] Because of this development in the government, there is less of a dichotomy. In Larry Scanlon's insightful synthesis, we should view public literature as the place of meeting between "the court, and the sub-noble groups that were coming to share its power."[22] Chaucer's coterie is paradigmatic. Several critics analyze the group of men who are associated with him, either because he mentions them in his poems or because they mention him, including a few of Richard II's chamber-knights, like Sir Lewis Clifford and Sir Philip de la Vache, several men in royal service, like Sir Peter Bukton and Henry Scogan, the Oxford philosopher (or London lawyer and official) Ralph Strode, and the poets John Gower, Thomas Usk, and Thomas Hoccleve. Even the short list of poets is instructive, since Gower was rural gentry (with London and later court ties) and Usk and Hoccleve were civil servants.[23] These groups alone demonstrate Middleton's and Scanlon's thesis, that the new members of court and government who were expanding participation in politics were also a natural audience for the poets who address public themes.[24] The literature is elite and sometimes formally addressed to royalty, but the audience included not only rulers but also people who might be expected to be concerned with rulers' behavior and its consequences for the nation as a whole.

However, for Scanlon the meeting between court and gentry entailed

19. P. Strohm, "Chaucer's Fifteenth-Century Audience," 19. See also D. Pearsall, *Old English and Middle English Poetry*, 212–13.

20. By this term, I mean gentle but non-noble landowners.

21. C. Given-Wilson, *The Royal Household and the King's Affinity*, 265.

22. L. Scanlon, *Narrative, Authority, and Power*, 144.

23. D. Pearsall, *Old English and Middle English Poetry*, 194–97; "The *Troilus* Frontispiece and Chaucer's Audience"; P. Strohm, "Chaucer's Audience," "Chaucer's Fifteenth-Century Audience," and *Social Chaucer*, 21–23, 27–46, 50–64; V. J. Scattergood, "Literary Culture at the Court of Richard II"; L. Patterson, *Chaucer and the Subject of History*, 32–39.

24. For L. Patterson's view of Chaucer's discomfort with the role of court poet, see "'What Man Artow?'" and *Chaucer and the Subject of History*.

"accommodation," defined as the gentry's responding to its dependence on the nobility by adopting the nobility's aims. For him, the middle class "assumed its role precisely by entering courtly culture and making common political cause with the nobility."[25] There is a "common political cause" between gentry and magnates in the broad sense that the values of courtly culture included, first, the king as the center of society and the guarantor of its health; second, the *Fürstenspiegel*; and, third, the theme of advice in politics. But it is not the case that the only role available to the middle class was to adopt the program of the nobility. The two groups cooperated occasionally, especially when both opposed either the king (especially on taxes) or the peasants (especially on wages for laborers).[26] Lee Patterson, for example, emphasizes the "unity of the ruling classes" when he interprets the Rising of 1381 as a sign of the opposition of "independent peasant producers to the seigneurial attempt to contain their growth." For him, the "crucial ideological opposition is not between the seigneurial nobility and the urban merchant class but between both of these elements of the exploiting class and the increasingly independent and self-sufficient productive classes in the country."[27] But even on the issue of rising wages, the two groups were at odds because larger landowners could tolerate higher wages longer than smaller landowners could; small landowners took the lead in parliament on the enforcement of the Statute of Laborers.[28] The barons could not count on the support or allegiance of the middle class.

It is worth paying a little more attention to the members of this important segment of the middle class, the gentry, who advised both magnates and kings and are the subjects of a recent historical discussion to which I alluded in Chapter 1. Many have thought that they were so intertwined with the nobility that they did not perceive themselves as having distinct interests or a separate identity.[29] The two groups of landowners were, in fact, intertwined. Magnates with land in several counties depended on local gentry to administer their estates,[30] to participate in their councils to give them advice,[31] and to look out for their interests with local officials like sheriffs and representatives to the commons in parliament.[32] These

---

25. L. Scanlon, *Narrative, Authority, and Power*, 144.

26. N. Saul, *Knights and Esquires*, 261.

27. L. Patterson, *Chaucer and the Subject of History*, 253.

28. N. Saul, *Knights and Esquires*, 261.

29. S. Payling, *Political Society in Lancastrian England*, 2.

30. S. Payling, *Political Society in Lancastrian England*, 100; N. Saul, *Knights and Esquires*, 86.

31. N. Saul, *Knights and Esquires*, 85.

32. N. Saul, *Knights and Esquires*, chapter 4.

needs prompted them to enter into the relationship with gentry that historians have called "bastard feudalism," in which the magnate offered lifetime annuities to men who became his retainers and pledged to look out for his interests. This bond sometimes involved military service, the wearing of the magnate's livery or badge, and, occasionally, attempts to manipulate local officials and the court system, all of which made retaining notorious and the subject of complaints from less privileged classes and fostered the impression that the landowning classes were all one.[33]

Nevertheless, despite these reasons to merge nobility and gentry, it is also possible to see the signs of their separateness. For one thing, many members of the gentry were not retained by a magnate. No magnate's fortune was large enough to invite every local landowner into his affinity. Estimating generously in order to take account of lost records, Nigel Saul hypothesizes that, in the fourteenth century, at least a third of Gloucestershire gentry had no formal ties with magnates. Those who did were not concentrated in one area, but lived among the unindentured.[34] Looking at the question of numbers another way, Simon Payling counts fifty peers and more than twenty-one hundred nonbaronial landowners. Noting that only a few earls and dukes gave annuities to significant numbers of retainers, he argues that the majority of gentry were not retained.[35] Furthermore, some of those men who were retained "hedged their bets" by allying themselves with several lords at once or to both a lord and the king.[36] According to Chris Given-Wilson, "something close to ten percent of England's upper gentry" joined the affinities of Richard II and Henry IV.[37] These multiple allegiances kept any one lord from assuming a retainer's support.

All these factors help to explain why the parliamentary commons sometimes complained about the system of retaining and demanded reforms. They frequently opposed the peers in parliament on issues having to do with the conduct of affinities. Since they objected to having outsiders who were retained by a magnate imposed on them as officeholders in the shires, they passed laws requiring that the offices of sheriff, justice of the peace, and parliamentary representative be occupied only by substantial landholders who resided in the shire.[38] An additional reason for the de-

33. The nobles, too, were sometimes divided on important issues. For an excellent account of faction among the Ricardian nobility, see P. Strohm, "Politics and Poetics."

34. N. Saul, *Knights and Esquires*, 97–98.

35. S. Payling, *Political Society in Lancastrian England*, 106–7.

36. N. Saul, *Knights and Esquires*, 93–94.

37. C. Given-Wilson, *The Royal Household and the King's Affinity*, 266.

38. N. Saul, *Knights and Esquires*, 108–10, 159–60; S. Payling, *Political Society in Lancastrian England*, 184–85.

mand that sheriffs and JPs be men with clout in the region was that often
the chief disturbers of the peace were the rowdy retinues of magnates. Retainers were also often involved in attempts to influence and distort the
justice system, since nobles sometimes attempted to use them to corrupt
the courts. To keep the peace and to safeguard equal justice, administrators
had to be those with both the will and the means to confront the lord.[39]
Numerous parliamentary statutes show that the commons had the requisite
will to enact this kind of requirement, none so boldly as the one passed at
the parliament of September 1388, which attacked the practices of retainers
just when the Appellants were at the height of their power. Although some
of the MPs were probably retainers of the Appellants, they did not hesitate
to assert the principle of domestic order by attacking those they considered
responsible for disrupting it. Even those who accepted the system of retaining or participated in it were independent enough to set limits on what they
considered the nobles' illegitimate exercise of power.[40]

One striking example of such independence is the behavior of John
of Gaunt's affinity, since despite the fact that it was "the largest and most
expensive of its day," John of Gaunt did not use it to dominate local or
national politics or its members' actions. According to Simon Walker,
he never "packed" parliament, even in 1377, the year after the Good Parliament of 1376, whose chastisement of him might have led him to try
to dominate the next one. His men did not monopolize the commissions
of the peace,[41] they married whom they chose, and they crossed him
when their own interests were at stake. For all his wealth and power, John
of Gaunt, like other magnates with affinities—and indeed, like English
kings—was not a dictator, but shared sovereignty with a large group of
local men. According to Walker, "on examination, the relationship between
lord and man that [bastard feudalism] implies turns out to be as much one
of equality as of dependence."[42] In short, the gentry were not so dependent
on the nobility that they did not think of themselves as separate[43] and act
independently.

It may not be amiss to recall that their ability to oppose authority was
demonstrated not only in the shires but also in national politics, since, as
we saw in Chapter 7, the gentry's dissatisfaction with Richard II was what

39. N. Saul, *Knights and Esquires*, 165–66.
40. R. L. Storey, "Liveries and Commissions of the Peace 1388–90," 131–33.
41. S. Walker, *The Lancastrian Affinity*, 260, 238–39, 245.
42. S. Walker, *The Lancastrian Affinity*, 260–61.
43. N. Saul, *Knights and Esquires*, 259.

allowed him to be deposed in 1399.[44] According to M. J. Bennett, even some gentry from Cheshire, the county he had cultivated late in his reign, turned against him. Bennett also notes Lancashire gentry who refused to take Henry IV's part in the revolts against him early in his reign.[45] According to Simon Payling, gentry disaffection contributed to the deposition of Henry VI in 1461.[46] The gentry's involvement in government and capacity for political independence predisposed them to be an apt audience for the subtleties of mirrors for princes in English. They would have known enough about current events to catch topical allusions. Their understanding of the powers and limits of rulers and the powers and limits of subjects would have made them attuned to the way the mirrors for princes sometimes use tact and tradition to camouflage reprimand and lobbying.

But this analysis of the gentry, who were providing links between court and countryside,[47] and who would have been a fit audience for literature addressing public themes, is also part of the larger story of the development of the medieval English polity. Other groups were also participating more in government. According to Gerald Harriss, in addition to the county gentry who held the shire offices, and "parish gentry [who] served as coroners, hundred bailiffs, tax collectors and purveyors," husbandmen served as constables and jurymen — offices "which brought social recognition and were stepping-stones to gentry status."[48] And, as we have seen, professionals and members of the urban ruling class were drawn into government as well. Although some historians believe that this process weakened the monarchy,[49] and members of the nobility sometimes thought it weakened them (indeed it may have caused some of the trouble between Richard II and the magnates in the 1380s and may have been one of the spurs that motivated magnates to form affinities), it helped to create what Harriss calls a "political society" with broad awareness of and presence in government. The nobles, sometimes jealous of their right to advise the king, had more and more to countenance the active participation of the

44. C. Given-Wilson, *The Royal Household and the King's Affinity*, 255, 267; "The King and the Gentry," 96, 101–2; P. Morgan, *War and Society in Medieval Cheshire*, 203–6.

45. M. J. Bennett, *Community, Class and Careerism*, 212–13.

46. S. Payling, *Political Society in Lancastrian England*, 154–56, 219–20.

47. P. R. Coss, "Bastard Feudalism Revised," 45.

48. G. Harriss, "Political Society and the Growth of Government in Late Medieval England," 33–34.

49. For a cogent summary of the work of P. R. Coss, R. W. Kaueper, and J. R. Lander, see G. Harriss, "Political Society and the Growth of Government in Late Medieval England."

gentry and other groups. We have seen in earlier chapters that the idea of an inclusive polity, the nation as a whole, could be wielded by factions for self-interested purposes. But it should also be clear that this conception is the necessary condition for public discourse on civic issues and for what, following Anne Middleton, I have called "public literature."

There is evidence that there were readers of this literature among all these groups. As we have seen (above and in Chapter 7), Chaucer's audience included country gentry, Londoners, and professional clerks. Manuscripts of the *Confessio* and the *Regement of Princes* are decorated with coats of arms, some of which belong to aristocrats, but some of which could belong either to aristocrats or gentry.[50] Several critics think some manuscripts of the *Confessio* could well have been owned by gentry,[51] and it is not irrelevant that Gower takes the gentry's point of view when he chastises the "knyghthode" for the kind of corruption often associated with bastard feudalism: " . . . of here large retenue, / The lond is ful of maintenue . . ." (VII.3011–12). Derek Pearsall's picture of "Hoccleve's circle" includes both magnates and officials in their households.[52] According to A. I. Doyle, the autographs of his poems are dedicated to "a London stationer, the Town Clerk, several of the royal dukes, Joan Bohun, countess of Hereford and Joan Beaufort, countess of Westmorland"; other people at court and officers of state are mentioned.[53] Public literature was getting its public.

Among the political actors during the period I have been looking at, some of whom were reading vernacular literature, there were many overlapping and shifting alliances that allowed for relative independence of political action. This model makes the one suggested by some Renaissance new historicists — that anything that appeared to be opposition to the regime was really instigated by the regime for the purposes of augmenting its power to quell it (see Chapter 1) — inappropriate for the late Middle Ages. Political opposition was possible, as was literary opposition, both of which sometimes consisted of more subtle forms of resistance than the word "opposition" implies. The very conception of an inclusive polity reveals the recognition, albeit implicit, that governance is a collaborative process. Advice itself is the representation of other voices bearing on a ruler. The pre-

50. K. Harris, "Patrons, Buyers and Owners," 168–69.
51. Chapter 7 above, note 84.
52. D. Pearsall, "Hoccleve's *Regement of Princes*," 394–96.
53. A. I. Doyle, "English Books In and Out of Court," 172. See also M. C. Seymour, "The Manuscripts of Hoccleve's *Regiment of Princes*," 255–58.

rogative of violence the ruler possessed does not contradict this picture, for even while the tropes of advice acknowledge that the ruler has certain tools of violence at his command, they also recognize that using them has a political cost, even undermining his legitimacy.

For this reason and others (for instance, perpetual financial troubles), late medieval English kings and other leaders were susceptible to criticism, persuasion, and pressure. The language of advice is a good instrument for moving them because it encompasses the paradoxical nature of the ruler's position — that his power makes him subject to his subjects — and demonstrates a complex rhetoric of deference and challenge appropriate to enact that paradox. It also provides other concepts necessary to political action, including that of the nation as a whole, that of a ruler's accountability to the concerns of a circle wider than just his friends, and that of the subjects' ability and right to act in the political sphere. In a society in which the ruling ideology pictures authority as flowing from the higher strata to the lower rather than in the reverse direction, these ideas might even be called subversive. At the very least, they expose the tension and contradiction between the two different models of social power. By developing, extending, and disseminating the important ideas of the collective, rulers' responsibility to it, and subjects' agency within it, the engaging works I have discussed in this book helped to create the public they represented (in all senses of the word) and participated in the lively, sometimes dangerous conversation about its welfare.

Works Cited

Works are listed by author. Anonymous works are listed by title (except for the *Secretum Secretorum*, which is listed by title, by the name of the medieval translator, if known, and by the modern editors' names). Medieval names with particles are alphabetized by first name. If an article was published in an anthology by a different editor, it appears here under the name of the author. A few anthologies also have their own listings under the editor's name.

Abercrombie, Nicholas, Stephen Hill, and Bryan S. Turner. *Dominant Ideologies*. London: Unwin Hyman, 1990.
———. *The Dominant Ideology Thesis*. London: George Allen & Unwin, 1980.
Adae Murimuth: Continuatio Chronicarum. Robertus de Avesbury: De Gestis Mirabilibus Regis Edwardi Tertii. Ed. Edward Maunde Thompson. London: Eyre and Spottiswoode for Her Majesty's Stationery Office, 1889.
Adam of Usk. *Chronicon Adae de Usk: A.D. 1377–1404*. Ed. and trans. Edward Maunde Thompson. London: John Murray, 1876.
Aegidius Romanus (Giles of Rome). *De regimine principum libri III*. Ed. F. Hieronymum Samaritanium. Rome: Bartholomaum Zannettum, 1607. Reprinted, Darmstadt: Scientia Verlag Aalen, 1967.
Aers, David. *Chaucer*. Atlantic Highlands, NJ: Humanities Press International, Inc., 1986.
———. *Chaucer, Langland and the Creative Imagination*. London: Routledge & Kegan Paul, 1980.
———. *Community, Gender, and Individual Identity: English Writing 1360–1430*. London and New York: Routledge, 1988.
———. "The *Parliament of Fowls*: Authority, the Knower and the Known." *Chaucer Review* 16 (1981–82): 1–17.
Albertani Brixiensis [Albertano of Brescia]. *Albertani Brixiensis. Liber consolationis et consilii, ex quo hausta est fabula de Melibeo et Prudentia*. Ed. Thor Sundby. Havniae: Fred. Host & Filium, 1873.
Allmand, Christopher. *Henry V*. London: Methuen, 1992.
The Anonimalle Chronicle: 1333–1381. Ed. V. H. Galbraith. London/Manchester: Longmans, Green & Co./University of Manchester Press, 1927.
Askins, William. "*The Tale of Melibee* and the Crisis at Westminster, November, 1387." *Studies in the Age of Chaucer: Proceedings, No. 2, 1986, Fifth International*

Congress, 20–23 March 1986, Philadelphia, Pennsylvania. Knoxville: The New Chaucer Society (1987), 103–12.

Aspin, Isabel S. T., ed. *Anglo-Norman Political Songs*. Oxford: Basil Blackwell for the Anglo-Norman Text Society, 1953.

Aston, M. E. "Lollardy and Sedition 1381–1431." *Past and Present* 17 (1960): 1–44.

Bacon, Sir Francis. *The Essayes or Counsells, Civill and Morall*. Ed. Michael Kiernan. Cambridge, MA: Harvard University Press, 1985.

Bacon, Roger. *Opera hactenus inedita Rogeri Baconi, Fasc. V: Secretum Secretorum cum Glossis et Notulis . . . [and] Versio Anglicana ex Arabico. . . .* Ed. Robert Steele and A. S. Fulton. Oxford: Oxford University Press, 1920.

Baldwin, James Fosdick. *The King's Council in England During the Middle Ages*. Oxford: Oxford University Press, 1913. Repr. Gloucester, MA: Peter Smith, 1965.

Barnes, Geraldine. *Counsel and Strategy in Middle English Romance*. Cambridge: D. S. Brewer, 1993.

Barnie, John. *War in Medieval English Society: Social Values in the Hundred Years War, 1337–99*. Ithaca, NY: Cornell University Press, 1974.

Barr, Helen, ed. *The Piers Plowman Tradition: A Critical Edition of "Pierce the Ploughman's Creed," "Richard the Redeless," "Mum and the Sothsegger" and "The Crowned King."* London: J. M. Dent; Rutland, VT: Charles E. Tuttle Co., Everyman's Library, 1993.

Barron, Caroline. "The Quarrel of Richard II with London 1392–7." In *The Reign of Richard II: Essays in Honour of May McKisack*, 173–201. Ed. F. R. H. Du Boulay and Caroline M. Barron. London: University of London, The Athlone Press, 1971.

Bellamy, John G. *The Law of Treason in England in the Later Middle Ages*. Cambridge: Cambridge University Press, 1970.

Bennett, M. J. *Community, Class and Careerism: Cheshire and Lancashire Society in the Age of "Sir Gawain and the Green Knight."* Cambridge: Cambridge University Press, 1983.

Benson, Larry D., ed. *The Riverside Chaucer*. 3rd ed. Boston: Houghton Mifflin Co., 1987.

Berges, Wilhelm. *Die Fürstenspiegel des hohen und späten Mittelalters*. Leipzig: Verlag Karl W. Hiersemann, 1938.

Biblia Sacra juxta Vulgatam Clementinam: divisionibus, summariis et concordantiis ornata. Septima Editio. Madrid: Biblioteca de Autores Cristianos, 1985. For English translation, see *The Holy Bible*.

Blyth, Charles. "Thomas Hoccleve's Other Master." *Mediaevalia* 16 (1993 for 1990): 349–59.

Boas, George. *Vox Populi: Essays in the History of an Idea*. Baltimore: Johns Hopkins University Press, 1969.

"British Anti-German Sentiment." *All Things Considered*. National Public Radio, July 17, 1990.

Brown, A. L. "The Commons and the Council in the Reign of Henry IV." *The English Historical Review* 79 (1964): 1–30.

———. *The Governance of Late Medieval England, 1272–1461*. Stanford, CA: Stanford University Press, 1989.

———. "The King's Councillors in Fifteenth-Century England." *Transactions of the Royal Historical Society*, 5th series, 19 (1969): 95–118.

———. "Parliament, c. 1377–1422." In *The English Parliament in the Middle Ages*. Ed. R. G. Davies and J. H. Denton. Philadelphia: University of Pennsylvania Press, 1981.

Bryan, W. F., and Germaine Dempster, eds. *Sources and Analogues of Chaucer's "Canterbury Tales."* Chicago: University of Chicago Press, 1941.

Burrow, J. A. "Autobiographical Poetry in the Middle Ages: The Case of Thomas Hoccleve." *Proceedings of the British Academy* 68 (1982): 389–412.

Cam, H[elen] M. *Law-Finders and Law-Makers in Medieval England: Collected Studies in Legal and Constitutional History*. London: Merlin Press, 1962.

———. *Liberties & Communities in Medieval England: Collected Studies in Local Administration and Topography*. Cambridge: Cambridge University Press, 1944. Reprinted, New York: Barnes & Noble, 1963.

———. "The Theory and Practice of Representation in Medieval England." In *Historical Studies of the English Parliament*. vol. I: *Origins to 1399*, 263–78. Ed. E. B. Fryde and Edward Miller. Cambridge: Cambridge University Press, 1970.

Carpenter, D. A. "English Peasants in Politics 1258–1267." *Past and Present* 136 (1992): 3–42.

Catto, Jeremy. "The King's Servants." In *Henry V: The Practice of Kingship*, 75–95. Ed. G. L. Harriss. Oxford: Oxford University Press, 1985.

Chabod, Federico. *Machiavelli and the Renaissance*. Trans. David Moore. Cambridge, MA: Harvard University Press, 1958.

Chaplais, Pierre. *Piers Gaveston: Edward II's Adoptive Brother*. Oxford: Clarendon Press, 1994.

Chaucer, Geoffrey. *The Riverside Chaucer*. Ed. Larry D. Benson. 3rd ed. Boston: Houghton Mifflin, 1987.

Chomsky, Noam. *Necessary Illusions: Thought Control in Democratic Societies*. Boston: South End Press, 1989.

Chrimes, S. B. *English Constitutional Ideas in the Fifteenth Century*. Cambridge: Cambridge University Press, 1936.

Chrimes, S. B., and A. L. Brown, eds. *Select Documents of English Constitutional History: 1307–1485*. London: Adam & Charles Black, 1961.

Clarke, M. V. *Medieval Representation and Consent: A Study of Early Parliaments in England and Ireland, with special Reference to the "Modus Tenendi Parliamentum."* 1936. Reissued, New York: Russell & Russell, 1964.

Clarke, M. V. *Fourteenth Century Studies*. Ed. L. S. Sutherland and M. McKisack. Oxford: Clarendon Press, 1937.

Clifford, Clark. *Counsel to the President: A Memoir*. New York: Random House, 1991.

Coffman, George. "John Gower, Mentor for Royalty: Richard II." *PMLA* 69 (1954): 953–64.

Coleman, Janet. *Medieval Readers and Writers: 1350–1400*. New York: Columbia University Press, 1981.

———. "English Culture in the Fourteenth Century." In *Chaucer and the Italian Trecento*, 33–63. Ed. Piero Boitani. Cambridge: Cambridge University Press, 1983.

Cook, Albert. *History/Writing*. Cambridge: Cambridge University Press, 1988.

Cooper, Helen. *Oxford Guides to Chaucer: "The Canterbury Tales."* Oxford: Oxford University Press, 1989.

Copeland, Rita. *Rhetoric, Hermeneutics, and Translation in the Middle Ages: Academic Traditions and Vernacular Texts*. Cambridge: Cambridge University Press, 1991.

Corrigan, Philip, and Derek Sayer. *The Great Arch: English State Formation as Cultural Revolution*. Oxford: Basil Blackwell, 1985.

Coss, P. R. "Aspects of Cultural Diffusion in Medieval England: The Early Romances, Local Society and Robin Hood." *Past and Present* 108 (1985): 35–79.

———. "Bastard Feudalism Revised." *Past and Present* 125 (1989): 27–64.

Curtis, Edmund. *A History of Medieval Ireland from 1086 to 1513*. 2nd ed. London: Methuen & Co. Ltd., 1938.

Davies, R. G., and J. H. Denton. *The English Parliament in the Middle Ages*. Philadelphia: University of Pennsylvania Press, 1981.

Delany, Sheila. "Politics and Paralysis of Poetic Imagination in *The Physician's Tale*." *Studies in the Age of Chaucer* 3 (1981): 47–60.

Dictionary of the Middle Ages. Ed. Joseph R. Strayer. New York: Scribner, 1982–89.

Dietz, Mary G. "Machiavelli's Paradox: Trapping or Teaching the *Prince*." See Langton, John, and Mary G. Dietz.

———. "Trapping the Prince: Machiavelli and the Politics of Deception." *American Political Science Review* 80 (1986): 777–800.

Dobson, R. B., ed. *The Peasants' Revolt of 1381*. 2nd ed. London: Macmillan Press, 1983.

Dollimore, Jonathan, and Alan Sinfield, eds. *Political Shakespeare: New Essays in Cultural Materialism*. Ithaca, NY: Cornell University Press, 1985.

Doob, Penelope. *Nebuchadnezzar's Children: Conventions of Madness in Middle English Literature*. New Haven, CT: Yale University Press, 1974.

Doyle, A. I. "English Books In and Out of Court from Edward III to Henry VII." In *English Court Culture in the Later Middle Ages*, 162–81. Ed. V. J. Scattergood and J. W. Sherborne. New York: St. Martin's Press, 1983.

Doyle, A. I., and M. B. Parkes. "The Production of Copies of the *Canterbury Tales* and the *Confessio Amantis* in the Early Fifteenth Century." In *Medieval Scribes, Manuscripts & Libraries: Essays presented to N. R. Ker*, 163–210. Ed. M. B. Parkes and Andrew G. Watson. London: Scolar Press, 1978.

Dunham, William Huse, Jr., and Charles T. Wood. "The Right to Rule in England: Depositions and the Kingdom's Authority, 1327–1485." *American Historical Review* 81 (1976): 738–61.

Eagleton, Terry. *Criticism and Ideology: A Study in Marxist Literary Theory*. London, New York: Verso, 1978.

Edwards, J. G. "The *Plena Potestas* of English Parliamentary Representatives." In *Historical Studies of the English Parliament*. vol. I: *Origins to 1399*, 136–49. Ed. E. B. Fryde and Edward Miller. Cambridge: Cambridge University Press, 1970.

Fabyan, Robert. *The New Chronicles of England and France*. Ed. Henry Ellis. London: Printed for F. C. & J. Rivington; T. Payne; Wilkie & Robinson;

Longman, Hurst, Rees, Orme and Co.; Cadell and Davies; J. Mawman; and J. Johnson and Co., 1811.

Ferguson, Arthur B. *The Articulate Citizen and the English Renaissance*. Durham, NC: Duke University Press, 1965.

Ferster, Judith. *Chaucer on Interpretation*. Cambridge: Cambridge University Press, 1985.

The First English Life of King Henry the Fifth written in 1513 by an anonymous Author known commonly as The Translator of Livius. Ed. Charles Lethbridge Kingsford. Oxford: Clarendon Press, 1905, 1911.

Fisher, John H. *The Importance of Chaucer*. Carbondale and Edwardsville: Southern Illinois University Press, 1992.

———. *John Gower: Moral Philosopher and Friend of Chaucer*. New York: New York University Press, 1964.

Flynn, James. "Reconstructing *Melibee*: Another Look at Chaucer's Translation of *Le Livre de Mellibee*." Paper presented at the Southeastern Medieval Association meeting, September 1990.

Foucault, Michel. *Discipline and Punish: The Birth of the Prison*. Trans. Alan Sheridan. New York: Pantheon Books, 1977.

Fradenburg, Louise. "The Manciple's Servant Tongue: Politics and Poetry in *The Canterbury Tales*." *ELH* 52 (1985): 85–118.

———. "Spectacular Fictions: The Body Politic in Chaucer and Dunbar." *Poetics Today* 5 (1984): 493–517.

Fryde, E. B., and Edward Miller, eds. *Historical Studies of the English Parliament*. Vol. I: *Origins to 1399*. Cambridge: Cambridge University Press, 1970.

Fryde, Natalie. "Edward III's Removal of His Ministers and Judges, 1340–41." *Bulletin of the Institute of Historical Research* 48 (1975): 149–61.

———. *The Tyranny and Fall of Edward II, 1321–1326*. Cambridge: Cambridge University Press, 1979.

Fulton, A. S. "The Secret of Secrets." See *Secretum Secretorum*. Steele, Robert, and A. S. Fulton, eds.

Galbraith, V. H. *Kings and Chroniclers: Essays in English Medieval History*. London: Hambledon Press, 1982.

Genet, Jean-Philippe. *Four English Political Tracts of the Later Middle Ages*. Camden 4th Ser., Vol. 18. London: Royal Historical Society, 1977.

Gewirth, Alan. *Marsilius of Padua: The Defender of Peace*. Vol. I of *Marsilius of Padua and Medieval Political Philosophy*. New York: Columbia University Press, 1951.

Giddens, Anthony. *Central Problems in Social Theory: Action, Structure and Contradiction in Social Analysis*. Berkeley: University of California Press, 1979.

Gilbert, Allan. *Machiavelli's Prince and Its Forerunners: The Prince as a Typical Book de Regimine Principum*. Durham, NC: Duke University Press, 1938. Reprint, New York: Barnes & Noble, 1968.

Gilbert, Felix. *Machiavelli and Guicciardini: Politics and History in Sixteenth-Century Florence*. Princeton, NJ: Princeton University Press, 1965.

Given-Wilson, Chris. "The King and the Gentry in Fourteenth-Century England." *Transactions of the Royal Historical Society*, 5th Ser., 37 (1987): 87–102.

————. *The Royal Household and the King's Affinity: Service, Politics and Finance in England 1360–1413*. New Haven, CT: Yale University Press, 1986.

Goodman, A. *The Loyal Conspiracy: The Lords Appellant Under Richard II*. London: Routledge and Kegan Paul, 1971.

Gower, John. *The Complete Works of John Gower*. 4 volumes. Ed. G. C. Macaulay. Oxford: The Clarendon Press, 1899–1902.

————. *The Major Latin Works of John Gower: "The Voice of One Crying" and "The Tripartite Chronicle."* Trans. Eric W. Stockton. Seattle: University of Washington Press, 1962.

————. *Mirour de l'Omme (The Mirror of Mankind)*. Trans. William Burton Wilson. Rev. Nancy Wilson Van Bank. East Lansing, MI: Colleagues Press, 1992.

Gramsci, Antonio. *Selections from the Prison Notebooks of Antonio Gramsci*. Ed. and trans. Quintin Hoare and Geoffrey Nowell Smith. London: Lawrence & Wishart, 1971.

Gransden, Antonia. *Historical Writing in England*. Vol. II. *c. 1307 to the Early Sixteenth Century*. Ithaca, NY: Cornell University Press, 1982.

Green, Richard Firth. *Poets and Princepleasers: Literature and the English Court in the Late Middle Ages*. Toronto: University of Toronto Press, 1980.

Greenblatt, Stephen. "Invisible Bullets: Renaissance Authority and Its Subversion, *Henry IV* and *Henry V*." In *Political Shakespeare: New Essays in Cultural Materialism*, 18–47. Ed. Jonathan Dollimore and Alan Sinfield. Ithaca, NY: Cornell University Press, 1985. Reprinted as "Invisible Bullets" in *Shakespearean Negotiations*, 21–65.

————. *Shakespearean Negotiations: The Circulation of Social Energy in Renaissance England*. Berkeley: University of California Press, 1988.

Greetham, D. C. "Self-Referential Artifacts: Hoccleve's Persona as a Literary Device." *Modern Philololgy: A Journal Devoted to Research in Medieval and Modern Literature* 86 (1989): 242–51.

Guenée, Bernard. *States and Rulers in Later Medieval Europe*. Trans. Juliet Vale. Oxford: Basil Blackwell, 1985 [French editions, 1971–1981].

Haines, Roy Martin. *Archbishop John Stratford: Political Revolutionary and Champion of the Liberties of the English Church ca. 1275/80–1348*. Toronto: Pontifical Institute of Medieval Studies, 1986.

Haldeman, H. R. *The Haldeman Diaries: Inside the Nixon White House*. New York: G. P. Putnam's Sons, 1994.

Hamilton, J. S. *Piers Gaveston: Earl of Cornwall, 1307–1312: Politics and Patronage in the Reign of Edward II*. Detroit/London: Wayne State University Press/Harvester-Wheatsheaf, 1988.

Hanawalt, Barbara. "Peasant Resistance to Royal and Seignorial Impositions." In *Social Unrest in the Late Middle Ages: Papers of the Fifteenth Annual Conference of the Center for Medieval and Early Renaissance Studies*, 23–47. Ed. Francis X. Newman. Binghamton, NY: Medieval and Renaissance Texts & Studies, 1986.

Hanna, Ralph III. "Pilate's Voice/Shirley's Case." *South Atlantic Quarterly* 91 (1992): 793–812.

Harris, Kate. "Patrons, Buyers and Owners: The Evidence for Ownership, and the Rôle of Book Owners in Book Production and the Book Trade." In *Book Pro-

duction and Publishing in Britain, 1375–1475, 163–99. Ed. Jeremy Griffiths and Derek Pearsall. Cambridge: Cambridge University Press, 1989.

Harriss, G. L. "Financial Policy." In *Henry V: The Practice of Kingship*, 159–79. Ed. G. L. Harriss. Oxford: Oxford University Press, 1985.

———, ed. *Henry V: The Practice of Kingship*. Oxford: Oxford University Press, 1985.

———. "Introduction: the Exemplar of Kingship." In *Henry V: The Practice of Kingship*, 1–29. Ed. G. L. Harriss. Oxford: Oxford University Press, 1985.

———. "The Management of Parliament." In *Henry V: The Practice of Kingship*, 137–58. Ed. G. L. Harriss. Oxford: Oxford University Press, 1985.

Harriss, Gerald. "Political Society and the Growth of Government in Late Medieval England." *Past and Present* 138 (1993): 28–57.

Hasler, Anthony J. "Hoccleve's Unregimented Body." *Paragraph* 13 (1990): 164–83.

Hector, L. C., and Barbara F. Harvey, trans. and eds. *The Westminster Chronicle, 1381–1394*. Oxford: Clarendon Press, 1982.

Helgerson, Richard. "Recent Studies in the English Renaissance." *Studies in English Literature* 26 (1986): 145–99.

Helmholz, R. H., ed. *Select Cases on Defamation to 1600*. Volume 101 of a series. London: Selden Society, 1985.

Henwood, Doug. "Putting Bondholders First." *Left Business Observer* 57 (February 16, 1993): 1.

Herman, Edward S., and Noam Chomsky. *Manufacturing Consent: The Political Economy of the Mass Media*. New York: Pantheon Books, 1988.

Higden, Ranulf. *Polychronicon Ranulfi Higden Monachi Cestrensis . . .* Vol. IX. Ed. Joseph Rawson Lumby. London: Longman & Co., Trübner & Co., 1886.

Hilton, Rodney. *Bond Men Made Free: Medieval Peasant Movements and the English Rising of 1381*. London: Methuen, 1973.

Hoccleve, Thomas. *Hoccleve's Works: The Minor Poems in the Ashburnham Ms. Addit. 133*. Ed. Frederick J. Furnivall and I. Gollancz. Rev. by Jerome Mitchell and A. I. Doyle. London: Oxford University Press for the Early English Text Society, Extra Series Nos. 61 and 73, Revised reprint 1970.

———. *Hoccleve's Works: III. The Regement of Princes A.D. 1411–12 from the Harleian MS. 4866, and Fourteen of Hoccleve's Minor Poems from the Egerton MS. 615*. Ed. Frederick J. Furnivall. London: Kegan Paul, Trench, Trübner & Co., for the Early English Text Society, 1897.

Selections from Hoccleve. Ed. M. C. Seymour. Oxford: Clarendon Press, 1981.

Holdsworth, Sir William. *A History of English Law*. London: Methuen & Co., 1922–52.

Holquist, Michael. "Introduction. Corrupt Originals: The Paradox of Censorship." *PMLA* 109.1 (1994): 14–25.

Holstun, James. "Ranting at the New Historicism." *English Literary Renaissance* 19 (1989): 189–225.

The Holy Bible: Douay Rheims Version. Baltimore: John Murphy Company, 1899. Repr., Rockford, IL: Tan Books, 1971.

Hotson, J. Leslie. "The *Tale of Melibeus* and John of Gaunt." *Studies in Philology* 18 (1921): 429–52.

Howard, Jean E. "The New Historicism in Renaissance Studies." *English Literary Renaissance* 16 (1986): 13–43.

Hulliung, Mark. *Citizen Machiavelli*. Princeton, NJ: Princeton University Press, 1983.

Hürnheim, Hiltgart von, ed. *Mittelhochdeutsche Prosaübersetzung des "Secretum Secretorum."* Berlin: Akademie-Verlag, 1963.

Jacob, E. F. *The Fifteenth Century, 1399–1485*. Oxford: Clarendon Press of Oxford University Press, 1961.

John of Salisbury. *Policraticus: On the Frivolities of Courtiers and the Footprints of Philosophers*. Ed. and trans. Cary J. Nederman. Cambridge: Cambridge University Press, 1990.

Johnson, Lynn Staley. "Inverse Counsel: Contexts for the *Melibee*." *Studies in Philology* 87 (1990): 137–55.

Jones, Richard H. *The Royal Policy of Richard II: Absolutism in the Later Middle Ages*. Oxford: Blackwell, 1968.

Justice, Steven. *Writing and Rebellion: England in 1381*. Berkeley: University of California Press, 1994.

Justman, Stewart. "'Auctoritee' and the *Knight's Tale*." *Modern Language Quarterly* 39 (1978): 3–14.

———. "Medieval Monism and Abuse of Authority in Chaucer." *Chaucer Review* 11 (1976–77): 95–111.

Kaeuper, Richard W. *War, Justice and Public Order: England and France in the Later Middle Ages*. Oxford: Clarendon Press, 1988.

Kail, J., ed. *Twenty-Six Political and Other Poems (Including "Petty Job") from the Oxford MSS Digby 102 and Douce 322*. Part I. London: Kegan Paul, Trench, Trübner & Co., Ltd. for the Early English Text Society, 1904.

Kempton, Daniel. "Chaucer's Tale of Melibee: 'A Litel Thyng in Prose.'" *Genre* 21 (1988): 263–78.

Kendrick, Laura. "Criticism of the Ruler, 1100–1400, in Provençal, Old French, and Middle English Verse." Ph.D. diss., Columbia University, 1978.

Kern, F. *Kingship and Law in the Middle Ages:* [Part I] *The Divine Right of Kings and the Right of Resistance in the Early Middle Ages:* [Part II] *Law and Constitution in the Middle Ages*. Oxford: Oxford University Press, 1939.

Kingsford, Charles Lethbridge, ed. *English Historical Literature in the Fifteenth Century*. Oxford: Oxford University Press, 1913. Repr., New York: Burt Franklin. Burt Franklin Bibliographical and Reference Series No. 37. [No date given].

———, ed. *The First English Life of King Henry the Fifth written in 1513 by an anonymous Author known commonly as The Translator of Livius*. Oxford: Clarendon Press, 1905, 1911.

Knapp, Peggy. *Chaucer and the Social Contest*. New York: Routledge, 1990.

Knight, Stephen. *Geoffrey Chaucer*. Oxford: Basil Blackwell, 1986.

Knighton, Henry. *Chronicon Henrici Knighton vel Cnitthon: Monachi Leycestrensis*. Ed. Joseph Rawson Lumby. Vol. II. London: Eyre and Spottiswoode, 1895.

Kohl, Stephan. "More than Virtues and Vices; Self-Analysis in Hoccleve's 'Autobiographies.'" *Fifteenth-Century Studies* 14 (1988): 115–27.

Kretzmann, Gregory, and James Simpson, eds. *Medieval English Religious and Ethi-*

cal Literature: Essays in Honor of G. H. Russell. Cambridge, UK; Dover, NH: D. S. Brewer, 1986.

Labarge, Margaret Wade. *Henry V: The Cautious Conqueror*. New York: Stein and Day, 1976.

Lander, J. R. *The Limitations of English Monarchy in the Later Middle Ages*. Toronto: University of Toronto Press, 1989.

Lane, Robert. *Shepheards Devises: Edmund Spenser's "Shepheardes Calender" and the Institutions of Elizabethan Society*. Athens: University of Georgia Press, 1993.

Langland, William. *Piers Plowman: The B Version. Will's Visions of Piers Plowman, Do-Well, Do-Better and Do-Best*. Revised edition. Ed. George Kane and E. Talbot Donaldson. London, Berkeley: The Athlone Press, University of California Press, 1988.

Langton, John, and Mary G. Dietz. "Machiavelli's Paradox: Trapping or Teaching the *Prince*." *American Political Science Review* 81 (1987): 1277–88.

Lawton, David. "Dullness and the Fifteenth Century." *English Literary History* 54 (1987): 761–99.

Leicester, H. Marshall, Jr. *The Disenchanted Self: Representing the Subject in the Canterbury Tales*. Berkeley: University of California Press, 1990.

———. "Our Tonges *Différance*: Textuality and Deconstruction in Chaucer." In *Medieval Texts and Contemporary Readers*, 15–26. Ed. Laurie A. Finke and Martin B. Shichtman. Ithaca, NY: Cornell University Press, 1987.

Lentricchia, Frank. *Ariel and the Police: Michel Foucault, William James, Wallace Stevens*. Madison: University of Wisconsin Press, 1988.

———. *Criticism and Social Change*. Chicago: University of Chicago Press, 1983.

Lerer, Seth. *Chaucer and His Readers: Imagining the Author in Late-Medieval England*. Princeton, NJ: Princeton University Press, 1993.

Lindahl, Carl. *Earnest Games: Folkloric Patterns in the Canterbury Tales*. Bloomington: Indiana University Press, 1987.

Livy. *Early History of Rome*. Trans. Aubrey de Sélincourt. Harmondsworth: Penguin Books, 1960.

Lodge, Eleanor, and Gladys A. Thornton, eds. *English Constitutional Documents: 1307–1485*. Cambridge: Cambridge University Press, 1935. Reprint, New York: Octagon Books, 1972.

Lomperis, Linda. "Unruly Bodies and Ruling Practices: Chaucer's *Physician's Tale* as Socially Symbolic Act." In *Feminist Approaches to the Body in Medieval Literature*, 21–37. Ed. Linda Lomperis and Sarah Stanbury. Philadelphia: University of Pennsylvania Press, 1993.

Lyon, Bryce. *A Constitutional and Legal History of Medieval England*. 2nd ed. New York: W.W. Norton & Co., 1980.

Macaulay, G. C. ed., *The Complete Works of John Gower*, 4 vols: *The French Works, The Latin Works, The English Works of John Gower*, vols. 1 & 2. Oxford: Clarendon Press, 1899–1902.

McCanles, Michael. *The Discourse of Il Principe*. Malibu: Udena Publications under the auspices of The Center for Medieval and Renaissance Studies, UCLA, Humana Civilitas, Vol. 8, 1983.

MacDonald, Donald. "Proverbs, *Sententiae*, and *Exempla* in Chaucer's Comic Tales: The Function of Comic Misapplication." *Speculum* 41 (1966): 453–65.

McFarlane, K. B. *Lancastrian Kings and Lollard Knights*. Oxford: Clarendon Press, Oxford University Press, 1972.

Macherey, Pierre. *A Theory of Literary Production*. Trans. Geoffrey Wall. London: Routedge & Kegan Paul, 1978.

Machiavelli, Niccolò. *Machiavelli: The Prince*. Ed. Quentin Skinner and Russell Price. [Trans. Russell Price.] Cambridge: Cambridge University Press, 1988.

———. *The Prince and The Discourses*. Trans. Luigi Ricci. Rev. E. R. P. Vincent. Introduction by Max Lerner. New York: The Modern Library (Random House), 1950.

McKisack, May. *The Fourteenth Century, 1307–1399*. Oxford: The Clarendon Press, 1959.

McNamara, Robert. *In Retrospect: The Tragedy and Lessons of Vietnam*. New York: Times Books, 1995.

Maddicott, J. R. "The County Community and the Making of Public Opinion in Fourteenth-Century England." *Transactions of the Royal Historical Society*, 5th ser., 28 (1978): 27–43.

———. "Parliament and the Constituencies, 1272–1377." In *The English Parliament in the Middle Ages*, 61–87. Ed. R. G. Davies and J. H. Denton. Philadelphia: University of Pennsylvania Press, 1981.

Manzalaoui, M. A. "'Noght in the Registre of Venus': Gower's English Mirror for Princes." In *Medieval Studies for J. A. W. Bennett Aetatis Suae LXX*, 159–83. Ed. P. L. Heyworth. Oxford: Clarendon Press, 1981.

———, ed. *Secretum Secretorum: Nine English Versions*. Vol. I. Text. Oxford: Oxford University Press for the Early English Text Society, 1977.

Marsilius of Padua. *The Defensor Pacis*. Vol. II of *Marsilius of Padua: The Defender of Peace*. Trans. Alan Gewirth. New York: Columbia University Press, 1956.

Mathew, Gervase. *The Court of Richard II*. London: John Murray, 1968.

Matthews, Lloyd J. "The Date of Chaucer's *Melibee* and the Stages of the Tale's Incorporation in the *Canterbury Tales*." *Chaucer Review* 20 (1985–86): 221–34.

Meale, Carol. "Patrons, Buyers and Owners: Book Production and Social Status." In *Book Production and Publishing in Britain, 1375–1475*, 201–38. Ed. Jeremy Griffiths and Derek Pearsall. Cambridge: Cambridge University Press, 1989.

Medcalf, Stephen. "Inner and Outer." In *The Later Middle Ages*, 108–69. Ed. Stephen Medcalf. New York: Holmes & Meier Publishers Inc., 1981.

Metlitzki, Dorothee. *The Matter of Araby in Medieval England*. New Haven, CT: Yale University Press, 1977.

Middle English Dictionary. Ed. Sherman M. Kuhn. Ann Arbor: University of Michigan Press, 1952– .

Middleton, Anne. "The Idea of Public Poetry in the Reign of Richard II." *Speculum* 53 (1978): 94–114.

Mitchell, Jerome. *Thomas Hoccleve: A Study in Early Fifteenth-Century English Poetic*. Urbana: University of Illinois Press, 1968.

Monahan, Arthur, P. *Consent, Coercion, and Limit: The Medieval Origins of Parlia-*

mentary Democracy. Kingston and Montreal: McGill-Queen's University Press, 1987.

Morgan, Philip. *War and Society in Medieval Cheshire 1277–1403*. Manchester: Manchester University Press for the Chetham Society, 1987.

Mum and the Sothsegger. See Helen Barr.

Mum and the Sothsegger. Ed. Mabel Day and Robert Steele. London: Humphrey Milford, Oxford University Press, 1936.

Myers, A. R., ed. *English Historical Documents: 1327–1485*. Volume 4 in the series, *English Historical Documents*, David C. Douglas, gen. ed. New York: Oxford University Press, 1969.

Neale, J. E. "The Commons' Privilege of Free Speech in Parliament." In *Tudor Studies Presented by the Board of Studies in History in the University of London to Albert Frederick Pollard, Being the Work of Twelve of his Colleagues and Pupils*. Ed. R. W. Seton-Watson. 1924. Reissued, New York: Russell & Russell, 1970. Also in *Historical Studies of the English Parliament*, Vol. II, 147–76. Edited by E. B. Fryde and Edward Miller. Cambridge: Cambridge University Press, 1970.

Norbrook, David. "Life and Death of Renaissance Man." *Raritan* 8 (1989): 89–110.

Oakley, Francis. "Celestial Hierarchies Revisited: Walter Ullmann's Vision of Medieval Politics." *Past and Present* 60 (1973): 3–48.

Olson, Paul A. *The "Canterbury Tales" and the Good Society*. Princeton, NJ: Princeton University Press, 1986.

Olsson, Kurt. *John Gower and the Structures of Conversion: A Reading of the Confessio Amantis*. Cambridge: D. S. Brewer, 1992.

Orme, Nicholas. *From Childhood to Chivalry: The Education of the English Kings and Aristocracy, 1066–1530*. London: Methuen, 1984.

Ormrod, W. M. *The Reign of Edward III: Crown and Political Society in England, 1327–1377*. New Haven, CT: Yale University Press, 1990.

Otway-Ruthven, A. J. *A History of Medieval Ireland*. London/New York: Ernest Benn Limited/Barnes & Noble, 1968.

Ovid. *The Fasti, Tristia, Pontic Epistles, Ibis, and Halieuticon*. Trans. Henry T. Riley. London: George Bell & Sons, 1879.

Owen, Charles A., Jr. "The *Tale of Melibee*." *Chaucer Review* 7 (1972–73): 267–80.

Palmer, J[ohn] J[oseph] N[orman]. *England, France and Christendom, 1377–99*. Chapel Hill: University of North Carolina Press, 1972.

Palomo, Dolores. "What Chaucer Really Did to Le Livre de Mellibee." *Philological Quarterly* 53 (1974): 304–20.

Paris, Matthew. *Matthew Paris's English History from the Year 1235–1273*. London: Henry G. Bohn, 1854. Repr. New York: AMS Press, 1968.

Patterson, Annabel. *Censorship and Interpretation: The Conditions of Writing and Reading in Early Modern England*. Madison: University of Wisconsin Press, 1984.

Patterson, Lee. *Chaucer and the Subject of History*. Madison: University of Wisconsin Press, 1991.

———, ed. *Literary Practice and Social Change in Britain, 1380–1530*. Berkeley: University of California Press, 1990.

————. "Making Identities in Fifteenth-Century England: Henry V and John Lydgate." In *New Historical Study: Essays on Reproducing Texts, Representing History*, 69–107. Ed. Jeffrey N. Cox and Larry J. Reynolds. Princeton, NJ: Princeton University Press, 1993.

————. *Negotiating the Past: The Historical Understanding of Medieval Literature*. Madison: University of Wisconsin Press, 1987.

————. "'No Man His Reson Herde': Peasant Consciousness, Chaucer's Miller, and the Structure of the *Canterbury Tales*." In *Literary Practice and Social Change in Britain, 1380–1530*, 113–55. Ed. Lee Patterson. Revised in *Chaucer and the Subject of History*, 244–79.

————. "Rev. of *Social Chaucer* by Paul Strohm." *Speculum* 67 (1992): 485–88.

————. "'What Man Artow?': Authorial Self-Definition in *The Tale of Sir Thopas* and *The Tale of Melibee*." *Studies in the Age of Chaucer* 11 (1989): 117–75.

Payling, Simon. *Political Society in Lancastrian England: The Greater Gentry of Nottinghamshire*. Oxford: Clarendon Press, 1991.

Payne, Robert O. *The Key of Remembrance: A Study of Chaucer's Poetics*. New Haven, CT: Yale University Press for the University of Cincinati, 1963.

Pearsall, Derek. "Gower's Latin in the *Confessio Amantis*." In *Latin and Vernacular: Studies in Late-Medieval Texts and Manuscripts*, 13–25. Ed. A. J. Minnis. Cambridge: D. S. Brewer, 1989.

————. "Hoccleve's *Regement of Princes*: The Poetics of Royal Self-Representation." *Speculum* 69 (1994): 386–410.

————. *The Life of Geoffrey Chaucer: A Critical Biography*. Oxford: Blackwell Publishers, 1992.

————. *Old English and Middle English Poetry*. London: Routledge & Kegan Paul, 1977.

————. "The 'Troilus' Frontispiece and Chaucer's Audience." *Yearbook of English Studies* 7 (1977): 68–74.

Peck, Russell A. *Kingship & Common Profit in Gower's "Confessio Amantis."* Carbondale: Southern Illinois University Press, 1978.

Pocock, J. G. A. "Languages and their Implications: The Transformation of the Study of Political Thought." In *Politics, Language, and Time: Essays on Political Thought and History*, 3–41. New York: Atheneum, 1971.

————. *The Machiavellian Moment: Florentine Political Thought and the Atlantic Republican Tradition*. Princeton, NJ: Princeton University Press, 1975.

————. "Texts as Events: Reflections on the History of Political Thought." In *Politics of Discourse: The Literature and History of Seventeenth-Century England*, 21–34. Ed. Kevin Sharpe and Steven N. Zwicker. Berkeley: University of California Press, 1987.

Pollitt, Daniel. "Courts Have Taken Many 'Threats' Seriously." *The* (Raleigh) *News and Observer*, December 2, 1994, 15A.

Polychronicon Ranulphi Higden Monachi Cestrensis. . . . Ed. Joseph Rawson Lumby. Vol. IX. London: Longman & Co., Trübner & Co., 1886.

Porter, Carolyn. "History and Literature: 'After the New Historicism.'" [with responses] *NLH* 21 (1990): 253–81.

Porter, Elizabeth. "Gower's Ethical Microcosm and Political Macrocosm." In *Gower's*

"Confessio Amantis:" Responses and Reassessments, 135–62. Ed. A. J. Minnis. Totowa, NJ: D. S. Brewer, 1983.

Redlich, Josef. *The Procedure of the House of Commons: A Study of Its History and Present Form*. Trans. A. Ernest Steinthal. London: Constable & Co., Ltd. Repr. New York: AMS Press, 1969.

Reed, Thomas L., Jr. *Middle English Debate Poetry and the Aesthetics of Irresolution*. Columbia: University of Missouri Press, 1990.

Reeves, A. Compton. "Thomas Hoccleve, Bureaucrat." *Medievalia et Humanistica: Studies in Medieval & Renaissance Culture*, n.s. 5. *Medieval Historiography* (1974): 201–14.

Renaud de Louens. "Le Livre de Melibee et Prudence." Ed. J. Burke Severs. In *Sources and Analogues of Chaucer's Canterbury Tales*, 568–614. Ed. W. F. Bryan and Germaine Dempster. Chicago: University of Chicago Press, 1941.

Rezneck, Samuel. "Constructive Treason by Words in the Fifteenth Century." *American Historical Review* 33 (1927–28): 544–52.

Richard the Redeless. See Helen Barr.

Richardson, H. G. "The Commons and Medieval Politics." *Transactions of the Royal Historical Society*, 4th series xxviii, 28 (1946): 21–45.

———. "Heresy and the Lay Power Under Richard II." *The English Historical Review* 51 (1936): 1–28.

Richardson, Malcolm. "Henry V, the English Chancery, and Chancery English." *Speculum* 55 (1980): 726–50.

———. "Hoccleve in His Social Context." *Chaucer Review* 20 (1986): 313–22.

Richmond, Colin. "Hand and Mouth: Information Gathering and Use in England in the Later Middle Ages." *Journal of Historical Sociology* 1 (1988): 233–52.

Ridolfi, Roberto. *The Life of Niccolò Machiavelli*. Trans. C. Grayson. Chicago: University of Chicago Press, 1963. (Orig. pub. 1954.)

Robbins, Rossell Hope. "Dissent in Middle English Literature: The Spirit of (Thirteen) Seventy-Six." *Medievalia et Humanistica* 9 (1979): 25–51.

Robertus de Avesbury. *De Gestis Mirabilibus Regis Edwardi Tertii*. See *Adae Murimuth*. . . .

Roskell, J. S. *The Commons and Their Speakers in English Parliaments, 1376–1523*. New York: Barnes & Noble, 1965.

———. *Parliament and Politics in Late Medieval England*. 3 vols. London: Hambledon Press, 1981–83.

Ross, C. "Rumour, Propaganda and Popular Opinion During the Wars of the Roses." In *Patronage, the Crown and the Provinces in Later Medieval England*, 15–32. Ed. R. A. Griffiths. Gloucester, UK/Atlantic Highlands, NJ: Alan Sutton/Humanities Press, 1981.

Rotuli Parliamentorum. Ed. J. Strachey. 6 vols. London, 1767–77.

Rousseau, Jean Jacques. *On the Social Contract*. Ed. Roger D. Masters. Trans. Judith Masters. New York: St. Martin's Press, 1978. (Orig. pub. 1782.)

Sanderlin, S. "Chaucer and Ricardian Politics." *Chaucer Review* 22 (1988): 171–84.

Saul, Nigel. *Knights and Esquires: The Gloucestershire Gentry in the Fourteenth Century*. Oxford: Clarendon Press, 1981.

Sayles, George O. *The King's Parliament of England*. New York: W. W. Norton, 1974.

Scanlon, Larry. "The King's Two Voices: Narrative and Power in Hoccleve's *Regement of Princes*." In *Literary Practice and Social Change in Britain, 1380–1530*, 216–47. Ed. Lee Patterson. Berkeley: University of California Press, 1990.

———. *Narrative, Authority, and Power: The Medieval Exemplum and the Chaucerian Tradition*. Cambridge: Cambridge University Press, 1994.

Scattergood, V. J. "Chaucer and the French War: *Sir Thopas* and *Melibee*." In *Court and Poet*, 287–96. Ed. Glyn S. Burgess. Liverpool: Francis Cairns, 1981.

———. "Literary Culture at the Court of Richard II." In *English Court Culture in the Later Middle Ages*, 29–43. Ed. V. J. Scattergood and J. W. Sherborne. New York: St. Martin's Press, 1983.

———. *Politics and Poetry in the Fifteenth Century*. London: Blandford Press, 1971; New York: Barnes and Noble, 1972.

Schmitt, Charles B., and Dilwyn Knox, compilers. *Pseudo-Aristoteles Latinus: A Guide to Latin Works Falsely Attributed to Aristotle before 1500*. London: Warburg Institute, University of London, 1985.

Scott, James C. *Weapons of the Weak: Everyday Forms of Peasant Resistance*. New Haven, CT: Yale University Press, 1985.

———. *Domination and the Arts of Resistance: Hidden Transcripts*. New Haven: Yale University Press, 1990.

"The Secret of Secrets." See *Secretum Secretorum*. Ed. Robert Steele and A. S. Fulton.

Secretum Secretorum. Ed. Hiltgart von Hürnheim. *Mittelhochdeutsche Prosaübersetzun des "Secretum Secretorum."* Berlin: Akademie-Verlag, 1963.

———. Ed. M. A. Manzalaoui, *Secretum Secretorum: Nine English Versions*. Vol. I. Text. Oxford: Oxford University Press for the Early English Text Society, 1977.

———. Ed. Robert Steele. *Three Prose Versions of the Secreta Secretorum*. Part I. Glossary by T. Henderson. London: Kegan Paul, Trench, Trübner & Co. for the Early English Text Society, 1898.

———. Ed. Robert Steele and A. S. Fulton. *Opera hactenus inedita Rogeri Baconi, Fasc. V: Secretum Secretorum cum Glossis et Notulis . . . [and] Versio Anglicana ex Arabico. . . .* Oxford: Oxford University Press, 1920.

Seymour, M.C. "The Manuscripts of Hoccleve's *Regiment of Princes*." *Transactions: Edinburgh Bibliographical Society* 4.7 (1974): 255–97.

———, ed. *Selections from Hoccleve*. Oxford: Clarendon Press, 1981.

Shakespeare, William. *The Complete Works of Shakespeare*. Ed. David Bevington. 4th ed. New York: HarperCollins Publishers, 1992.

Shultz, George P. *Turmoil and Triumph: My Years as Secretary of State*. New York: Scribner's, 1993.

Skinner, Quentin. *The Foundations of Modern Political Thought*. Vol. I: *The Renaissance*. Cambridge: Cambridge University Press, 1978.

———. *Machiavelli*. New York: Hill and Wang, 1981.

Spiegel, Gabrielle M. *Romancing the Past: The Rise of Vernacular Prose Historiography in Thirteenth-Century France*. Berkeley: University of California Press, 1993.

Statutes of the Realm. London: Dawsons, 1963.

Steel, Anthony. *The Receipt of the Exchequer, 1377–1485*. Cambridge: Cambridge University Press, 1954.

Steele, Robert, ed. *Three Prose Versions of the Secreta Secretorum*. Part I. Glossary by

T. Henderson. London: Kegan Paul, Trench, Trübner & Co. for the Early English Text Society, 1898.

Steele, Robert, and A. S. Fulton, eds. *Opera hactenus inedita Rogeri Baconi, Fasc. V: Secretum Secretorum cum Glossis et Notulis . . . [and] Versio Anglicana ex Arabico. . . .* Oxford: Oxford University Press, 1920.

Stephenson, Carl, and Frederick George Marcham, eds. and trans. *Sources of English Constitutional History: A Selection of Documents from A.D. 600 to the Present.* New York: Harper and Brothers, 1937. Rev. ed. *Sources of English Constitutional History: A Selection of Documents from A.D. 600 to the Interregnum.* New York: Harper & Row Publishers, 1972.

Stillwell, Gardiner. "The Political Meaning of Chaucer's *Tale of Melibee.*" *Speculum* 19 (1944): 433–44.

Stock, Brian. *Listening for the Text: On the Uses of the Past.* Baltimore: Johns Hopkins University Press, 1990.

Stockton Eric W., trans. *The Major Latin Works of John Gower: "The Voice of One Crying" and the "Tripartite Chronicle."* Seattle: University of Washington Press, 1962.

Storey, R. L. "Liveries and Commissions of the Peace 1388–90." In *The Reign of Richard II: Essays in Honour of May McKisack*, 131–52. Ed. F. R. H. Du Boulay and Caroline M. Barron. London: University of London, The Athlone Press, 1971.

Stow, George B. "Richard II in John Gower's *Confessio Amantis*: Some Historical Perspectives." *Mediaevalia* 16 (1993 for 1990): 3–31.

Strohm, Paul. "Chaucer's Audience." *Literature & History* 5 (1977): 26–41.

———. "Chaucer's Fifteenth-Century Audience and the Narrowing of the 'Chaucer Tradition.'" *Studies in the Age of Chaucer* 4 (1982): 3–32.

———. "Form and Social Statement in *Confessio Amantis* and *The Canterbury Tales.*" *Studies in the Age of Chaucer* 1 (1979): 17–40.

———. *Hochon's Arrow: The Social Imagination of Fourteenth-Century Texts.* Princeton, NJ: Princeton University Press, 1992.

———. "Politics and Poetics: Usk and Chaucer in the 1380s." In *Literary Practice and Social Change in Britain, 1380–1530*, 83–112. Ed. Lee Patterson. Berkeley: University of California Press, 1990.

———. *Social Chaucer.* Cambridge, MA: Harvard University Press, 1989.

Stubbs, Bishop William. *Chronicles of the Reigns of Edward I and Edward II.* Vol. I: *Annales Londonienses and Annales Paulini. . . .* London: Longman & Co.: Trübner & Co., 1882.

———. *The Constitutional History of England in its Origin and Development.* 3 Vols. 5th ed. Oxford: Clarendon Press, 1898.

Tatlock, John S. P. *The Development and Chronology of Chaucer's Works.* Chaucer Society, 2d ser. Vol. 37. London: Kegan Paul, Trench and Trübner, 1907. Repr. Gloucester, MA: Peter Smith, 1963.

Thompson, Faith. *The First Century of Magna Carta: Why It Persisted as a Document.* Minneapolis: University of Minnesota, 1925.

Tuck, Anthony. *Crown and Nobility, 1272–1461: Political Conflict in Late Medieval England.* Totowa, NJ: Barnes and Noble Books, 1986 [first published, 1985].

———. *Richard II and the English Nobility.* London: Edward Arnold, Ltd., 1973.

Ullmann, Walter. *The Individual and Society in the Middle Ages*. Baltimore: Johns Hopkins University Press, 1966.

Walker, Simon. *The Lancastrian Affinity, 1361–1399*. Oxford: Clarendon Press, 1990.

Wallace, David. "'Whan She Translated Was': A Chaucerian Critique of the Petrarchan Academy." In *Literary Practice and Social Change in Britain, 1380–1530*, 156–215. Ed. Lee Patterson. Berkeley: University of California Press, 1990.

Walsingham, Thomas. *Chronica Monasterii S. Albani. Thomae Walsingham, Quondam Monachi S. Albani, Historia Anglicana*. Vol. I: *A.D. 1272–1381*. Vol II: *A.D. 1381–1422*. Ed. Henry Thomas Riley. London: Longman, Green, Longman, Roberts, and Green, 1863 (Vol. I) and 1864 (Vol. II).

Warren, W. L. *The Governance of Norman and Angevin England, 1086–1272*. Stanford, CA: Stanford University Press, 1987.

Wasserman, Julian N., and Robert J. Blanch, eds. *Chaucer in the Eighties*. Syracuse, NY: Syracuse University Press, 1986.

Waterhouse, Ruth, and Gwen Griffiths. "'Sweete Wordes' of Non-Sense: The Deconstruction of the Moral Melibee (Part I)." *Chaucer Review* 23 (1989): 338–61.

———. "'Sweete Wordes' of Non-Sense: The Deconstruction of the Moral Melibee (Part II)." *Chaucer Review* 24 (1989): 53–63.

"We're Not Naming Names." FYI, *The News and Observer*. Raleigh, April 21, 1993.

The Westminster Chronicle, 1381–1394. Ed. and trans. L. C. Hector and Barbara F. Harvey. Oxford: Clarendon Press, 1982.

Wilson, William Burton, trans. See John Gower. *Mirour de l'Omme*.

Wilkinson, B[ertie]. *Constitutional History of England in the Fifteenth Century (1399–1485) With Illustrative Documents*. New York: Barnes & Noble, 1964.

———. *Constitutional History of Medieval England, 1216–1399*. Vol. II: *Politics and the Constitution, 1307–1399*. Vol. III: *The Development of the Constitution, 1216–1399*. London: Longmans, Green and Co., Ltd., 1952, 1958.

———. *The Later Middle Ages in England, 1216–1485*. London: Longman, 1969.

Wright, Thomas, ed. *Political Poems and Songs Relating to English History Composed during the Period from the Accession of Edw. III to that of Ric. III*. London: Longman, Green, Longman, and Roberts, 1859.

———. *Political Songs of England from the Reign of John to that of Edward II*. London: John Bowyer Nichols & Sons for the Camden Society, 1839.

Yeager, R. F. *John Gower's Poetic: The Search for a New Arion*. Cambridge: D. S. Brewer, 1990.

———. "*Pax Poetica*: On the Pacifism of Chaucer and Gower." *Studies in the Age of Chaucer* 9 (1987): 97–121.

Yoder, Edwin, M., Jr. "Gergen May Change Clinton for the Better." *The News and Observer* (Raleigh, North Carolina), June 3, 1993. Washington Post Writers Group.

Yonge, James. "The Gouernaunce of Prynces." See *Secretum Secretorum*, ed. R. Steele and A. S. Fulton.

Index

Abercrombie, N., 5n

Adam of Usk, 33, 126

advice: as alternative to deposition, 82–83, 144; use of, for political purposes, 67–88, 110, 118–34, 155, 176, 186–87. *See also* Advisers; Mirrors for princes

advisers (to kings): actual, 17, 25, 26, 68–73, 76, 80–83, 93, 103, 111, 120, 124, 126, 133; bad, 5n, 63, 70–72, 74, 75, 78–79, 81–83, 85, 124–26, 176–77; criticism directed at, rather than at king, 2–3, 12, 28–29, 34, 63, 67–68, 78, 81–82, 110, 122–23, 125–27; of different religion, 42, 52–53; elevation of, 44, 56–57; excommunication threats to actual, 73, 76; fifteen virtues of, 43, 46–47, 53, 75; flatterers among, 10, 63, 78, 86, 113, 114, 127, 167; and Magna Carta, 17; necessity of following correct, 39–40, 44–49, 71, 74; the people as king's best, 126–32; removal of, 28, 83; selection of, 45–47, 50–53, 58–59, 76–77, 87, 94–97, 103, 168–69; self-interested, 71, 72, 75, 78–79, 168–69; tests for, 41, 50, 53, 64, 75, 168; truth-telling among, 113–17, 150, 151; who should select, 72–77, 81, 83–84, 91–92; women as, 17, 19, 41, 92, 94–98, 102–3, 106, 110–11, 165, 167n, 168, 175; writers as, 111, 131–32, 138, 141, 145, 147–50, 158–59; young, 10, 76, 77n, 93, 103, 111, 123–26, 148–49, 176. *See also* Kings; Mirrors for princes

advisers (to patrons), 60, 63, 65–66

advisers (to presidents), 174–75

Aegidius Romanus, 139n, 142n

Aers, David, 104, 105

"Against the King's Taxes" (anonymous), 15, 18, 67–68

Ahab and Micheas story, 115–18

Albertano of Brescia, 89n, 91

Alcuin, 129

Alexander the Great: Aristotle as adviser of, 2, 35–36, 39, 41–45, 49–53, 55–57, 112, 118, 139n, 155; and Persians, 42–44, 66n

Allmand, C., 64n, 141n, 150nn, 157n, 158n

Althusser, Louis, 5

Alvisi, 169n, 170n

ambiguity: to avoid censure, 8, 9, 54, 113–18, 162; and Machiavelli, 162–73; in mirrors for princes, 89, 110, 162–73; in *Tale of Melibee*, 89–90, 102–6, 176. *See also* "Hidden transcript"

ancient examples. *See* Historical examples

Annales Paulini, 69

Anonimalle Chronicle, 27, 28nn, 78nn, 122n

anonymity, 7, 10, 36

Apius story, 119–21, 131, 134n

Appellants (Richard's rebellious lords), 79n; attack on Richard II's advisers by, 23, 33, 79, 85, 99–100, 164n; challenge and deference toward Richard II by, 1, 3, 34, 79–85, 107, 109–11, 119, 124, 128, 143, 157, 176–77; and Chaucer, 101, 103, 107; takeover of government by, 175–76, 184; in *Tale of Melibee*, 90, 103, 104, 107, 176. *See also* Arundel, Richard; Beauchamp, Thomas; Henry IV: as Henry of Bolingbroke; Mowbray, Thomas; Thomas of Woodstock

Arabic language. *See* *Kitab sirr al-asrar*

Archbishop of Canterbury, 30. *See also* Arundel, Thomas; Becket, Thomas; Simon of Sudbury; Stratford, John

Archbishop of York, 80

aristocrats. *See* Magnates

Aristotle, 59, 60, 64–65, 156, 165; advice of, to Alexander, 2, 35–36, 41–43, 51–53, 118, 128–29; as Alexander's adviser, 39, 44–45, 49–50, 54, 55–57, 112, 139n

Arrons and Tarquin story, 114–15, 117

Arundel, Richard (earl of Arundel), 63, 79n. *See also* Appellants

Arundel, Thomas (Archbishop of Canterbury), 86–87, 144n, 157
Ashmole manuscript (Bodleian Library manuscript Ashmole 396: "The Secrete of Secretes"), 44, 47n, 49nn, 50n, 51n, 79n. See also *Secretum Secretorum*
Askins, W., 92n
Aspin, I. S. T., 15n, 18n, 68n
Aston, M. E., 35n
audience: Chaucer's, 186; courtly, 180–82; interpretation of "hidden transcript" by, 8; king as, 19, 61–66, 85; Machiavelli's, 165–72; for mirrors for princes, 4, 13, 178–85; for particular languages, 113; women as, 150n; for Yonge's version of *Secretum Secretorum*, 55, 61–64
authority: Gower's, 113; John Stratford's, 73; of Latin, 112; medieval obsession with, 172; in mirrors for princes, 165; of translator, 59–60; of writers, 140, 148

Bacon, Sir Francis, 39, 47
Bacon, Roger, 71n, 74n, 75n, 77n
Badby, John, 138, 152–53
Bakhtin, Mikhail, 4–5
Baldwin, J. F., 3n, 68n
Ball, John, 13n, 23, 35
Barclay, George, 108, 112
Barnes, G., 14n
Barnie, J., 32n, 91n, 92n, 102n
Barr, Helen, 37n
Barre, Lucas de la, 34
Barron, C., 33n
bastard feudalism, 6, 183–84, 186
Baston, Roger, 34
Beauchamp, Thomas (earl of Warwick), 79n, 101. See also Appellants
Beauchamp, Sir William, 100
Beaufort, Bishop, 158
Beaufort, Joan (countess of Westmorland), 186
Becket, Thomas, 29, 73, 139n
Bellamy, J. G., 25n, 26, 33n, 34nn, 93n
Bennett, M. J., 185
Berges, W., 1n, 12n, 162n
Bernard (Saint), 59
Biblical examples. *See* Historical examples
Bishop of Bangor, 31–32, 34
Bishop of London, 29
Black Prince, 77n

Blyth, Charles, 145n, 148n, 153, 154n
Boas, George, 108, 129n
Bohun, Joan (countess of Hereford), 186
Book of the Duchess (Chaucer), 151n
The Book of the Secret of Secrets. See Secretum Secretorum
Borgia, Cesare, 167–68
Bracton, Henry de, 11n
Brembre, Nicholas, 80, 101
broadsides, 23
Brown, A. L., 29n, 68n, 82n, 86n, 87n, 134n, 136n, 149n
Bryan, W. F., 91n, 92n
Bukton, Sir Peter, 181
Burke, Walter, 61n
Burrow, J., 137n
Bush, George, 175
Busoni, G. B., 171
Butler, James (earl of Ormonde), 12, 55–56, 60, 61, 139n, 154n, 166, 178

Cam, Helen, 19, 22nn
Canterbury Tales (Chaucer), 12, 41n, 90, 99n, 105, 106, 119. See also *titles of specific tales*
Carpenter, D. A., 18
Catto, Jeremy, 140, 180n
Cavendish, John, 32
censorship, 7–9, 11, 15, 176
Chabod, Federico, 169n, 170n
Chaplais, P., 120n
Charlemagne, 129
Charles I (king of England), 8
chastity, 115
Chaucer, Geoffrey, 3, 41n, 89–107, 120n, 148n, 150n, 152n, 165; associates of, 101, 181; audience for works by, 186; support of, for Richard II, 12–13, 101–3, 106, 109, 139n, 178; *Tale of Melibee* of, as mirror for princes, 89–107, 167n. See also *titles of works by*
Chaucer and the Subject of History (Patterson), 106
Chomsky, Noam, 8
Chrimes, S. B., 24n, 26, 29n, 82n, 86n, 134n, 136n
Christianity, 161, 163n
Chronicon Henrici Knighton, 15
Cicero (Tully), 56
Clarke, M. V., 20n, 82n, 122

class: advisers', 45–46, 58–59, 75, 76–77,
    147–48; and slander laws, 32–33. *See also*
    Gentry; Kings; Magnates; Peasants;
    People
classical examples. *See* Historical examples
clerks, 59, 138, 140, 180. *See also* Translators;
    Writers
Clifford, Clark, 175
Clifford, Sir Lewis, 181
Clinton, Bill, 34n, 123n, 149n
Coffman, George, 108
Coleman, Janet, 10, 24n, 36n, 123, 124n,
    134n, 179–80
Collyngbourne, Wyllyam, 34
common counsel ("comun conseil"), 20, 121,
    134, 136
commons (parliament): during Good Par-
    liament, 19, 28, 77–79, 122, 124n; and
    Henry IV, 87n, 144; increasing power of,
    6, 11, 17, 20, 21, 28; political speech in, 27–
    31, 125; on retaining system, 183–84; and
    Richard II, 83, 88, 100
"community of the realm," 16–22, 24, 87,
    122n, 131, 187. *See also* Unanimity
"comun conseil" (common counsel), 20, 121,
    134, 136
Confessio Amantis (Gower), 108, 110, 113–26,
    131–33, 138, 147, 153–55, 179; audience for,
    180–81, 186; change of dedicatee in, 108n,
    109, 111, 134; death and removal of rulers
    in, 84, 114, 117, 119–20, 123–26; as mirror
    for princes, 3, 13, 112, 176
conservatism, 5
constitutionalism (in England), 6, 11n, 24,
    25, 69, 87n
contradictions. *See* Ambiguity
Cook, Albert, 89n
Cooper, H., 90n, 93n
Copeland, Rita, 112, 118, 129n
Corrigan, Philip, 20
Cosimo de' Medici, 171
Coss, P. R., 24n, 129n, 133n, 185nn
council (king's), 25; development of, 2–3,
    68–69, 77; under Edward III, 2, 28, 68n,
    76, 77; under Henry IV, 144; Prince of
    Wales's participation on, 139, 140–41, 144,
    147, 149, 150, 157; under Richard II, 2,
    68n, 69, 80, 82, 85, 100, 143
counsel/counsellors. *See* Advice; Advisers
Counsel to the President (Clifford), 175

courts, 32
Cronica Tripertita (Gower), 109, 110, 130–31
Curtis, E., 55n, 60n–62n

dating (of medieval literature), 11, 90, 93n,
    111, 112, 133n, 138–39, 150
Day, M., 37n
death: imagining king's, 33–34, 38; of kings,
    84, 155; as leveler, 57–59
decemvirs, 119, 121, 131
deception. *See* Truth
deconstruction, 9n, 13, 91, 93, 103, 105–7,
    163, 175, 176; of advice ideology, 49–54,
    118
defamation. *See* Slander law
de Gaulle, Charles, 129n
Delany, S., 120n
Dempster, G., 91n, 92n
deposition (of kings), 25–26, 122, 132–34;
    advice as alternative to, 82–83, 144; of
    Edward II, 22, 26, 34, 69n, 70–72, 74, 75,
    82, 83, 87, 120–22n, 156, 175; of Henry VI,
    185; of Richard II, 22n, 26, 63, 64, 82,
    85–87, 109, 121, 122n, 129, 130, 133–34,
    141, 157, 175, 184–85; threats of, against
    Edward III, 121
De Regimine Principum, 142
Despenser, Hugh (the elder), 71, 72, 76
Despenser, Hugh (the younger), 71, 72, 76
Deuteronomy (Bible), 59
Dietz, Mary, 170
Diogenes and Aristippus story, 114, 118
Discipline and Punish: The Birth of the Prison
    (Foucault), 45, 151
Discourses on the First Ten Books of Titus Livius
    (Machiavelli), 169n, 170
disguise. *See* "Hidden transcript"
Dobson, R. B., 35nn, 122nn, 124n
"doctrine of restraint," 83. *See also* Kings:
    limitations on
Dollimore, J., 4n
Doob, P., 137n
downward pressures, 11, 15, 16, 63, 138, 151
Doyle, A. I., 133n, 180n, 186
Dunham, William Huse, Jr., 25, 82, 83

Eagleton, T., 9n
Early History of Rome (Livy), 119–20
Ecclesiastes (Bible), 73
Edward I (king of England), 19, 21

Edward II (king of England), 77n; advisers of, 69–72, 74, 75, 80, 87, 120; coronation oath of, 21n, 70, 74, 156; deposition of, 22, 26, 34, 69n, 70–72, 74, 75, 82, 83, 87, 120–22n, 156, 175

Edward III (king of England), 22, 26, 70, 124, 149; advisers of, 87, 126, 148; and Alice Perrers, 92, 110, 120; political speech under, 32; power of king's council under, 2, 28, 68n; threats to, 72–79, 121

Edwards, J. G., 20n, 21n

Edwy (Anglo-Saxon king), 125n

egalitarianism: in ideological language, 17; in mirrors for princes, 12, 46–47, 54, 58–59, 155–56

England: constitutionalism in, 6, 11n, 24, 25, 69, 87n; and Ireland, 62; local governments in, 18–24, 37n; no alternative to monarchy in medieval, 120; as a political nation, 15–24, 87, 185–86; variety of languages in, 23, 110

"English Culture in the Fourteenth Century" (Coleman), 180

English language: Gower's writings in, 110, 112, 118, 129n, 132; as language of England, 23; mirrors for princes in, 179; Secretum Secretorum translated into, 11–12, 40n, 41, 45, 179. See also Idioms; Literature: vernacular

exchequer, 143

exempla (in Regiment of Princes), 140, 142, 145–46. See also Historical examples

Fabyan, Robert, 35n

Fall of Princes (Lydgate), 179

"false consciousness," 17, 18

Fasti (Ovid), 115

feminism, 5n

Ferguson, Arthur B., 2n, 127n, 137n, 162

Ferster, Judith, 54n, 98n, 105n

feudalism: concept of king under, 24–25; law associated with, 26; lords' roles under, 79–80, 87. See also Bastard feudalism

"fictitious loans," 143

The First English Life of King Henry the Fifth (ed. Kingsford), 39, 60n

Fisher, John H., 108, 131–33n, 179n

Florence (Italy), 165–66, 169, 170–71

Flynn, J., 98n

foreign examples. See Historical examples

forgiveness, 98

formalism, 12–13, 90, 93–98, 102, 104

Foucault, Michel, 5, 45, 151

Fradenburg, Louise, 151n

France, 18, 64, 157–58; attempts to make peace with, 99–100, 103, 123, 133, 157–58; England's war with, 22, 72, 76, 79, 82, 92. See also French language; Taxation

Frederick II (Holy Roman emperor), 91

Frederick the Great (of Prussia), 170, 171

free men, 17, 19

French language, 179; Gower's writings in, 110–12; Secretum Secretorum in, 12n. See also Literature: vernacular

Froissart, Jean, 122

Fryde, Natalie, 69n, 72, 77n

Fulton, A. S., 36nn, 41n–43nn, 45nn, 46nn, 49n, 50nn, 51n, 57n, 64n, 71n, 74n, 75n, 77n, 79n, 129n, 137n, 142nn, 147n, 162n, 163n

Furnivall, Frederick J., 138n, 139, 146nn, 149

Fürstenspiegel. See Mirrors for princes

the Gabiens, 114–15, 117

Galbraith, V. H., 28nn, 33n, 78nn, 122n

Gaveston, Piers (Edward II's favorite), 69, 71, 72, 76, 80, 120

Genet, Jean-Philippe, 2n

Genius, 114, 127, 165

gentry, 106n; defined, 181n; and kings, 87, 133–34, 184–85; vs. magnates, 182–84; in parliament, 6, 19–20, 180, 182, 184–86; as readers, 179–82, 186

Gergen, David, 123n

Germany, 18, 24–26

Gewirth, A., 26n

Giddens, Anthony, 17

Gilbert, Allan, 161, 162, 163nn, 164, 167n, 168nn, 172, 173

Gilbert, Felix, 161n, 162, 163, 166n

Gingrich, Newt, 145

Giuliano de' Medici, 160n, 167

Given-Wilson, Chris, 68n, 77n, 80nn, 87n, 124n, 157nn, 185n; on deposition of kings, 82–83, 133; on gentry, 183

Gollancz, Israel, 146nn, 149

Goodman, A., 79n

Good Parliament, 31–32, 81, 111, 184; re-

moval of kings' advisers by, 77–79, 120, 122, 175; role of commons in, 19, 27–28, 77–79, 122; and taxes, 124n
"good Samaritan" story, 53
"The Gouernaunce of Prynces" (Rawl. B. 490 manuscript), 55–66, 85
"The Governance of Lordschipes" (Lambeth 501 manuscript), 40nn, 41, 42n, 44, 45, 47, 50n, 60, 179. See also *Secretum Secretorum*
Gower, John, 77n, 84, 104, 165, 176; audience of, 179–80, 186; and Chaucer, 181; *Mirour de l'Omme* by, 110–13; political ideas of, 3, 13, 87, 108–9, 126–32, 138, 147, 178; use of historical examples by, 113–26, 155. See also *Confessio Amantis*; *Cronica Tripertita*; *Vox Clamantis*
Gramsci, Antonio, 169
Gransden, Antonia, 1n
"grant," 146
"grante ous," 125, 136
Green, Richard Firth, 3n, 24n, 36n, 57n, 90n, 92n, 102n, 140n; on advice writers and readers, 10, 178–80
Greenblatt, Stephen, 4–5
Greetham, D. C., 138n
Griffiths, G., 93n
Guenée, Bernard, 6n, 15, 16n, 25n, 162n
Guicciardini, Francesco, 89, 98
Gunlicks, L. F., 171n

Haines, R. M., 73nn, 76n, 126n
Haldeman, H. R., 129n, 175
Hamilton, J. S., 69n
Hanawalt, Barbara, 5–6
Hanna, Ralph, III, 35
Harris, K., 179n, 186n
Harriss, G. L., 140nn, 141n, 143, 144, 157
Harriss, Gerald, 185
Harvey, B. F., 34n, 81n, 84n, 99n, 100n
Hasler, Anthony J., 151, 152–53
Haxey, Thomas, 29–31, 157
Hector, L. C., 34n, 81n, 84n, 99n, 100n
Helgerson, R., 9n
Helmholz, R. H., 32n
Helms, Jesse, 34n
Henry II (king of England), 62, 73
Henry IV (king of England, formerly Henry of Bolingbroke [earl of Derby]), 37, 158, 179, 183, 185; advisers of, 86–87; claims of,

to throne, 33, 133; death of, 138, 159; deposition of Richard II by, 26, 108, 109; finances of, 143–45, 155, 157; and Gower, 108n, 134, 139; as Henry of Bolingbroke, 79n, 101n, 103n, 109; and Hoccleve, 13, 14n, 145, 178; parliamentary limitations placed on, 176; people's support for, 130, 131; political speech under, 29n, 30, 31; power of king's council under, 2, 68n; and Statute of Treasons, 34. See also Appellants
Henry IV, Part I (Shakespeare), 128, 168
Henry of Bolingbroke. See Henry IV
Henry of Derby. See Henry IV
Henry of Keighley, 27
Henry V (king of England, formerly Prince of Wales), 13, 134n, 159, 179; advice to, 39n; and James Yonge, 55, 61–66, 85; as Prince of Wales, 138–42, 144, 145, 147, 149–52, 157–58, 176, 178
Henry VI (king of England), 2, 68n, 185
Henwood, D., 149n
Herman, Edward S., 8
Hermes, 47
"hidden transcript" (camouflaged texts), 4, 7–8, 36–38, 49–50, 102, 151, 156. See also Ambiguity
Higden, Ranulf, 1n
Hill, S., 5n
Hilton, R., 120n
Hippocratic oath, 95
historical examples: for authority, 148; to avoid censure, 8, 9, 38; as justification for tyrannicide, 25; as means of political speech, 13, 110, 114–26, 131, 132–33, 150–59, 176–78. See also Exempla; Knowledge; *specific stories*
historicism, 12–13, 90, 91–93, 98, 99, 102, 104–6; Renaissance new, 4, 5, 186
History of Florence (Machiavelli), 171
Histriomastix (Prynne), 8
Hoccleve, Thomas, 3, 13, 40n, 104, 137–59, 164, 165, 178, 180; annuity of, 138, 139, 141, 145–47, 150, 152, 159, 163; audience for works by, 186; and Chaucer, 181. See also *Regement of Princes*
Holdsworth, W., 32nn
Holquist, Michael, 34n
Holstun, James, 5
Holton, John, 34
Hotson, J. L., 92n

household (king's), 68; Richard II's, 29–30, 80n, 82, 100, 157
Howard, J., 5n
Hulliung, Mark, 161, 162n, 170n
"humble speche," 125, 135
Hussein, Saddam, 175

"The Idea of Public Poetry in the Reign of Richard II" (Middleton), 180
ideology, 154; and Chaucer, 104–5; and deconstruction, 106–7; definition of, 17; "dominant ideology thesis," 5; faultlines in, of advice, 12, 40, 49–54, 104, 113–18, 163; literature as test of, 104, 174; theories of, 7
idioms, 121, 133, 134–36, 146
imperialism, 162, 170n
In Retrospect (McNamara), 175
"Invisible Bullets" (Greenblatt), 4
Iran-Contra hearings, 174
Ireland, 12, 55–66, 178
irony (in *Tale of Melibee*), 90, 93
Italy, 18

Jacob, E. F., 143nn, 144n, 149n, 150n, 157n, 158n
Johannes de Caritate, 47
John (duke of Bedford), 62
John of Bridlington (pseudonym), 36
John of Canace story, 145–46
John of Gaunt (duke of Lancaster), 28, 29, 31–32, 34, 77, 92, 100n, 101, 184
John of Paris, 26n
John of Salisbury, 25, 123n, 139n, 153
Johnson, Lynn Staley, 92n, 102
Jones, Richard H., 23n, 69, 80n, 88
Jonson, Ben, 8
Julius II (pope), 166–68, 170
justice, 115; in Edward II's coronation oath, 70; in *Secretum Secretorum*, 42–43, 54
Justice, Steven, 13n, 18n, 19n, 23, 130n
justiciar (of Ireland), 63
Justman, Stewart, 105n

Kail, J., 10n
Kaueper, R. W., 79n, 185n
Kempton, Daniel, 91, 93, 96
Kendrick, L., 7n
Kern, F., 24–25

kings (rulers): actual advisers for, 17, 25, 26, 68–72, 80–83, 93, 103, 111, 120, 124, 126, 133; as audience, 19, 61–66, 85; dangers of criticizing, 2–4, 27–29, 33, 34–35, 37, 63, 67–68, 73, 106–7, 127, 133, 134, 150–52; discipline of, 12, 150–59; finances of, 61, 64–65, 72–73, 141–45, 149, 157, 163–64; limitations on, 6, 15–17, 21, 24–26, 68, 69–70, 83, 115; link between self-rule and good governance by, 109, 111, 120, 121n, 127, 140; necessity of, to be ruled, 40, 44–49, 54, 81–84, 115, 139–40, 174, 187; need for immoral behavior by, 162, 165; need of, for information, 36–37, 81, 113; no alternatives to, in medieval England, 120; nonhereditary, 162, 164n, 166, 168; opposition to, in advice manuals, 72, 84–85, 113–18, 126, 133, 134, 155–60, 171, 175–76; as own best adviser, 56, 97–98, 147; point of view of, in mirrors for princes, 1–2, 40–44, 54, 68, 78; struggles of, with magnates, 3, 79–85; and subjects, 9, 15–18, 21, 24–25, 27–29, 37–38, 151–54, 165, 186–87; winning obedience of, 42–43, 54, 66n, 156; youthful, 91–92. *See also* Advisers; Council (king's); Household (king's); Mirrors for princes; Patronage; *specific kings*
Kingsford, C. L., 39n, 60n, 150n
Kitab sirr al-asrar (*The Book of the Secret of Secrets*), 2, 39, 41, 42, 45, 162n. See also *Secretum Secretorum*
Knapp, Peggy, 104, 105n
Knight, Stephen, 105, 106
Knighton, Henry, 15, 23n, 69n, 83n
knowledge (power of), 59–60, 66. *See also* Authority; Historical examples
Kohl, S., 137n

Labarge, M. W., 141n, 157n
Lambeth 501 manuscript ("The Governance of Lordschipes"), 40nn, 41, 42n, 44, 45, 47, 50n, 60, 179. See also *Secretum Secretorum*
Lancaster. *See* John of Gaunt
Lander, J. R., 21n, 24n, 185n
Lane, Robert, 4
Langland, William, 36, 180
Langton, John, 170n
Latimer, Lord William, 28, 77, 79, 122

Latin language, 2, 179; Gower's writings in, 110–12, 118, 129; *Secretum Secretorum* in, 12, 40n, 41, 45, 71n, 75n, 77n
laws, 26, 153–54. *See also* Statute(s)
Lawton, David, 3, 102n, 158
learning. *See* Knowledge
Legend of Good Women (Chaucer), 150n
Leicester, H. Marshall, Jr., 93, 104, 154
Lentricchia, Frank, 4n, 5n
Lerer, S., 13n, 49n, 99n
Lerner, M., 170n, 171n
letters (circulation of), 23, 73–75, 126
liberality, 115
Liber Consolationis et Consilii, 89n, 91
Lichfield Chronicle, 122n
"liege lord," 125, 135
Lindahl, Carl, 32
literacy, 23, 179
literature: dating of medieval, 11, 90, 93n, 111, 112, 133n, 138–39, 150; historical actors becoming, 84–85; historicizing of, 9–12, 175–77; in medieval England, 15; of political engagement, 9–10; as test of ideology, 104, 174; vernacular, 2, 112, 118, 178–85. *See also* Audience; Mirrors for princes; Translators; Writers; *specific authors and works*
Livy, 119–20, 123
local government, 18–24, 37n
Lodge, E., 29n–31n, 33n
Lomperis, L., 120n
London, 32–33
lords (parliament), 20, 28, 30, 122. *See also* Magnates
Lorenzo de' Medici, 160n, 169n, 170
Louis XII (king of France), 167
Luke (Bible), 53
Lumby, J. R., 15n
Lycurgus (Athenian ruler), 153–54
Lydgate, John, 179, 180
Lyon, Bryce, 3n, 6n, 16n, 22n, 28n, 31, 37n, 68n, 77n
Lyons, Richard, 28, 77, 79, 122

Macaulay, G. C., 110n, 111n, 113n, 125n, 129n
McCanles, Michael, 163
MacDonald, D., 93n
McFarlane, K. B., 143nn, 144
Macherey, Pierre, 9n, 104, 174n

Machiavelli, Niccolò, 4, 13, 160–73
The Machiavellian Manager's Handbook for Success (Gunlicks), 171n
Machiavelli's Prince and Its Forerunners (Gilbert), 161, 173
McKisack, May, 28n, 30n, 32n, 73n, 120n, 124nn; on Edward II, 26n; on Edward III, 75n, 123; on Latimer and Lyons, 79
McMirgh, Arthur, 61
McNamara, Robert, 175
Maddicott, J. R., 19, 21n, 22n, 23nn
madness, 129–30, 156
magic, 42–44
Magna Carta, 76, 99; allegations about violations of, 73, 74; coverage of, 17; language of, 18, 121; as limitation on king, 15, 16, 25
magnates (aristocrats; lords; nobles; peers): as advisers to king, 17, 25, 69–72, 75, 76–77, 87, 99; *vs.* gentry, 182–84; laws against speech critical of, 32–34, 36; and parliament, 6, 19–20, 83; as readers of mirrors for princes, 178–79, 182, 186; Richard II's support from, 133; self-interest of, 71, 72, 75, 79–80, 99–100, 133, 185–86; struggles of, with kings, 3, 26, 69–72, 79–85. *See also* Appellants; *specific individuals*
the Magus and the Jew story, 42, 52–53, 61, 175
majority rule, 122
"Making Identities in Fifteenth-Century England" (Patterson), 106
Manzalaoui, M. A., 44n, 45n, 47nn, 49nn, 51n, 57n, 64n, 66n, 79n, 108n, 138n, 160n
Marcham, F. G., 16n, 21nn, 23n, 28n, 29n, 30nn, 33n, 86n, 157n
Marcus Regulus, 154–55
Mare, Sir Peter de la, 27–29, 31, 77n
Marsilius of Padua, 25
martyrdom, 73
Marxism, 5, 17, 18
Mathew, Gervase, 108, 118
Matthew (Bible), 53
Matthews, L. J., 90n
Meale, C., 134n
Medcalf, S., 137n
Medici family, 160, 166–72
medicine. *See* Physicians
Medieval Readers and Writers (Coleman), 10

Medieval Representation and Consent (Clarke), 122

Melibee. See Tale of Melibee

Merciless Parliament, 80, 85, 100, 101, 103, 176

mercy, 164

Metlitzki, Dorothee, 2n

Middle Ages: deposition of English kings during, 25; individualism in, 137n; influence of, on Renaissance mirrors for princes, 161–65; political speech in, 8–9, 11, 15. *See also* England; Mirrors for princes

Middleton, Anne, 15n, 131n, 180, 181, 186

Mildenhall, William, 33

The Miller's Tale (Chaucer), 106

"minora," 112

Mirour de l'Omme (Gower), 110–13

mirrors for princes (advice manuals; *Fürstenspiegel*): challenge and deference in, 1, 3, 7–9, 12, 54, 55–60, 65–66, 88, 132, 138, 140–41, 158–60, 171–73, 176, 187; characteristics of, 1–4, 10, 12, 40, 68, 71, 73–75, 81, 97, 109, 111, 149, 155, 173; contributions of medieval, to Renaissance, 161–65; genre conflicts in, 139–42, 147; historical use of advice from, 67–88, 176–77; ideological faultlines in, 12, 40, 49–54, 93, 104, 113–18, 163; opposition to rulers in, 72, 84–85, 113–18, 126, 133, 134, 155–60, 171; origins of, 2; paradox of advice in [rulers must be ruled], 40, 44–49, 83–84, 174, 187; rulers' point of view in, 1–2, 40–44, 54, 68, 78; social functions of, 63, 65–66, 110–13, 118–34, 169–70, 178; themes of, 10, 12. *See also* Advisers; Audience; Kings; Political speech; *specific mirrors for princes*

Mitchell, J., 137n

Modus Tenendi Parliamentum, 20, 62n, 122

Monahan, A., 26n

monarchy. *See* Kings

Morgan, P., 133n, 157n, 185n

Mowbray, John (duke of Norfolk), 179

Mowbray, Thomas (earl of Nottingham), 79n, 103n. *See also* Appellants

MS Lambeth 501, 40n. *See* "Governance of Lordschipes"

MS Reg. 18 A. *See* Royal 18 A vii manuscript

Mum and the Sothsegger (anonymous), 36–38, 78n, 134n, 150, 180

Myers, A. R., 1n, 28n, 30n, 69n, 74n, 83n, 84n, 99n, 134n

nationalism, 170n

Neale, J. E., 27n

Nero, 57n

news, 22–24, 26, 35, 37n

Nixon, Richard M., 129n, 175

nobility. *See* Magnates

Norbrook, David, 5

novelty claims, 164–66, 169, 172–73

Oakley, Francis, 11n

old man (in *Regement of Princes*), 140, 142, 145n, 148n, 151–52, 165

Olson, Paul, 91, 92nn, 105n

Olsson, K., 113n

"On the Times" (anonymous), 36

opposition. *See* Kings: opposition to, in advice manuals; Resistance

Ordinances of 1311, 21n

Orme, N., 12n

Ormonde, earl of. *See* Butler, James

Ormrod, W. M., 73n, 76nn

Otway-Ruthven, A. J., 61nn, 62nn, 63n, 64n

Ovid, 115

Owen, Charles, 98

Palmer, J. J. N., 100nn, 103n

Palomo, D., 90n

Paris, Matthew, 67, 71, 78

Parkes, M. B., 133n, 180n

parliament, 128; development of, 3, 19–20, 24, 69n, 70, 87n; gentry in, 6, 19–20, 180, 182, 184–86; Good Parliament, 19, 27–28, 31–32, 77–80, 111, 120, 122, 124n, 175, 184; Irish, 61; and king's advisers, 25, 69, 76, 77, 83; and kings' finances, 143–44; and limitations on speech, 26–34; majority rule in, 122; Merciless Parliament, 80, 85, 100, 101, 103, 176; news about, 22–24, 26; Peter de la Mare's 1377 speech before, 28; petitions in, 19–22, 27, 68, 101; on Richard II's deposition, 85–86; and *scandalum magnatum* law, 32–34; and taxation, 16, 22, 75, 124–25; Wonderful Parliament, 101, 102, 175–76. *See also* Commons; Lords

"patente," 146

patronage, 69, 77, 80–81, 85, 86, 99n, 100, 101, 133, 152, 158–59
patrons, 12, 13, 55–56, 60, 178; advisers' relations with, 47–49, 60, 63, 65–66; rulers as, of writers and translators, 139–40, 165–72
Patterson, Annabel, 7–9, 54, 132, 165n
Patterson, Lee, 5n, 89n, 90n, 92n, 129n; on Chaucer, 101n, 102; on deconstruction, 9n, 13; on resistance, 4, 182; on *Tale of Melibee*, 94, 98–99, 105–6
Payling, Simon, 182nn, 183, 185
Payne, Robert O., 105n
peace. *See* Wars
Pearsall, Derek, 101, 109, 112, 129n, 139n, 140–41, 145n, 157, 179n, 186
peasants, 19, 106, 108, 180, 182; Gower on, 129–32; in Peatling Magna uprising, 17, 18; and resistance, 6. *See also* Rising of 1381
Peatling Magna, 17–18
Peck, Russell, 109–11n, 123
people, 138; and king, 87, 110, 125–33, 147–49, 178; limitations on king by, 16, 25. *See also* Kings: and subjects
Perrers, Alice (Edward III's mistress), 28, 92, 110–12, 120, 175
Persian Gulf war, 175
Philip the Fair, 139n
physicians, 41, 51, 95–96
The Physician's Tale (Chaucer), 119, 120n
Piers Plowman (Langland), 36
pity, 115, 123, 164
plena potestas (power of attorney), 20–22, 132
Pocock, J. G. A., 9n, 14, 161, 164n
poems of complaint, 10
poets, 57. *See also* Writers
Poets and Princepleasers (Green), 10
poison, 41
Pole, Michael de la, 32, 80, 82, 101
Policraticus (John of Salisbury), 153
political speech: dangers of, 27–38, 67–68, 110; limitations on, 11, 16, 26–36, 114, 150; mirrors for princes' role in, 13, 67–88, 110, 118–34, 155, 176, 186–87; subversive ways of expressing, 3–4, 7–10, 13, 54, 102, 113–34, 150–51, 155, 176–78, 187; use of historical examples in, 13, 110, 114–26, 131, 132–33, 150–59, 176–78. *See also* Censorship; Kings: dangers of criticizing

Politics and Poetry in the Fifteenth Century (Scattergood), 10
Pollitt, Daniel, 34n
Polychronicon Ranulphi Higden Monachi Cestrensis, 1, 3, 49–54, 84, 99n
Porter, Carolyn, 4, 5nn
Porter, Elizabeth, 109
power of attorney. *See Plena potestas*
prayer, 60, 62
"preiden," 124, 135
presidents (U.S.), 34n, 123n, 129n, 149n, 174, 175
Preston, Sir Christopher, 62
The Prince (Machiavelli), 13, 160–73
Prince of Wales. *See* Henry V
proclamations, 22–23, 33
Prophecies (John of Bridlington), 36
prophecies (political), 34
Proverbs (Bible), 51
Prudence (from *Tale of Melibee*), 94–98, 102–3, 106, 165, 167n, 168, 175
Prynne, William, 8
pseudonyms, 36

Raleigh *News and Observer,* 34n, 171n
Reagan, Ronald, 174
Redlich, J., 122n
Reeves, A. C., 137n
Reg. 18 A vii manuscript. *See* Royal 18 A vii manuscript
The Regement of Princes (Hoccleve), 137–59, 162n, 179, 186; autobiographical elements in, 137–39, 147, 148–49; as mirror for princes, 3; old man in, 140, 142, 145n, 148n, 151–52, 165; pun in title of, 40n; Roman consul in, 154, 155
Rehoboam story, 77n, 123–29, 131–34, 148, 177
Reilly, Donald, 176
Renaissance new historicism, 4, 5, 186
Renaud de Louens, 91, 92n
representation (concept of), 17, 19–20, 22, 132, 147, 186
republicanism, 165–66, 170–71
resistance, 4–10, 25, 31, 152–53, 156–57, 176, 186. *See also* Deposition; Kings: opposition to, in advice manuals; Rising of 1381
"reson," 125, 136
retainers, 183–84, 186

Rezneck, S., 34nn

Richard II (king of England), 28, 70, 90n, 183; advisers of, 25, 63–64, 69, 80–83, 85–88, 93, 99–100, 103, 111, 119, 120, 124, 126, 133, 148; after deposition of, 33, 37, 38, 176; Appellants' challenge to, 1, 3, 33, 34, 75, 79–85, 107, 109–11, 119, 128, 133, 143, 164n, 176–77; assumption of control over government by, 32, 100, 133, 143; Chaucer's support for, 12–13, 101–3, 106, 109, 139n, 178; deposition of, 22n, 26, 63, 64, 82, 85–87, 109, 121, 122n, 129, 130, 133–34, 141, 157, 175, 184–85; and Gower, 108n, 109, 131, 132, 139n, 179; household of, 29–30, 80n, 82, 100, 157; political speech under, 29–31; power of king's council under, 2, 68n, 92–93, 143–44; rebels' 1381 allegiance to, 19n; reburial of, 141n; taxation under, 123; threats to depose, 82, 83, 99; and unanimity, 122

Richardson, H. G., 6, 27n, 35n, 147n, 179n

Richard the Redeless (anonymous), 36, 37

Richmond, Colin, 24

Ridolfi, R., 166nn, 171n, 172n

Rising of 1381, 11, 13n, 35, 108, 120, 122, 131, 132; motivations for, 21, 79, 100, 123–24, 129; as resistance, 5–6, 156, 182; and *Vox Clamantis,* 109

Robbins, R. H., 36n

Robertus de Avesbury, 74n, 75nn

Roman consul (in *Regement of Princes*), 154, 155

Roman law, 26

Roskell, J. S., 28nn, 29nn, 30n, 31, 32n

Ross, C., 24n

Rousseau, Jean Jacques, 169–70

Royal 18 A vii manuscript (Reg. 18 A manuscript; "The Secrete of Secretes"), 43, 50n, 51n, 79n, 81, 84–85. See also *Secretum Secretorum*

rulers. *See* Kings

St. Albans chronicler, 29

Sanderlin, S., 101n

Saul, Nigel, 6n, 182nn, 183, 184n

Savage, Sir Arnold, 29n

Sayer, Derek, 20

Sayles, George O., 6, 22, 27n

scandalum magnatum, 32–34

Scanlon, Larry, 105, 121n, 142n, 181–82; on

Regement of Princes, 139–41, 151, 154, 158

Scattergood, V. J., 10, 24n, 32n, 34–35, 92n, 109n, 137n, 179n

Scogan, Henry, 181

Scott, James C., 7, 9, 36n, 132, 151

Scrope, Sir Stephen, 61

Secretum Secretorum, 39–66, *48,* 89, 115, 118, 154n, 158, 160, 168; additions to, about Richard II, 84–85; advice in, 11–12, 35–36, 45, 49–54, 71, 75–78, 83, 87, 113, 128–29, 174, 175; as influence on Fürstenspiegel tradition, 2, 3, 74, 93, 94, 110, 112, 138, 142, 147n, 148–49, 156, 163, 164; themes of, 10, 40–49, 54, 75, 76–78, 83, 86, 97, 98; translations of, 11–12, 40n, 41, 45, 71n, 75n, 77n, 166, 179; on war, 162n; Yonge's additions to, 57, 59, 61–66. *See also* Ashmole manuscript; "Gouernaunce of Prynces"; *Kitab sirr al-asrar*; Lambeth 501 manuscript; Royal 18 A vii. manuscript; University College, Oxford, manuscript 85

Sejanus (Jonson), 8

Selections from Hoccleve (Seymour), 138

Selections from the Prison Notebooks of Antonio Gramsci, 169

self-consuming artifacts, 34, 89, 97, 99, 102, 163

Seneca, 57n, 59

"serauntes," 146

"seruiens noster," 146

Severs, I. Burke, 91n

sexual excess, 45

Seymour, M. C., 138–39, 186n

Shakespeare, William, 128, 168

Shirle, John, 35

Shultz, George, 174, 175

Simon of Sudbury (Archbishop of Canterbury), 131

Sir Thopas (Chaucer), 90, 99

Skinner, Quentin, 2n, 40n, 167, 170n, 171n; on *The Prince,* 161, 163n, 166n, 169n

slander laws, 29n, 32–34

Soderini, Pietro, 165–66

soldiers, 150

Solomon (Biblical figure), 95, 96–97, 123, 124, 126

speech. *See* Political speech

Spiegel, Gabrielle M., 14n

statute(s): of 1361, 23; of 1386, 84n; as re-

placement for vengeance, 105. *See also*
Laws
Statute of Laborers, 182
Statute of Treasons, 29n, 33–34
Statute of York, 21n
Steel, A. B., 143n
Steele, R., 36nn, 37n, 40nn, 41nn, 42n,
43nn, 46n, 50nn, 51n, 55n, 57n, 59n, 64nn,
66n, 71n, 74n, 75n, 77n, 79n, 81n, 129n,
137n, 142nn, 147n, 148n, 163n
Stephenson, C., 16n, 21nn, 23n, 28n–30nn,
33n, 86nn, 157n
Stillwell, Gardiner, 91–93n, 102n
Stock, Brian, 11, 161n
Stockton, Eric, 108, 111nn, 129n, 130, 131,
132n
Storey, R. L., 184n
Stow, G. B., 109n
Stratford, John (Archbishop of Canterbury),
72–78, 126
Strode, Ralph, 181
Strohm, Paul, 92n, 101, 104, 105, 106n, 109n,
181, 183n
Stubbs, Bishop W., 6, 11n, 69n, 87n, 125n
Sundby, T., 91nn

"taillage," 124
Talbot, John, 61–64, 178
Tale of Melibee (Chaucer), 54n, 109, 115, 118,
127n, 175; dating of, 90; as mirror for
princes, 3, 12–13, 89–107, 113, 167n, 168,
176; Prudence in, 94–98, 102–3, 106, 165,
167n, 168, 175
Tarquin and Arrons story, 114–15, 117
Tatlock, J. S. P., 90n
taxation: Machiavelli on, 163, 164n; par-
liamentary consent to, 16, 21, 22; in
Rehoboam story, 123–24; resistance
to, 6, 76, 182; under Richard II, 86, 100,
123, 129; for war, 22, 72–73, 76, 79,
100, 123
"Ten of War," 166n
texts (camouflaged). *See* "Hidden transcript"
Thatcher, Margaret, 71n
Thomas Aquinas, 26n
Thomas of Woodstock (duke of Gloucester),
63, 79. *See also* Appellants
Thompson, E. M., 74n, 126nn
Thompson, F., 16n, 23n, 33n
Thornton, G. A., 29n–31n, 33n

Tiptoft, Sir John, 29n, 179
translators: constraints on, 139, 176; self-
representations as, to avoid censure, 8–9,
102; status of, 44, 56–60, 63, 65. *See also*
Yonge, James
treason, 8; activities considered as, 32, 33, 76;
Appellants' charges of, against Richard's
advisers, 79–85, 99–100, 103, 124; and
members of parliament, 31; proverb linked
to, 93n. *See also* Statute of Treasons
Tresilian, Robert, 80, 101
Trinity College manuscript RIII 2, 180
trust, 49–54, 97
truth, 113–17, 150, 151
Tuck, Anthony, 76n, 80nn, 82, 100, 133n
Tully (Cicero), 56
Turmoil and Triumph (Shultz), 175
Turner, B. S., 5n

Ullmann, Walter, 11n, 49n
unanimity, 121–22, 125, 130–31. *See also*
"Community of the realm"
University College, Oxford, manuscript 85
("The Secrete of Secretes"), 45n, 47, 48,
49. See also *Secretum Secretorum*
upward pressures, 11, 15, 16, 26, 63, 138, 151
Usk, Thomas, 101, 181

Vache, Sir Philip de la, 181
Vere, Robert de, 80, 93, 103, 111, 120, 124,
126, 133
Vere of Valance, Guy de (Bishop of Tripoli),
41, 47, 55n
villeins, 17, 122
Virginia and Apius story, 119–21, 123, 125,
126, 132
Voltaire, 171
Vox Clamantis (Gower), 108, 110, 112, 180;
deriding of king in, 111; as reaction to Rising of 1381, 109, 123, 129–32; unanimity in,
122
"Vox populi, vox dei," 129

Walker, Simon, 184
Wallace, David, 104, 105n
Walsingham, Thomas, 69n, 120n, 126n
Warren, W. L., 18n
wars: England's, against France, 22, 72, 76,
79, 82, 92, 123, 133; mirrors for princes on,
162n; in Persian Gulf, 175; in *Tale of Meli-*

wars: (*continued*)
  bee, 89–93, 99–100, 102–4, 106. *See also*
  Wars of the Roses; Welsh uprisings
Wars of the Roses, 34
Waterhouse, R., 93n
Welsh uprisings, 143, 144, 150
The Westminster Chronicle, 33n, 34, 80–82n,
  84, 99n
Wilkinson, Bertie, 16n, 19n, 20nn, 22n, 25nn,
  28n, 69n, 71n, 74n–76n, 78nn, 86nn,
  87nn, 122n, 126n, 134n, 136nn, 156n; on
  England as political nation, 18, 87; on limited monarchy, 69n
Williams, Raymond, 4
women: as advisers, 17, 19, 41, 92, 94–98,
  102–3, 106, 110–11, 165, 167n, 168, 175; as
  causes of men's behavior, 61; as readers,
  186

Wonderful Parliament, 101, 102, 175–76
Wood, Charles, 25, 82, 83
Wright, T., 15n, 18n, 36nn
writers, 57; as advisers to kings, 111, 131–32,
  138, 141, 145, 147–50, 158–59; authority of,
  59–60; constraints on, 16, 27, 31, 32, 106–
  7, 110, 139; punishments for, 34–35; use of
  advice by, for political purposes, 67–88,
  110–13, 176. *See also* "Hidden transcript";
  Mirrors for princes; Political speech;
  Translators
Wyclif, John, 29
Wynnere and Wastoure, 134n

Yeager, R. F., 92n, 125n
Yoder, E., Jr., 123n
Yonge, James, 12, 40n, 55–60, 74n, 85, 104,
  139n, 154n, 166, 178